CHOOSING THE LEADER

MATTHEW N. GREEN AND DOUGLAS B. HARRIS

Choosing
the
Leader

Leadership Elections in the

U.S. House of Representatives

Yale UNIVERSITY PRESS

NEW HAVEN AND LONDON

Published with assistance from the
Louis Stern Memorial Fund.

Yale University Press books may be purchased in quantity
for educational, business, or promotional use. For
information, please e-mail salespress@yale.edu (U.S. office)
or sales@yaleup.co.uk (U.K. office).

Set in Janson Oldstyle type by Newgen North America, Austin, Texas.
Printed in the United States of America.

Library of Congress Control Number: 2018944215
ISBN 978-0-300-22257-9 (pbk: alk. paper)

A catalogue record for this book is available from the
British Library.

This paper meets the requirements of ANSI/NISO Z39.48-1992
(Permanence of Paper).

10 9 8 7 6 5 4 3 2 1

CONTENTS

PREFACE

The November 2016 elections were a major disappointment for Democrats in the U.S. House of Representatives. Fully expecting to start the next year with Hillary Clinton in the White House—if not with control of their chamber—they instead would be without a majority in either the House or Senate and forced to deal with a neophyte Republican populist president, Donald Trump. In addition, Democrats hoping to move past the elections and present a unified front to the public faced two potentially divisive races for party leadership posts. A pair of House members had been campaigning for months for the vacant position of caucus vice chair in a race many believed was too close to call. Then, in mid-November, Congressman Tim Ryan (D-OH) declared that he would challenge Nancy Pelosi (D-CA) for the office of minority leader, which she had held since 2011 (Lillis 2016).

The outcomes of both elections promised longer-term consequences for the party. Linda Sánchez (D-CA) won the first race, narrowly defeating fellow Californian Barbara Lee by a vote of 98 to 96 and putting her in an advantageous position to move up in the ranks of leadership. The election for minority leader, held two weeks later, was not as close—Pelosi soundly defeated Ryan, 134 to 63—but it was the most votes cast against Pelosi since she first ran for leadership in 2001, and it reflected "a growing anxiety" among younger Democrats that Pelosi was excluding them from power and failing to provide the direction needed to win future elections (Caygle 2016; Cottle 2016; Kane and O'Keefe 2016).

These two races—one for an open seat, the other a revolt against an incumbent—exemplify an important but little-understood element of congressional politics. Party leaders in Congress are widely understood to be critical to legislative outcomes, and their selection is not always consensual. In fact, they can be the result of difficult and divisive contests decided by a small handful of lawmakers. But while journalists occasionally cover the ins and outs of these races, there has been little systematic analysis of how legislators make the decisions about whom to support in these elections and, by extension, who is selected to lead them.

We offer such an analysis in this book. In so doing, we reject the conventional wisdom that these elections can be boiled down to ideological preferences, and we disagree with the equally prevalent notion that legislators' votes are so individualistic and personality-driven as to preclude generalization. Instead, we argue that two key factors help explain the leadership choice of members of the U.S. House of Representatives: their professional connections with particular candidates, and the extent to which they expect each candidate to help them achieve their goals. We test this new theoretical argument using qualitative and quantitative data, including material collected from over twenty congressional archives around the country, for fourteen leadership races in both political parties over the past six decades.

We have many people to thank for helping bring this study to fruition. A number of current and former lawmakers and congressional staff were willing to sit down for interviews to share their priceless knowledge of leadership races, for which we are most grateful. Attendees at Georgetown University's American Government Seminar Series offered valuable suggestions and critiques for part of our research, including Michael Bailey, Jonathan Ladd, Hans Noel, and Michele Swers. Special thanks to the Historian of the U.S. House of Representatives, Matthew Wasniewski, for his beneficial ideas and for inviting us to present our research to members of the House Historian's office. We are indebted to Michael Hanmer for his statistical advice, Sean Kelly and Scott Frisch for generously sharing data on the 2006 majority leader race, and Sarah Treul for kindly providing us her then-unpublished manuscript on congressional state delegations. Additional helpful advice and suggestions came from Brian Alexander,

Emily Baer, Stephanie Burkhalter, Anthony Champagne, Maurice Cunningham, Bill D'Antonio, Victoria Farrar-Myers, Danny Hayes, Soren Jordan, Nathan Kalmoe, David Karol, Ken Kato, Jennifer Lawless, Eric Lawrence, Frances Lee, Jeffrey Lewis, Bryan Marshall, David Mayhew, Scott Meinke, Garrison Nelson, Hong Min Park, Keith Poole, Eric Powers, Paul Quirk, Jim Riddlesperger, John Sides, Steve Wenzel, Don Wolfensberger, and Antoine Yoshinaka. Doug Harris would especially like to thank, in memoriam, Sukie Hammond and Bob Peabody, who first taught him the importance and excitement of studying legislative leadership selection.

We are most grateful for the help from staff and archivists at the many congressional collections where we gathered data. They include, but are not limited to, John Atteberry, Laura Berfield, Kristen Chinery, Brad Coffield, Janet Dotterer, Amara Edwards, Jeffrey Flannery, Nathan Gerth, Teresa Gipson, Chris Gordon, Carolyn Hanneman, Rachel Henson, Myron House, Frank Mackaman, Roger Myers, Charles Niles, Sean Noel, John O'Connell, Marilyn Parrish, Lisa Peña, Geoffrey Reynolds, Jill Severn, Jeffrey Thomas, and Lori Tretheway. Financial assistance was provided by the Everett McKinley Dirksen Congressional Research Center, the Carl Albert Congressional Research and Studies Center, the Morris K. Udall Research Grant program, and the summer research grant program at Loyola University Maryland.

We are especially grateful to Bill Frucht of Yale University Press, who not only endorsed our project but guided it through the review process with diligence and enduring patience. The anonymous reviewers of our manuscript provided trenchant critiques and valuable guidance, which we greatly appreciate.

Finally, we want to thank our families for their support. Matthew thanks his wife, Holly, and children, Joshua and Olivia (the uncredited cover photographer of his previous book), who silently endured the many hours he sat hunched over a laptop and his occasional disappearances to distant archives. Doug thanks his wife, Christine Kempf, and daughters, Zoe and Maya Kempf-Harris, for the daily entertainment, patience, and love.

CHOOSING THE LEADER

CHOOSING THE LEADER

Party leaders in Congress matter. They shape the agenda and the rules of their chamber, control lawmakers' access to internal information, and assemble and enforce collective agreements within the legislature. They negotiate on behalf of their colleagues with interest groups and elected officials outside of Congress, and they serve as their party's public face to other branches of government, the press, and the public. They also participate in electoral politics, developing partisan messages, raising campaign funds, and recruiting electoral candidates (Cox and McCubbins 2005; Curry 2015; Harris 1998; Mayhew 1974; Peabody 1976; Sinclair 1995; S. Smith 2007; Strahan 2007).

Deciding who will serve as a party leader can therefore have both immediate and enduring consequences for congressional politics and American public policy. Yet despite its importance, leadership selection in the U.S. Congress is a topic few have studied in depth. Though there is a substantial body of research on what congressional party leaders do, why they do it, their influence, and how their powers have changed over time (e.g. Green 2010; Meinke 2016; Pearson 2015; Strahan 2007), no comprehensive study of the *selection* of those leaders has been written in the past four decades, apart from occasional analyses of individual races or trends in the relative divisiveness of elections over time (e.g., Brown and Peabody 1992; Green 2006, 2008; Green and Harris 2007; Harris 2006; Jenkins and Stewart 2013).

Our purpose is to fill this gap in our understanding of how congressional leaders are chosen. We offer the first systematic analysis of party leadership elections in Congress since the 1970s, looking in particular at how election campaigns unfold and the factors driving lawmakers' vote choice when vacancies occur or challenges erupt against sitting leaders.[1] Drawing upon a diversity of data, including press reports, interviews with former lawmakers and staff, and archival records, we provide detailed accounts of fourteen different races between 1965 and 2013, explaining the mechanics and politics of each one from the moment a candidate decided to run to the count of the final ballot. We also examine vote tallies from over twenty archival collections—many never-before analyzed—to overcome one of the biggest hurdles to studying these races: the use of secret ballots to determine the outcome.[2] Using regression analysis to test the independent effect of several factors on the vote choice of lawmakers in each race, we uncover a generalizable logic that goes beyond the conventional wisdom that voting in party leadership elections is determined by ideology or ties of friendship.

In this chapter, after briefly reviewing the House's major elected party leadership positions, we discuss the common wisdom about congressional leadership elections and the limits of early research on the topic. Next, we introduce a new theory of leadership selection and explain how candidates, campaigns, and political context contribute to the factors that shape legislators' vote choice for a leader. We then introduce the empirical data we use to test our theory, describe our testing methodology, and outline the chapters that follow.

Party Leadership Positions in the U.S. House of Representatives

Both parties in the House of Representatives have a number of elected leadership positions. The *Speaker of the House* is the highest office in the chamber: the sole House leadership post mentioned in the Constitution and, since 1947, in the line of presidential succession just after the vice president. The Speaker's responsibilities include representing the chamber as a whole, presiding over sessions (or selecting a designee to do so), helping set the majority party's agenda and protect its majority status, appointing lawmakers to certain committees, and serving as the party's top spokesperson. It is the only elected leadership position for which candidates are first nominated by each party and then selected by the entire chamber, typically on the first day of a new Congress.

Each party also has a floor leader. The *majority leader*, second in party rank to the Speaker, is responsible for setting the legislative agenda, scheduling and monitoring floor deliberations, and helping lobby for votes, while the *minority leader* is his or her party's highest ranking officer and has responsibilities that include serving as party spokesperson, providing leadership on the chamber floor, and appointing fellow partisans to particular committees. Majority and minority floor leaders have been selected within each party caucus since the early twentieth century (Nelson 1977). Another set of leaders are the *majority whip* and *minority whip*, each chiefly responsible for building support for (or against) bills and amendments on behalf of their party and facilitating communication on legislation between rank-and-file lawmakers and other leaders. The Democratic whip was appointed by the majority leader (in consultation with the Speaker) until 1986, when it became an elected office, while Republicans have elected their whip since the 1960s (Nelson 1977; Ripley 1967). (When in the minority, both parties tend to refer to their leader and whip positions as "Democratic" or "Republican," rather than the less-appealing "minority.")

There are additional leadership posts, also elected by secret ballot within each party, which we refer to occasionally in this study. They include various officers affiliated with each party organization, such as the chairs of the Democratic Caucus and Republican Conference, the Democratic Caucus vice chair (formerly secretary), and the Republican Conference vice chair and secretary. Also included are the chair of the GOP's campaign arm, the National Republican Campaign Committee (NRCC); the Republican Policy Committee, a party advisory group; and, prior to its elimination in 1995, another GOP advisory body, the Republican Research (or Planning and Research) Committee.[3]

In chapter 2, we discuss in more detail the reasons why individuals might seek any of these leadership posts. For now it is worth noting two consequences of their shared features. First, their relatively large number—not to mention the scores of unelected leadership offices that also exist, such as the two parties' assistant, deputy, and regional whips—underscores the significant and expansive responsibilities of party leadership in the modern Congress, especially during the present-day period of heightened party polarization and reduced influence of legislative committees. Second, while they vary in duties and tasks, ambitious members of Congress see them collectively as useful vehicles for influencing policy and expanding their district, state, and even national visibility. Legislators may occasionally seek a specific leadership post for its own sake, but more often they pursue one position in the belief that, if they prove successful in that office, they will be well positioned to run for a higher-ranked leadership office later. The idea of a hierarchy or *ladder* of leadership positions is an important one, and although the ranking of positions on the ladder is often imprecise and subject to change over time, it means that the decision of whom to support for a particular leadership office often depends less on a candidate's qualifications for that office— as important as they might be to some lawmakers in individual instances—than on whether the candidate is generally well suited to serve in leadership.

The Conventional Wisdom: Ideology and Personal Relationships

Much of what scholars and observers have come to accept as true about leadership elections originates in the research of two influential political scientists. David B. Truman suggested in his book *The Congressional Party* (1959) that lawmakers choose leaders who are close to the ideological midpoint of their parties. This so-called "middleman hypothesis" held that legislators are more inclined to select candidates who are aligned with neither ideological wing of their party and thus can broker agreements between them. Though some researchers have since come to different conclusions about the ideological moderation of party leaders,[4] the idea that ideology—one's broad set of beliefs and principles about politics (Noel 2013)—is the basis for selecting leaders in Congress is still widely accepted today. Specifically, many assume that lawmakers pick the candidate in a contested leadership race who is closer to them ideologically. We call this the *ideology hypothesis* of leadership selection.

> *Ideology hypothesis:* Legislators are more likely to vote for the candidate in a contested leadership election who is closer to their preferences along the traditional "left-right" ideological spectrum.

The second conventional school of thought about leadership voting decisions was most thoroughly elaborated by Robert L. Peabody, a pioneering student of leadership elections. In his book *Leadership in Congress*, Peabody insisted that most of the factors that could influence leadership elections "do not lend themselves to clear-cut isolation, easy operationalization, assignment of weights, or sophisticated causal orderings" (Peabody 1976, 470). One such variable was the strength and nature of personal relationships between candidates and lawmakers (Peabody 1976, 299–300, 498). Other researchers and observers have concurred that personal relationships are central. Nelson Polsby, for instance, suggested that the outcome of one leadership race in the early 1960s hinged upon "the mysteries of how men interact with one another, of what leads people into enmity, jealousy, [and] friendship," and another pair of political scientists deemed leadership races to be "family affairs" (Bibby and Davidson 1967, 143; Polsby 1962 [1992], 265). Decades after Peabody's book, this claim remains the standard explanation of voting behavior offered by many contemporary journalists and lawmakers (e.g., Gehrke 2015; Goldstein 1994). We call it the *personal-relationship hypothesis* of leadership selection.

> *Personal-relationship hypothesis:* Legislators are more likely to vote for the candidate in a contested leadership election with whom they have a closer, more positive personal relationship.

Although both the ideology and personal-relationship hypotheses have an element of truth to them, there are theoretical and empirical reasons to question their utility as parsimonious theories of leadership vote choice. Take first the claim that ideology drives a legislator's choice of party leader. By assuming that general left-right ideological compatibility is what lawmakers care about, it neglects potentially important nuances with causal significance, such as cross-cutting ideological cleavages or candidates' positions on specific issues, and other plausible—and arguably more relevant—criteria for selecting leaders, like the ability to provide benefits and services to the rank-and-file. It also leaves unexplained precisely why ideology should matter at all, assuming the winning candidate is not a "middleman" chosen to bridge the gap between opposing ideological wings of the party. Indeed, some legislators we interviewed expressed skepticism of the ideology hypothesis. Though one former Democratic Party leader told us that ideology "is still significant" in leadership races, another erstwhile leader insisted that "it would be overly simplistic to say people felt they had to do something ideologically," and a former Republican lawmaker noted that "the philosophical thing is not as deep" when it comes to leadership selection.[5] One could thus make a strong case that the ideology hypothesis is an undertheorized and incomplete explanation of vote choice.

The personal-relationship hypothesis also rests on somewhat shaky ground. It presumes that the responsibilities of leaders are immaterial and that lawmaker self-interest—a foundational explanation of congressional behavior (Mayhew 1974)—is largely irrelevant when it comes to a task as weighty as choosing leaders. It also takes as a given that each member of Congress has a personal relationship with at least one leadership candidate or, if not, is implausibly indifferent toward the outcome of the election. Anecdotal and interview data further suggest that friendships are frequently trumped by other considerations. One former congressman recalled that he was a close friend to a candidate for Republican whip but, because the other candidate was from his state and "I'd given a commitment" to him, he could not vote for his comrade.[6] In the election for GOP leader that same year, Barber Conable (R-NY) wrote to one of the candidates that while "I value your leadership, your friendship and your judgment," he believed the other candidate better prepared for the post.[7] Barbara Vucanovich (R-NV) had wanted to vote for her "friend" Susan Molinari (R-NY), who was running for Conference vice chairman in 1994, but could not because she had already agreed to support another colleague (Vucanovich and Cafferata 2005, 160). Even Peabody admitted that "personality is likely to be decisive only when other factors such as ideology and regional strength are neutralized" (Peabody 1976, 300–302).

We do not reject the notion that ideology, personal relationships, or both may shape some lawmakers' voting decisions in certain leadership elections. However, a careful consideration of the distinguishing features of leadership offices and elections for those offices suggests a more nuanced and comprehensive theoretical model of vote choice.

The Mixed-Motive Model

The factors that shape vote choice derive from two central characteristics of leader elections and behavior. First, the electorate is relatively small: in the House, candidates need the support of half of their party in the chamber plus one (usually between 80 and 140 legislators). This means lawmakers may not necessarily be friends with the candidates, but they are likely to be familiar with their political positions and prior legislative behavior. Second, most party leadership posts carry with them an expectation of service. Depending on the post, that service may include assisting partisan colleagues win reelection, serving as the public face of their party and the chamber, providing colleagues with scarce resources and promotions to positions of influence, shaping the legislative agenda and guiding its enactment, and otherwise helping the rank-and-file achieve their goals (Aldrich 1995; Sinclair 1995). Lawmakers and staff concur that service is a central function of leadership and therefore of utmost importance in the choice of party leaders. In a leadership race, "members will have to decide who they think can help them with their problems," as former party leader Martin Frost (D-TX) put it (Cassidy 2002). Jim Cooper (D-TN) explained that "what matters when you come here is who's been nice to you, who's helped you out on all the petty day-to-day issues" (Calmes 1986), and a one-time candidate remarked to us that lawmakers evaluate "whether, when they need you, you'll be available to them."[8] According to former leadership aide John Lawrence, "leadership decisions are driven . . . by the answer to the time-honored question: 'What can you do for me?'" (Lawrence 2016).

The relatively small scale of leadership elections and the service-oriented expectations members have of party leaders have several implications for voting decisions in those elections. For one thing, professional connections forged through shared working environments will be a stronger foundation for evaluating candidates than personal friendships alone, because they allow representatives an opportunity to evaluate candidates, their skills, and their characteristics closely and regularly (e.g., Barry 1989, 20; Sinclair 1995, 232). For another, lawmakers are likely to look for—and expect—demonstrable evidence that candidates, if elected, will help them achieve their objectives. Finally, since individual lawmakers have different goals, and not all will have equally strong relationships with the candidates, we should expect to see different groups of legislators supporting the same candidate for different reasons, just as we see in elections more generally (Lippmann 1922; Sides et al. 2012).[9]

We distill these axioms about leadership selection politics into a "mixed-motive" model of vote choice composed of two specific hypotheses, one relational and the other instrumental. The first, the *professional connection hypothesis*, states that a lawmaker is more likely to vote for the candidate with whom she shares a working professional relationship. Two spheres in Congress are particularly fruitful for developing such relationships.[10] One is a shared state delegation. Until the 1970s or so, a lawmaker's state delegation was his principal social and political organization, often voting as a unit and deferring to the dictates of their senior-most member. Their influence is "not necessarily as controlling" nowadays, as a former House member put it to us,[11] but state delegations are still important for cultivating professional relationships in Congress. Remarked one recent Democratic lawmaker, your delegation "becomes your house . . . it's essentially a club within the congressional family" where "you get to know folks [who are] mutually supportive of each other."[12] Legislators from the same state often work together on bills and administrative requests to advance common geographical interests, lobby jointly to secure choice committee seats for their delegation, support each other for reelection, cosponsor the same legislation, and meet regularly at state society events and other informal gatherings (Bullock 1971; Fiellin 1963; Fowler 2006; Pellegrini and Grant 1999; Ripley 1967; Treul 2017). Noted one former candidate for leadership, "state delegations are a big deal" because they "will often stick together" and "vote as a bloc."[13] As a result, according to a Republican aide with leadership campaign experience, "your state delegation—you go there first" for support if you are a candidate.[14]

The other environment in which professional relationships develop and serve as a reservoir of votes for leadership candidates is their committees. The smaller scale of committees and their centrality in the bill-crafting process create favorable opportunities for committee colleagues to become familiar with one another, attending hearings and legislative mark-up sessions together and forming coalitions to enact or defeat bills. Some committees may even develop their own internal norms of behavior that in turn enforce stronger professional ties among their members (Fenno 1963). "The committee is your team, so to speak," observed one member of Congress. "You get to know those people better than anyone else in Congress."[15] During the 1965 race for Republican leader, Don Rumsfeld (R-IL) remarked that one should lobby for votes among those "who you know on committees," and a more recent GOP leadership candidate acknowledged that "committees can be a factor [in vote choice], especially if there are close working relationships" between the candidate and fellow committee members.[16] When he ran for Research Committee chair in April 1987, Mickey Edwards (R-OK) wrote to Newt Gingrich (R-GA) to solicit his support, complaining that "too many" of their colleagues were voting for candidates who were "in some other way related to them (committee assignment, same state delegation, etc.)."[17]

> *Professional connection hypothesis:* Legislators are more likely to vote for the candidate in a contested leadership election with whom they share a professional connection, in particular a committee assignment or state delegation.

The mixed-motive model includes a second supposition, the *goal salience hypothesis.* It posits that a member of Congress is more likely to vote for the candidate seen as most disposed to help him achieve his core individual goals of reelection, policy enactment, and internal influence (Fenno 1973; Mayhew 1974; Sinclair 1995).[18] Those goals will vary in importance for each member from one context to the next. Certain goals may be made salient by the political context —e.g., recent election results—as well as candidates themselves, based on their particular traits or past behaviors, key themes they emphasize in their campaigns, or scarce goods they provide to indicate support for lawmakers' interests. We have found evidence for this hypothesis in several contested leadership races (Green 2006, 2008; Green and Harris 2007), and other work suggests its validity as well (e.g., Harris 2006; Kelly n.d.; S. Smith 2007).

> *Goal salience hypothesis:* Legislators are more likely to vote for the candidate in a contested leadership election whom they expect will satisfy their electoral, policy, or influence goals as made salient by the candidate, her campaign, or the context of the race.

Note that, while the goal salience hypothesis is compatible with the ideology hypothesis, we posit that ideology does not matter in and of itself but as a signal that a candidate will help achieve legislators' broad policy goals (Peabody 1967). Furthermore, because a candidate's ideology is associated with just one potentially salient goal, it is neither necessary nor sufficient to explain vote choice. In other words, the mixed-motive model establishes the condition under which ideology should help influence voting decisions—when it is made salient in the leadership election—while positing that factors associated with other legislator goals may be salient as well.

Nor do our twin hypotheses preclude the possibility that personal relationships may play a role in leadership selection. Such relationships obviously exist in, and are significant to, the legislature (see e.g., Champagne et al. 2009; Clapp 1963; Green 2016), and candidates are certain to try to exploit such connections if they think doing so will yield votes.[19] The extreme difficulty in measuring personal relationships prevents us from systematically testing the personal-relationship hypothesis, a matter we return to in chapter 7. If the mixed-motive model holds true, however, such relationships will not be the only factor that explains vote choice. Choosing a leader is serious business, and we assume the archetypical lawmaker will be strategic when deciding whom to vote for, rather than selecting a candidate solely on the basis of who is a closer comrade.

The 3 C's: Candidates, Campaigns, and Context

One advantage of our approach is that it takes into account the flavors of different leadership races, recognizing that who runs, how candidates compete, and the environment in which they run shape vote choice. We elaborate on these "3 C's" of leadership selection in Congress—candidates, campaigns, and context—below.

1. The candidates. Like any election, an election for congressional party leader presents a comparative choice determined by the pool of announced candidates (Bradshaw 1995). Candidate emergence is thus a key precursor to leadership elections, framing the choice that members confront and unlocking some constellations of goals and relationships at the expense of others. Once candidates emerge, their professional relationships are likely to translate into electoral support, and just as in elections more generally, their distinctive characteristics and prior records serve as cues to voters (Sides et al. 2012). Characteristics that are potentially salient to legislator goals include age, seniority, gender, region, electoral cohort, and overall ideology,[20] while prior records may include specific political positions, votes on salient matters, and past service to lawmakers. We therefore look closely at key candidate characteristics in leadership elections when testing the mixed-motive model, especially if those characteristics are emphasized by the candidates themselves or made salient by the political environment.

2. *The campaigns.* Campaigns can steer some lawmakers toward one leadership candidate or another in the same way they do in elections for public office (Brady, Johnston, and Sides 2006; Jacobson 2015; Sides et al. 2012). One aide explained that "a lot of it [campaigning] is based on first trying to discern what the driving factors are to gain a person's support . . . figuring out what the hot button issues are that matter to members." Running for leadership, noted another aide, is "like a traditional campaign. Where's my base?"[21]

Campaigns can influence voting decisions in at least two ways. The first is through broad-based appeals, making certain goals salient through framing, priming, reinforcement, and other messaging tactics, analogous to what candidates in mass-based elections do (e.g., Carsey 2000; Finkel 1993; Franklin 1991; Petrocik 1996; Sellers 1998). Press conferences, "Dear Colleague" letters, endorsements by influential party members or interest groups, and other devices are commonly employed to emphasize certain themes, ideas, candidate characteristics, and prior legislative and leadership records in an effort to win votes and imply future attention to core legislator goals. The second way campaigns matter is through individually targeted appeals, which may take the form of persuasion or providing particularized side-payments like campaign donations (S. Smith 2007).[22] Even the simple act of asking for someone's vote can make a difference, and failure to do so can be fatal.[23] When observers insist that leadership elections are personal, they are often referring not to intraparty relationships but to this kind of one-on-one campaigning. "They are such personal affairs," said one House aide; "they are member-to-member, secret affairs. . . . So much of it is 'under the Dome.'"[24] "Any leadership race is as personal as you can get," as leadership candidate Guy Vander Jagt (R-MI) once remarked. "It's eyeball to eyeball. Promises and rewards are nothing unusual" (Hornblower 1980).

Three things should be mentioned about leadership campaigns. First, in theory (though seldom in practice), a candidate could campaign so poorly, or be at such a disadvantage against her rivals, that lawmakers who would "naturally" vote for her due to professional relationships or salient goals do not. Second, campaigns can be shaped by outsiders who editorialize, offer endorsements, or lobby for votes, like interest groups, other elected officials, and media outlets. These external influences are often beyond the control of campaigns, but sometimes candidates employ an explicit "outsider" strategy of garnering help from actors external to the chamber. Third, a campaign-related tactic that sometimes matters, especially for close elections, is maximizing turnout. One candidate for a Democratic leadership post told us that he "knew which of my supporters might not be there" on election day, and he renegotiated the scheduling commitments of two of them to ensure their attendance.[25] A House Democrat who worked on Nancy Pelosi's (D-CA) campaign for whip in 2001 recalled that "she had members assigned to call two or three other members . . . at 7:30 in the morning, to make sure they were awake" before the vote.[26]

Though campaigns are a major feature of leadership elections, and we assume that they can influence voting decisions, ours is not a study of campaign effects per se. Sometimes campaigns try, without success, to neutralize the perceived advantages of their opponents or emphasize particular issues or personal traits. However, one can reasonably infer that a campaign has made a difference in an election when one finds a strong correlation between the vote choice of certain lawmakers and a campaign's themes and tactics. Accordingly, we estimate the importance of campaigns—especially for making some lawmaker goals salient over others—by looking at such data as statements of candidacy; how candidates frame themselves, their campaigns, and their opponents; which groups and individuals they seek support from, and how; and endorsements and lobbying by outsiders.

3. The context. The third and final "C" of congressional leadership races is the political context, the broader environment within which the race takes place. A few contextual elements can be noteworthy. The *number of candidates* running for a given office—itself a result of the ambitions of would-be candidates—matters. If there are more than two candidates, the election—which is determined by majority vote—may be decided by multiple ballots, and the winning candidate may be the person who can persuade supporters of his weaker opponents to give him their votes after their first-choice candidate is eliminated. Also important is *whether the party is in the majority or the minority:* leadership candidates from the former may feel more pressure to show they will carry out policy goals, while those from the latter may be expected to put a greater focus on winning elections, particularly in a competitive electoral environment (Lee 2016). Another significant contextual element is *other leadership races or incumbent leaders.* If the party's current set of leaders are all from the same background or region, for instance, a candidate may emphasize his distinctiveness as an asset to the party.[27] Also, incumbent leaders can overtly or covertly express their preferences in an election, thereby changing the decision calculus of some colleagues. In the event of multiple races, one candidate may pursue a logrolling agreement with another candidate in a different race, each one asking his supporters to vote for the other. Finally, the *most recent election results* may make certain goals more salient and alter the composition of the party in ways that benefit particular candidates. For example, lawmakers who barely won reelection may be especially sensitive to collective concerns that the party is in electoral trouble and needs new leadership to improve its image (Cox and McCubbins 1993; Peabody 1976).[28] Unexpectedly large seat losses may also encourage lawmakers to support candidates seeking to remove an incumbent leader.

The effect of contextual variables on outcomes and vote choice is hard to test, and they may not impact individual lawmakers' votes in many races. Nonetheless, we discuss those variables in instances where observers believed they were important enough to have influenced the election results.[29]

Testing the Model

In chapters 3 through 6, we test our two hypotheses on fourteen leadership races in the U.S. House of Representatives between 1961 and 2013. For each one we describe the basic characteristics of the candidates, the terms of the campaigns they waged, and the context within which the race took place. We also identify the professional relationships and salient goals that were present in the race. While the state delegation and committee assignments shared with candidates are readily identifiable, goals that are salient to lawmakers are somewhat trickier to ascertain. Accordingly, we consider a goal to be salient if it is made so by at least two of the three C's of leadership races— candidates, campaigns, and context—with the exception of campaign donations by candidates (which are important in and of themselves without necessarily being a function of candidate traits or the political context). For instance, policy goals may be salient if a candidate's campaign emphasizes that goal, provided the candidate is distinctive ideologically or the political context is one in which policy goals are particularly salient. This allows us to discount the effect of mere campaign rhetoric unsupported by either the context or a candidate's attributes. As control variables, we include in all of our analyses measures of goals that are assumed to matter in leadership races generally, even if not salient in a particular race (see table 1.1).[30] Recognizing that each leadership race has its own unique characteristics, we also test additional, case-specific variables made salient by the candidates, the campaign, or the context, as appropriate. To estimate how lawmakers voted in each election, we draw primarily on pre- or postelection whip tallies kept by the candidates themselves and obtained from various historical archives.[31] We then use regression analysis (probit for two-candidate elections, multinomial logit for elections with three or more candidates) to see whether professional connections and the goals made salient by candidate traits and campaign tactics help explain vote choice. In addition, we employ the observed value approach (Hanmer and Kalkan 2013) to estimate the average effect of each variable on the probability of voting for each candidate.[32]

Table 1.1. Member-Level Variables Used in Regression Models

Explanation for Vote	Variables Common to All Analyses	Variables Specific to Particular Candidates and Campaigns
Professional Connection	• Shared committee • Shared state delegation	n/a
Reelection Goal	• Seat marginality (% of 2-party vote)	• Campaign resources received from candidate(s)
Policy Goal	• Ideology (DW-NOMINATE)	• (Dis)agreement with candidate(s)' votes or positions • (Dis)agreement with issues emphasized by campaign(s)
Influence Goal	• Serves as leader • Serves as committee chair or ranking member	• Shared region, background • Membership in certain groups emphasized or targeted by the campaign(s)

Testing our hypotheses with regression analysis is not without its limitations. A standard log-likelihood regression model is often unable to estimate the effect of certain variables if they perfectly predict (or, put another way, are completely separated by) a vote for or against a candidate, creating a "quasicomplete" separation problem (Albert and Anderson 1984). (As we show in subsequent chapters, this is most commonly a problem with shared committee and state delegation, because all the members of a candidate's committee or state delegation often commit to that candidate.) There is also the danger of omitted variable bias, especially if candidates systematically provide unrecorded and unadvertised goods or services to lawmakers in exchange for their vote. Failure to include a measure of those benefits could result in biased coefficients for other variables in a regression model as well as an artificially large error term (Bailey 2016; Menard 2010).[33] And regression analysis cannot readily test the personal-relationship hypothesis, since personal relationships are by nature private and thus nearly impossible to measure.

Nonetheless, the ability to estimate the impact of a variety of variables on how lawmakers decide to vote makes regression analysis an advantageous method for testing our hypotheses.[34] To address the quasicomplete separation problem, we follow the conventional technique of noting when the problem arises and excluding variables whose coefficients cannot be estimated.[35] Since small committees or state delegations can result in statistically insignificant coefficients, particularly if they are correlated with other explanatory variables, we run alternative specifications that test professional connections alone. Though omitted variable bias is a possibility, we find a remarkable consistency in our findings across races and over time, suggesting a high degree of reliability and lack of bias in our estimates. (This is true even as the number of elected leadership positions, the amount of intraparty fundraising, and the growth of media attention to these races have grown, a point we return to in our final chapter.) Furthermore, while we cannot prove or disprove the personal-relationship hypothesis, we can at least infer that it is not a parsimonious explanation of voting behavior if the other variables we use to test the mixed-motive model prove statistically significant.

What serves as sufficient evidence for the mixed-motive model? We do not claim that it will explain all, or even most, of the variation in vote choice in a leadership race. As Peabody noted, in contests for power within a group as relatively small as a congressional party, there will doubtless be unique, unmeasurable factors that influence a number of lawmakers' vote choice. Furthermore, some lawmaker goals are either difficult to measure or estimated by multiple variables that are highly correlated, such as age and seniority, making it hard to tease out their discrete effects. We also do not expect professional connections to be explanations of voting decisions in every leadership race, since some candidates may be absentee members of their committee, refuse to associate with their fellow state legislators, fail to ask their professional colleagues for their vote, or come from the same state or committee as another candidate and thus split their colleagues' allegiances. We therefore take as reasonable evidence for our model in a given leadership race (a) a committee assignment or state delegation, uniquely shared with at least one leadership candidate, that is statistically significant in explaining vote choice (or must be omitted because it is completely separated by vote choice), and (b) the preponderance of uncorrelated goal-related variables, especially nonideological ones, that are statistically significant (or are completely separated by the vote).

The Reliability of Whip Counts

How can we be sure that private whip counts, which we use to estimate votes in most of our cases, are accurate? One could argue that there are at least three possible sources of error in such data. First, legislators may change their minds between a whip count and the vote itself. Second, candidates may record commitments incorrectly, either due to false information or because they do a poor job of counting votes. Third, lawmakers may misrepresent how they plan to vote. This last possibility is a common claim about leadership elections. "People lie to their mothers about their true intentions," according to Rep. Charlie Rose (D-NC) (Jacobs 1995, 304). During the 1976 Democratic Caucus debate over selecting a majority leader, Charlie Wilson (D-TX) wryly remarked to the nearly 300 Democrats gathered that "according to the tally sheet of the count for Majority Leader, we now have 860 members in this Caucus."[36] Peabody claimed there is "bound" to be "considerable 'slackness'" in [the] count" of voting commitments for a secret ballot, while Nelson Polsby argued that the secret ballot allows lawmakers to vote their "private preferences with impunity." More recently, one reporter asserted that "many members of Congress are two-timers," when it comes to vote pledges in leadership elections (Hohmann 2016; Peabody 1976, 178, 197; Polsby 1962 [1992], 282).

While we readily acknowledge that whip counts are an imperfect measure of actual vote choice, they are less prone to error than one might think. Some lawmakers' preferences are fluid over the course of a campaign, but the vast majority of the whip tallies we rely upon are either postelection estimates or completed within days of the election, when most party members have decided how they will vote. Candidates' private whip counts also tend to be quite close to final vote totals, suggesting they are fairly accurate.[37] Table 1.2 compares the private prevote tallies of several leadership races with the actual number of votes received by the candidate conducting the count. Though the differences vary widely, the mean difference between estimate and actual vote totals is small, with candidates receiving an average 5.1 percent fewer votes than expected.[38] Another reason for confidence in whip count data is that, assertions by some notwithstanding, there is strong evidence that lawmakers seldom explicitly promise their vote to multiple candidates. In the few races where we uncovered vote counts from more than one candidate, fewer than 8 percent of party members on average were counted as supporters by two or more people running for the same office (see table 1.2, last column). This low rate of multiple commitments is confirmed by the testimony of lawmakers and congressional aides involved in leadership races.[39] For instance, David Bonior wrote that while "some members might lie to you about their pledge of support," when he ran for whip in 1991 (and correctly predicted the exact number of votes he would get), "the number of members in that last category was minimal" (Bonior 2018, 320). When asked whether lawmakers might lie, a Republican aide surmised in an interview that "some of that happens" but "it doesn't happen as much as people think it would."[40]

In fact, despite the secret nature of the ballot, members of Congress have strong reasons to refrain from lying about their vote choice. For one thing, there is an incentive to advertise one's vote commitment widely in order to get credit from the candidate and demonstrate loyalty. Some even show their completed ballot to their desired candidate or her ally before casting it (e.g., Jacobs 1995, 318).[41] More importantly, there is a strong norm in Congress against violating one's commitments and deceiving fellow representatives (Barber 1965; Weingast 1979). Morris Udall (D-AZ) was told by dozens of

Table 1.2. Accuracy of Internal Whip Counts

Race	Source (pre- or postelection tally)	Predicted Vote (for self)	Actual Vote (for self)	Difference	% Making Multiple Commitments
GOP Leader (1965)[a]	Ford (pre)	80	73	−8.8%	n/a
Dem Speaker (1969)	Udall (post)	49	58	+18.4%	2.5% (6)[b]
Dem Leader (1971), 1st ballot	Udall (post)	69	69	0.0%	n/a
Dem Leader (1971), 2nd ballot	Udall (post)	81	88	+8.6%	
Dem Leader (1976), 1st ballot	Wright (pre)	94	77	−18.1%	6.8% (20)[c]
Dem Leader (1976), 2nd ballot	Wright (pre)	94	95	+1.1%	—
GOP Leader (1980)	Michel (pre)	115	103	−10.4%	14.2% (27)
GOP Leader (1980)	Vander Jagt (pre)	95	87	−8.4%	—

GOP Whip (1980)	Shuster (pre)	98	90	−8.2%	n/a
Dem Leader (1989)	Gephardt (pre)	181	156	−13.8%	n/a
GOP Whip (1989)	Gingrich (pre)	87	87	0.0%	n/a
GOP Whip (1994)[a]	Walker (pre)	92	80	−13.0%	n/a
GOP Leader (1998), 1st ballot[a]	Armey (pre)	105	100	−4.8%	n/a
GOP Leader (1998), 2nd ballot[a]	Armey (pre)	121	127	+5.0%	n/a
Dem Leader (2006)	Murtha (pre)	114	86	−24.6%	n/a

[a] Counting leaners as votes in favor.

[b] Comparing Udall's postvote tally to the names of those who sent telegrams to McCormack committing to vote for him.

[c] Comparing Wright's prevote tally to Burton's postvote tally. All 20 had pledged to Wright, but Burton believed they had voted for him.

Democrats that they could not support his challenge against Speaker John McCormack (D-MA) in 1968 because they had already pledged to vote for McCormack. When Jim Wright (D-TX) was asked if he, like other Texans, would support Bernie Sisk (D-CA) for majority leader in 1971 over Hale Boggs (D-LA), Wright replied, "I'm pledged to Boggs, and I'll stick." During the same race, another candidate, Morris Udall, received requests from some Democrats to be released from their pledges on the eve of the election (King 1971). In 2002, Ray LaHood (R-IL) abandoned his campaign for Republican whip against Roy Blunt (R-MO) because too many Republicans had already pledged support for Blunt and, he noted, "the truth is, people are going to stay by their commitments" (Kantin 2002).

Indicative of this norm is the degree to which lawmakers who do not wish to support a candidate will give tepid, vague promises of support rather than tell an untruth. Among the creative ways legislators have given "nonendorsement" endorsements: "You're a hell of a guy and I sure think you'd make a good" leader, "I've always admired the way you worked," "You know where I'll be on this one," and "You'd make a great whip."[42] "Politicians want to make everyone happy," explained one former leadership candidate, an instinct that extends even to their own colleagues. Recalled a lawmaker who won a number of contested leadership positions, "there's a lot of people who can't stand being in these positions—they hate conflict, they hate having to make choices."[43]

The dance that lawmakers follow to avoid hurting candidates' feelings without committing a falsehood underscores not only the scarcity of false vote commitments but also the onus put upon candidates to read their colleagues' true intentions accurately. As Udall remarked, "what one guy offers as a generality, another may accept as a specific," and "anything short of 'Yes, I'll vote for you' means they *aren't* going to vote for you" (King 1971). Effective candidates, explained one former lawmaker, must "look [colleagues] in the eye and get a visceral sense of whether they're telling you the truth or not."[44] In 1965, one Republican whip warned, "don't rely on what they tell you, whether they're for you or not. Listen to how he tells you."[45] Fifty years later, a Democratic leadership candidate noted in an interview that "you've got to really listen to the tone, the choice of words" that are used by lawmakers and take heed "if they're not taking your calls [or] they're not calling you back."[46] All of this suggests that the accuracy of a whip count may depend in part on how skillfully a candidate can count.[47]

The Plan of the Book

The remainder of the book is structured as follows. First, given the importance of candidate emergence in ultimately determining who becomes a party leader, we explore the nature and likely origins of ambition for leadership in chapter 2. We suggest some common factors that explain why individuals develop the nascent ambition to pursue a leadership office and why some of them express that ambition by actually running for office. We also discuss why some candidates drop out before an election, and why some seemingly hopeless candidates nonetheless campaign all the way to the finish.

The next four chapters test the mixed-motive model using a series of case studies of contested leadership races, divided into categories identified by Peabody (Peabody 1967, 1976). Each chapter opens with a detailed analysis of an especially noteworthy or significant race in a particular category of election, then proceeds to briefer studies of other races from the same category. For each contest we sketch the basic story of the race, from the emergence of candidates to the final outcome; underscore key candidate traits, campaign features, and contextual variables; identify lawmaker goals and professional relationships expected to influence vote choice, testing their influence using regression analysis; and highlight the election's subsequent significance for congressional (and, sometimes, national) politics.

Chapters 3 and 4 examine Peabody's first category of races, *open competition*, in which an incumbent leader is not running for reelection and there is no obvious successor below him. By far the most common type—74 of the 108 contested leadership elections between 1961 and 2016 were open competition races[48]—these are sometimes marked by intensely fought campaigns and the exacerbation of long-term intraparty rifts. Because of their frequency, we consider these cases in two separate chapters, dividing our analysis by party in order to consider whether each party's open competition elections were split along different dimensions during the period we examine: ideological and regional dimensions for Democrats, strategic or stylistic dimensions for Republicans (Brown and Peabody 1992; Connelly and Pitney 1994; Harris 2006; Lee 2016; Nelson 1977). Chapter 3 considers open races in the Democratic Party, featuring an extended analysis of the campaign for minority whip in 2001 between Nancy Pelosi and Steny Hoyer (D-MD) as well as examinations of Hale Boggs's victory in a five-way contest for majority leader in 1971[49] and Richard Gephardt's (D-MO) election as majority leader in 1989. The GOP's open races are the subject of chapter 4, starting with Newt Gingrich's fateful victory over Ed Madigan (R-IL) to be whip in 1989, then Bob Michel's successful run for minority leader in 1980, the race for Republican whip between Trent Lott (R-MS) and Bud Shuster (R-PA) that same year, and the 1994 race for Republican whip won by Tom DeLay (R-TX).

Chapter 5 is dedicated to *challenges to the heir apparent,* when, despite an established pattern of succession, a lawmaker wishing to ascend the so-called leadership ladder to a newly vacant position is challenged by another candidate. These types of races often occur when the heir apparent is politically vulnerable or a sizeable group of partisans support a rival on political or personal grounds. They include the four-way race for majority leader in 1976 that put Jim Wright in line to become Speaker, the 2006 race for Republican leader that brought future Speaker John Boehner back into the leadership, and the 2006 Democratic race for majority leader.

Chapter 6 considers intraparty *revolts:* races in which an incumbent is challenged in his bid to keep his leadership post. Though such races are uncommon and seldom successful, they often reveal important divisions within the congressional party and can be a harbinger of future changes to party leadership. Cases examined in this chapter include three Republicans who ran against Majority Leader

Dick Armey (R-TX) in 1998, Gerald Ford's (R-MI) successful challenge against minority leader Charlie Halleck (R-IN) in 1965, Morris Udall's effort to defeat incumbent Speaker John McCormack in 1969, and intraparty votes cast on the floor against John Boehner for Speaker of the House in 2013.

Finally, in chapter 7 we conclude with a review of our findings and their implications for understanding congressional politics and history. We also discuss alternative explanations of voting decisions in leadership races and touch upon the extent to which our model can explain vote choice in other legislatures, including the U.S. Senate.

In the autumn of 2015, it seemed that no one from the majority party—at least, no one viable—wanted to be Speaker of the House of Representatives. The incumbent Speaker, John Boehner (R-OH), announced on September 25 that he would step down from the position mid-Congress and retire from the House, following long-standing turmoil within the Republican Party. At first, Majority Leader Kevin McCarthy (R-CA) eyed the position, but after encountering significant resistance to his candidacy, he announced to a surprised GOP Conference and DC press corps that he was withdrawing from the race. Although there were other candidates, including Daniel Webster (R-FL) and Jason Chaffetz (R-UT), none were considered credible successors.

Speculation soon settled on Paul Ryan (R-WI), the young and charismatic conservative chairman of the Ways and Means Committee who had been his party's unsuccessful candidate for vice president in 2012. But Ryan insisted he would not run, perhaps because, as many observers noted, it would be "an enormous headache" to lead the restive and "quarrelsome" House GOP (Steinhauer 2015; Viebeck 2015). If Ryan seemed content to remain at Ways and Means, however, the Republican Conference was not content to let him. Boehner urged Ryan to run and had "other party leaders plead" with him as well (Herszenhorn and Huetteman 2015). Rather than Ryan seeking the position, the position seemed to be seeking him, making it what one GOP leadership aide called "the opposite of a leadership race."[1] Finally, after two weeks of intensive recruitment efforts and meetings between Ryan and key groups within the party, the Wisconsinite announced his intention to seek the post. Chaffetz quickly dropped out and endorsed Ryan, and on October 28—over a month following Boehner's declared departure—Ryan won a conference vote for the nomination, 200 to 43, over Daniel Webster. The next day, the full House elected him Speaker, albeit with nine Republicans casting ballots in favor of Webster (Costa and DeBonis 2015; Steinhauer and Huetteman 2015; Wong 2015).

Why did McCarthy throw his hat into the ring, only to withdraw it later? Why did speculation center on Ryan rather than any of the two-hundred-plus other Republicans in the House? Why did Chaffetz and Webster decide to run, despite the long odds against their election? These puzzles touch upon two broader questions of political ambition that occupy this chapter: what makes some lawmakers decide to run for leadership posts, and why some stay in a race until the end while others drop out. More generally, political ambition is foundational to the subject of vote choice in leadership elections because candidate emergence directly affects all three "C's" of leadership selection: the candidates, their campaigns, and the broader political context. Ambition shapes the candidate pool, which in turns makes a race a framed choice in which some professional relationships and member goals are likely to be more consequential than others in shaping vote choice. Understanding leadership selection thus requires at least some attention to the ambitions of would-be leaders and how those ambitions emerge.

Drawing upon interviews with current and former members of Congress and congressional staff, plus existing research on political ambition,[2] this chapter offers some tentative answers to the question of why certain lawmakers decide to be candidates for a party leadership post. Following the lead of political scientist Jennifer Lawless, we frame the discussion in terms of two kinds of ambition: nascent ambition, or the general "interest in seeking elective office," and expressive ambition, "the act of entering a specific race at a particular time" (Lawless 2012, 18–19).

Contemplating a Leadership Career: Nascent Ambition

One must have a great deal of political ambition to get to Congress. Once there, however, it seems that few legislators seriously contemplate formal party leadership careers, let alone decide to run for a leadership position.[3] What, then, makes a legislator contemplate running to be a leader in the first place?

For some, the answer defies easy generalization. Robert Peabody argued that what "winnows" the field of would-be candidates are "more or less intangible traits labeled 'leadership potential'" (Peabody 1976, 472). Former leadership candidates and staff whom we interviewed also cited imprecise personal qualities as determinants. One aide claimed that members who are more extroverted explore leadership possibilities more extensively than those who "keep to themselves."[4] Referring to a Republican member who reputedly was eyeing a leadership spot, he observed, "to see him on the floor, he's gregarious and backslapping." A former Democratic leadership staffer asserted in an interview that some legislators have "a leadership quality. They want to lead. . . . At every level of professional sports or whatever, some want to take the next step and lead."[5] Interviewees also noted how some individuals just seem to have a greater thirst for power. According to another leadership aide, "A lot of folks are content to be large fish in small ponds . . . They are royalty back in the district and for some that is perfectly fine." Others, by contrast, "have a different management style" and want to run things.[6] Arguing that "most politicians are inherently inclined to want . . . more power," one staff member cited the allure of "being on the big stage with proximity to the White House."[7] "The decision to run," said a former Republican lawmaker, "stems from whether or not you want to play a national role."[8] Influence, public prestige, and other benefits that come from serving in leadership—and which help encourage would-be managers of the institution to run for party leader (Mayhew 1974)—may be especially valued by certain lawmakers.

Beyond these general personal traits and motives—"leadership potential," extroversion, an inherent desire for more power or a higher profile—an important factor seems to be whether other aspects of the job of a representative, like helping constituents or enacting legislation, are sufficiently satisfying. As the same GOP legislator quoted above told us, "there are three kinds of members: constituency people, committee people, and floor people. . . . Floor-oriented people want to play a national role and they are the leadership people."[9] A leadership staffer speculated that "maybe one of the differences is wanting to work on shaping the broader agenda as opposed to digging down in the policy work of a committee. . . . You are more of a generalist [as leader]."[10] One erstwhile Democratic leader admitted that he found committee work "tedious": "I was getting bored to death sitting in those hearings and running from subcommittee [hearing] to subcommittee [hearing]." He preferred party leadership, he said, because "I'm more into making a decision . . . and doing the politics to make it happen."[11] Of course, someone unhappy in their career in the House may opt to leave the chamber altogether. A former party leader explained, for instance, that some members do not seek leadership positions due to their "external ambitions to run for governor or Senate," and that would-be leadership candidates face a choice between "external ambitions versus [if] you want to make a career in the House."[12] One does not preclude the other, however: House leaders such as Roy Blunt (R-MO), Trent Lott (R-MS), and Mike Pence (R-IN) later successfully sought other elected offices.

Nascent ambition can also be stoked by more senior colleagues. One study of leadership selection found that "the hand of past friendships" and a "system of mentor-protégé preferment . . . aided [protégés] in their quest for leadership in the House and provided often determinative advantages in securing their leadership posts" (Champagne et al. 2009, 14).[13] Many lawmakers in the House have been encouraged to run for elected posts by senior mentors, or appointed to lower-rung offices as a launching pad to pursue more prominent elected positions. Sam Rayburn (D-TX), for example, served as mentor to such future leadership candidates as Carl Albert (D-OK), Hale Boggs (D-LA), Jim Wright (D-TX), and Richard Bolling (D-MO). Democratic leader Richard Gephardt was himself a Bolling protégé, while Bob Michel (R-IL) promoted fellow Illinoisans Lynn Martin and Ed Madigan to leadership posts. This goes beyond mere recruitment: the protégé is someone who has a "quasi-filial relationship" with his or her mentor, taking the mentor's lead and gradually being introduced to the leadership sphere and the potentiality of joining it (Greenfield 2002, 45).

Certain career patterns and types of congressional districts seem to promote leadership aspirations as well. Members of Congress who achieve significant seniority by a relatively young age may be more likely to pursue legislative leadership posts (Peabody 1976, 11–15). Those from safer congressional districts may harbor aspirations for leadership because they have greater freedom to allocate time and attention to run for, and serve in, an elected leadership position, as well as conduct the time-consuming fundraising that allows them to distribute money to colleagues as part of a leadership campaign.[14] Many lawmakers and staff we interviewed noted this. According to a former party leader, to serve means that one must have a "willingness to work hard and have a broader interest than just getting re-elected. . . . For some, [re-election's] hard enough."[15] When asked about the disposition to seek a leadership office, an erstwhile Democratic leadership aide said, "They are obviously not doing it for their district. . . . For the most part, it's for the greater good of the Democratic Caucus."[16] One former Republican leader echoed this sentiment: "If you are a constituency person . . . [your job] eats up a lot of time," and playing a national role "makes you more controversial back home."[17] "Having a safe district that allows you to travel and raise money for the party is big," observed a GOP aide. "If you are not worried about your own reelection . . . you can more easily run for leadership."[18] That staffer recalled an instance that combined district safety with encouragement from a mentor and district predecessor: "Bill Thomas (D-CA) once told Kevin McCarthy that this is a leadership district. You're going to get reelected every time."[19]

Whether it creates or reflects nascent ambition, following certain paths of internal advancement is thought to promote a run for party leader. Appointments to key committees can help put one on a leadership path. For example, the Rules Committee is often a promising assignment because its members are selected by party leaders, and it is the only committee where lawmakers regularly come to testify on behalf of their bills and amendments, resulting in "exposure to a lot of other members," according to legislator who served on the committee.[20] Other committees with power and influence, like Appropriations and Ways and Means, may also be launching pads for a bid to run for leader.[21] Participation in extended party leadership organizations can also help promote one's chances of securing leadership posts (Meinke 2016). More generally, stringing together a career of advancing milestones and accomplishments provides credentials and momentum as colleagues come to take notice of one's achievements, temperament, and profile. In the words of one GOP leadership staff member, "People will get the reputation very quickly of being a workhorse, a showhorse, a whiner, or a team player. People will develop a certain profile . . . that might peg them on a leadership path. . . . [If, on a first assignment,] they play a good role and are cooperative and a team player, [they] might get another assignment and you go from there."[22] Recent high-profile successes might burnish a lawmaker's reputation with her colleagues and make them seriously consider her as a leadership candidate.

Lawmakers who follow a path of greater responsibility and higher profile might also be subject to recruitment by fellow party members, as was the case for Paul Ryan when the speakership became vacant.[23] Vic Fazio (D-CA) tells of state delegation colleagues imploring him to run for leadership when fellow Californian Tony Coelho stepped down as majority whip (Hook 1989c), for instance, and Charles Goodell (R-NY) and Robert Griffin (R-MI) drafted Gerald Ford to challenge Charles Hoeven (R-IA) and, later, Charlie Halleck (R-IN) in the 1960s (see chapter 6). Peer recruitment was also cited frequently in our elite interviews. One former Democratic leader noted, "About eight years in, I could see opportunities beginning to present themselves. People would say, 'If you ever run, I want to help you.'"[24] Another lawmaker recalled that he had assumed his vocation in the House would be committee-oriented, until the Speaker's chief of staff approached him and asked, "have you ever considered being on the Rules Committee?"—the first step in what would be a successful leadership career.[25] The corps of leadership aspirants, as one Republican leadership aide said, tends to be "members with a broad group of friends and interests—people who encourage them to run."[26] Sue Myrick (R-NC) later recalled that she ran for leadership "because other people encouraged me to do it," but regretfully noted, "that's the wrong reason to run. . . . You need to have a commitment on your own part to do it."[27]

Since nascent ambition is a necessary precondition for individuals to run for party leadership, it can have a major impact on the kinds of people who end up leading a congressional party. Historically, neither party in the House has had particularly diverse leadership teams. Women did not begin to appear in party leadership until the mid-1960s, and fewer than twenty of the nearly one hundred House members who have served in at least one elected party post between 1961 and 2016 have been women, most in lower-level positions. This is less the result of female candidates losing races than women choosing not to run at all: only thirty-five women have been candidates for competitive leadership contests in the House during that fifty-five-year time period.[28] Similarly, from 1961 through 2016, only eleven African-American members and even fewer Latinos have sought election to party leadership offices. Women and minorities have been historically underrepresented in Congress, reducing the number available to run for leadership, but the same factors that shape nascent ambition may have also discouraged those who are already in the House from running. For instance, mentor-protégé relationships tend to develop among colleagues with similar personal and political backgrounds, putting more junior lawmakers from smaller, nonmajority demographic categories at a disadvantage when the chamber's ranks of senior members and leaders are white-male-dominated. Minority lawmakers may thus feel discouraged from considering a run for leadership when denied the preferment given to others who fit the mold of past patterns of succession (Champagne et al. 2009; Rosenthal 2006).

In recent decades, however, the forces that drive nascent ambition have encouraged more minority lawmakers to consider entering leadership, especially as both parties perceive electoral advantages from diversity. When J. C. Watts (R-OK) was elected Conference chairman in 1998, ousting incumbent John Boehner (R-OH), Watts's colleagues saw collective political gain in advancing an African American to a high-profile leadership post (Watts 2003). Conference Vice Chair Susan Molinari's (R-NY) announcement that she would leave Congress led to speculation that as many as six different women could be elected to take her place as vice chair (Elving 1997). After Democratic women expressed disappointment that Rosa DeLauro (D-CT) lost her bid for caucus chair in 2000, Minority Leader Dick Gephardt (D-MO) appointed her to a newly created position, Assistant to the Leader. The race for Democratic Caucus vice chair in late 2016 saw, for the first time, a candidate pool consisting entirely of nonwhite women (Californians Linda Sánchez and Barbara Lee). Minority candidates themselves increasingly emphasize their background to appeal to these demands. In her campaign for Conference chair in 1997, for instance, Deborah Pryce's (R-OH) campaign talking points noted that she "is running for Conference Chair . . . as a woman (and moderate) who has the opportunity to break into the top tier of leadership."[29] It may be that, with the rise of women and minorities in party leadership in recent years, nonwhite, nonmale lawmakers have role models to further spur their nascent ambition.

In short, for members to pursue leadership careers they must first imagine themselves as potential leaders and/or believe that others see them as such. As with ambition for office in the broader political system, these crucial views of self result from a combination of personal inclinations for influence, "soft" factors of socialization that invite and spur ambition, and context, career paths, and recruitment that nurture and sustain it (Lawless 2012, 20–23). Importantly, this kind of nascent ambition for office might be harbored for years, awaiting a strategic opportunity or just good fortune, and ambitious lawmakers' underlying dispositions may well ebb and flow over time. Preparation is thus essential, since leadership vacancies can occur unexpectedly, with an incumbent leader making a surprise announcement that she will accept an appointment or seek election to another office or leave elective politics altogether.[30] As one former Democratic House leader put it, "If you are really ambitious to move on up, you can't do it from a standing start . . . you have to be thinking about it [for a long time], preparing for it."[31]

Running for Leadership: Expressive Ambition

However long a lawmaker has harbored leadership aspirations, it nevertheless still "takes the spark of opportunity to ignite the flame of congressional ambition" (Fowler and McClure 1989, 15). The nascent ambitions of individuals must find opportunities for expression: a vacancy, a vulnerable incumbent leader, or a leadership race with weak candidates. But when opportunities do present themselves, how do members calculate whether or not it is actually worth it to "jump in" and mount campaigns for legislative leadership positions?

The literature on ambition for public office identifies two key elements that go into a lawmaker's decision to run for office: the estimated chances of winning and the perceived opportunity costs associated with entering a race. The benefits of victory may be substantial: greater visibility and prestige, more political influence, and a launching pad from which to pursue higher office or a more lucrative career. Costs include time, effort, and other resources required to mount a credible campaign; the impact on one's reputation and relationships with peers by running and losing; and, if one already occupies a leadership office, surrendering that office to run for another one (Maisel and Stone 1997; see also Gaddie 2004).

There is good reason to believe the same cost-benefit analysis applies to lawmakers considering whether to pursue an elected party leadership post in the House of Representatives. Take, for instance, this account of Dan Rostenkowski's (D-IL) tentative, and ultimately abandoned, candidacy for the speakership after the 1984 elections, when incumbent Speaker Tip O'Neill announced his retirement: "Rostenkowski realized that a bid for speaker would require a grueling campaign with no guarantee of success. He could not count on a committee of bosses to declare him the most worthy contender, as had been the case decades ago in Chicago. . . . Might he have fought and won? Perhaps. Did he show a lack of political courage? Probably.

But he surely realized that a challenge to [the heir apparent, Jim] Wright would risk everything, including his Ways and Means chairmanship" (Cohen 1999, 156).

The power and influence of leadership positions are among the chief benefits at stake when one decides to run for a post. To be in party leadership means having a say in party policy and strategy, and those higher up in the leadership ladder can expect greater prominence and influence. Another benefit is the ability to provide broader collective and institutional goods. Reflecting on his failed bid to oust John McCormack, for instance, Morris Udall claimed that he ran to "breathe new life into" both his chamber and "the Democratic Party which may be on the decline if younger people of this country can't play more of a part in its leadership."[32] For others, those collective goods include stability, the prevention of change deemed premature or misguided, or the creation of greater representational diversity in their party's leadership.

Running for leadership is not without its costs, however. In addition to devoting time and effort to a campaign, one may risk losing another position of power in the House. For example, Jennifer Dunn (R-WA) surrendered her role as vice chair of the Republican Conference to challenge Dick Armey (R-TX) in 1998, and John Shadegg (R-AZ) gave up his chairmanship of the Republican Policy Committee in order to make a bid for majority leader in 2006. Both lost, leaving them out of leadership altogether (Green and Harris 2007; VandeHei 1998e). Another potential cost related to losing is being subject to retaliation by the victor and his devotees. Udall's 1969 challenge to John McCormack reportedly cost him the support of some senior Democrats in his 1971 race for majority leader, and McCormack himself aided Udall's principal rival, Hale Boggs (Peabody 1976; Maney 1998; and see also chapter 3). Even if it does not burn bridges, an embarrassing showing in a leadership race might weaken one's reputation within and outside Congress.

Given the considerable uncertainty in projecting election outcomes, there is no small amount of conjecture and guesswork involved in making these calculations. Further complicating this cost-benefit calculus is that the decision to run can expand or curtail subsequent opportunities to pursue leadership positions. At stake in leadership races is not only the position being contested but also the opportunity to join or climb a leadership ladder, the (often informal) hierarchy of party posts that can give lower-ranked leaders some advantage when running for higher-ranked positions (see chapter 1). A lawmaker with nascent ambition may campaign for a lower-level office, not because of the attractiveness of that office per se, but because she knows that being elected to it might make her a more formidable candidate for higher posts later. Still, even to put one's toe in the water reflects a choice with considerable consequences for one's congressional career. According to a former Democratic leader, "At some point early on you've got to figure out what path you want to take," either the committee route or the "structured leadership path."[33]

When making a cost-benefit calculation about whether to run for a given leadership position, strategic and ambitious lawmakers consider first and foremost whether the post is already occupied. Incumbents have many advantages—not least the benefits they have given other lawmakers in the past—making them difficult to remove. Running against an incumbent also risks incurring his wrath, those of his allies, and other rank-and-file legislators who fear tarnishing their party with a reputation for division and infighting. In addition, incumbents routinely try to dissuade would-be challengers. Speaker Tip O'Neill quelled multiple potential challenges during his tenure, for example (J. Farrell 2001), and when Minority Leader John Boehner worried that he might be challenged by Mike Pence (R-IN) in 2008, recalled a leadership aide, "there was a behind-the-scenes efforts to get him [Pence] a seat at the leadership table" to preclude such a move.[34] Minority Leader Nancy Pelosi undoubtedly had a potential challenge in mind when, shortly after the 2016 elections, she declared that two-thirds of the party supported her reelection (Caygle and Cheney 2016). Thus, unless the incumbent leader is "soiled by scandal, has lost touch with constituents, or narrowly won the previous election" (Gaddie and Bullock 2000, 7), most lawmakers with nascent ambition opt to wait for a leadership post to open up.

Unsurprisingly, the vast majority of competitive leadership races in the House have been for open seats.

An additional factor in the cost-benefit calculation is estimating who else is likely to run. If stronger candidates, or candidates with similar strengths, are likely to throw their hats in the ring, it may be a fruitless endeavor to do the same. Similarly, if there is an established pattern of succession, with someone lower on the leadership ladder seen as a natural heir to a departing incumbent, it may dissuade others from running. This is why some leadership offices are ultimately filled through routine advancement, "when a vacancy occurs in a top leadership position, a clear pattern of succession exists, and the next-ranking member in the party hierarchy is elevated without challenge" (Peabody 1976, 278).[35]

Lawmakers are not averse to manipulating the candidate pool by shaping the cost-benefit analyses of potential candidates. A would-be candidate might enter a race early in the hopes of discouraging strong rivals from doing the same, though that tactic comes with its own risks: it can convey an impression of excessive ambition and, if done before the incumbent leader officially steps down, be seen as a graceless, aggressive move that could cost the support of those loyal to that leader.[36] As one House Democrat put it, "it would be like dating a widow before the funeral" (Hook 1989c). A less overt approach is to seek out other possible rivals in advance and try to dissuade them from running. Robert Walker (R-PA) did this when eyeing the post of Republican whip in 1994 (see chapter 4), and when Dick Armey worried that either Bill McCollum or Gerald Solomon (R-NY) might, like him, run for GOP leader in 1994, his staff advised Armey to call these men "quickly" and "ask for their support. If you find out they are not running against you, you can use this in your other calls to colleagues. If they are thinking about running, you can talk them out of it, pointing out that you already have significant support lined up, etc."[37]

Sometimes a top party leader tries to influence the calculation of would-be candidates for other offices through recruitment or other means. For example, incoming Speaker Tom Foley (D-WA) made it easier for David Bonior to run against Bill Gray for whip in 1989 by confirming that "he would reappoint him [Bonior] for chief deputy whip" if Bonior lost the whip's race (Brown and Peabody 1992, 371). Bob Michel (R-IL), hoping to keep Newt Gingrich from becoming whip, not only supported Ed Madigan's run for the post but also urged Jerry Lewis (R-CA) not to be a candidate, in part to consolidate the anti-Gingrich vote. Five years later, Michel encouraged Robert Walker to run for whip against Tom DeLay (R-TX) and Bill McCollum (R-FL) because Walker was an "institutionalist" who would provide regional diversity in a southern-dominated leadership.[38]

To sum up, members with ambitions to enter or move up the ranks of party leadership might have to harbor those ambitions until the time is right—typically, but not necessarily, when a vacancy occurs. Members are more likely to feel constraints against expressing ambition when an heir is present or a stronger candidate has declared her candidacy already, but may also take steps to preclude a serious challenger from emerging. Party leaders themselves can also try to persuade or dissuade ambitious colleagues from seeking a particular post.

Quixotic Candidates

Though it is reasonable to assume that most lawmakers will approach the calculation of costs and benefits rationally, candidates for leadership posts periodically emerge who seemingly have no chance of winning. And they usually lose. Some examples: in 1971, John Conyers (D-MI) ran against Carl Albert for the party's nomination for Speaker, and lost, 220–20; he ran again two years later, and gained just five more votes; Harold Ford (D-TN) won a mere 29 votes in his race against Nancy Pelosi for Democratic leader in 2002; and Daniel Webster was badly beaten in his challenge against Paul Ryan to be his party's nominee for Speaker in 2015. Assuming these individuals were fully aware that their odds of victory were near zero, what motivated them to nonetheless make a long-shot bid for office?

Though it may seem irrational, there are logical reasons for quixotic candidates to emerge. Perhaps the single biggest reason is to bring attention to a cause, a group of colleagues, or the candidate himself. By throwing one's hat in the ring, an improbable candidate can gain media attention, which he or she may then leverage to achieve future ambitions in the chamber or outside of it. Dennis Hastert was a last-minute candidate against Dick Armey for majority leader in 1998 and came in last place, but his entry may have helped him—intentionally or not—to convince Republicans that he should be their next Speaker (see chapter 6). When Harold Ford declared his candidacy for Democratic leader against Nancy Pelosi in 2002, he did so on a talk radio show and, four years later, ran (albeit unsuccessfully) for the U.S. Senate (York 2002). Candidates can also use a longshot leadership bid to draw a spotlight on their particular subgroup in the party (be it ethnic, geographic, gender, or other), and there may be particular issues at stake too. For example, Conyers, an African American, ran in 1971 "to protest the way in which the challenge to the seating of the Mississippi delegation was being frustrated" by southern white Democrats (Peabody 1976, 208).

Quixotic candidates occasionally emerge who claim that they oppose a fait accompli, and if only one person is running for a leadership post, they feel compelled to do so too. This was reportedly the logic behind Richard Bolling's brief run against Carl Albert to be Democratic leader in 1961 (Bolling 1965a), and one reason Morris Udall challenged John McCormack as the Democratic nominee for Speaker seven years later (see chapter 6). Rarely, however, do these legislators hold a belief in competition for its own sake; more often they are driven by strong political or personal objections to the individual being anointed. When Heath Shuler (D-NC) opted to challenge Nancy Pelosi as party leader in 2010, it came in the wake of devastating seat losses for the party, particularly among southerners and moderates. Angry that, in his words, "the far edges [are] running the Congress," Shuler mounted no organized campaign but still picked up 43 votes in caucus against Pelosi's 150 (Robertson 2010). Six years later, another Democrat, Tim Ryan (D-OH), challenged

Pelosi—what one lawmaker called "kind of a sacrificial, suicidal mission"—because, while he claimed that "I love Nancy Pelosi . . . I personally don't believe we can win the House back with the current leadership" (Cottle 2016; Lillis 2016).

The Other Side of Ambition: Dropping Out

Sometimes a candidate with nascent ambition decides to enter a leadership race, only to withdraw before the election. This too likely reflects a cost-benefit calculation, based on one of two key changes. The first, and less common, is that the member is presented with another, better and/or more certain opportunity. Dan Rostenkowski's decision to turn down his party's whip post in 1980 in favor of a Ways and Means chairmanship is one example of this. Another occurred in 1986, when Martin Sabo (D-MN) abandoned his bid to be the party's first elected whip after he received a sought-after appointment to an Appropriations subcommittee (Hook and Towell 1986, 973). Later, Bob Livingston (R-LA) dropped out of the 1994 Conference chairman race when it became clear that he would "leapfrog over three more senior Republicans on the Appropriations Committee to become acting chairman" (Camia 1994a).

The second and more prevalent reason that a candidate withdraws from a leadership race is that he concludes he lacks the votes to be elected. When Richard Bolling abandoned his campaign for majority leader in 1962, he acknowledged that "developments of the last few days have convinced me that I don't have a chance to win'" (Polsby 1962 [1992], 272). Similarly, Albert Rains (D-AL) ended his challenge against John McCormack, who sought to become Speaker upon Rayburn's death in 1961, once McCormack announced he had the votes to be chosen (Nelson 2017).[39] Having sought votes to be caucus chair against Dick Gephardt in 1984, David Obey (D-WI) withdrew, after realizing that "he could not win because it was shaping up, in his words, as a 'personality contest'" (Granat 1984). In the wake of the disappointing 1998 midterm elections, Newt Gingrich sought reelection as Speaker and canvassed votes right up until the moment that he realized he almost certainly would lose. Dennis Hastert recalled, "it was a personal humiliation for him, but the fact is he stepped down when he found he didn't have the votes" (Hastert 2004, 161).[40] No doubt this consideration was behind Jason Chaffetz's withdrawal from the race for Speaker in 2015 when Paul Ryan decided to run.

Weak candidates who drop out are less intriguing than those whose chances dim over time but nonetheless stay in the running. Writing about the 1971 race for Democratic leader, for instance, Robert Peabody observed that a candidate who remains in a race despite long odds must worry about "'unnecessary' costs he may inflict upon his supporters. . . . Should the candidate subject his supporters to the wrath of the potential winner and his aides if his own cause is clearly lost?" (Peabody 1976, 198). Apart from the reasons given above for why quixotic candidates enter in the first place, serious candidates who realize they are bound to lose may find it difficult to admit defeat. There is also the ever-present element of uncertainty inherent in any cost-benefit calculation, so the chance of victory—however remote—may be enough to keep underdogs fighting through election day. In his long-shot campaign against John McCormack for Speaker, Udall reportedly gambled that he could still win votes even as he remained well behind in vote commitments (Carson and Johnson 2001; see also chapter 6).

Conclusion

Ambition is key to leadership selection. Who contemplates a leadership career, who gets into a race for leader, and who drops out all contribute to the choices that members face when choosing their leadership. Candidates must nurture their careers in ways that prepare them for opportunities. Such nascent ambition usually turns into expressive ambition when would-be candidates make a cost-benefit analysis that indicates their odds of victory in a winnable opportunity (usually an open seat) are worth the risks. Taken together, all of this individual-level ambition—nascent and expressive—shapes the House's "leadership class" and helps us understand the choices that members face in leadership campaigns. Ultimately, it determines who among all of its members leads the House, as well as the degree of stability and conflict that exists within both political parties.

The most common type of leadership race in the House of Representatives is the open competition race: when two or more candidates run for a vacant position and none of them occupies a leadership post considered the "natural" stepping stone to the position (Peabody 1976). The prevalence of such races, and the fact that they are especially likely to attract multiple candidates, makes intuitive sense, given the risks involved in challenging incumbents or those who can make a strong claim, based on tradition or party norms, to an open leadership position. Since a campaign for leadership entails a number of potential costs, as noted in the previous chapter, most ambitious lawmakers will wait for the most ideal circumstance: a vacancy with no heir apparent.

These races are the focus of this chapter and the next. We begin by examining open competition races in the House Democratic Party. Though we contend that the mixed-motive model applies to both parties' leadership elections, looking at just House Democrats allows us to document and test the significance of an important long-standing division within the party, between its conservative, often southern wing and its liberal, usually nonsouthern wing. This divide often framed the House Democrats' open leadership competitions and is generally believed to have influenced some Democrats' vote choice in leadership elections (Champagne et al. 2009). We begin with a detailed focus on one of the longest campaigns for leadership in the modern House: the 1998–2001 race for Democratic whip between Nancy Pelosi (D-CA) and Steny Hoyer (D-MD), which would put the winner in a prime position to later become Speaker of the House. We then discuss two additional open races, for majority leader in 1971 and majority leader in 1989. For all three, we use statistical analysis to test our claim that both professional connections and salient goals shape lawmakers' vote choice in leadership elections.

The Long Campaign: The 1998–2001 Race for Minority Whip

In July 1998, Nancy Pelosi made a fateful choice that would lead to a lengthy, but ultimately fruitful, campaign to join her party's leadership. Reminiscent of Dick Armey's (R-TX) precocious bid for majority leader in 1994 while his party was still in the minority, Pelosi campaigned for a post that might become available if Democrats took control of the chamber. In that scenario, she reckoned, Minority Leader Dick Gephardt (D-MO) would become Speaker and Minority Whip David Bonior (D-MI) would become majority leader, creating a vacancy for majority whip. It was an optimistic, but not unreasonable, assumption: though House Democrats had been out of power since 1994, they had gained a few seats in 1996 and were less than a dozen shy of a majority. However, she would have to settle for minority whip when her party came up short in the next two congressional elections and Bonior announced in 2001 that he would leave the chamber to run for governor of Michigan. The race for that post, which pitted Pelosi against Steny Hoyer (D-MD) and, for a time, John Lewis (D-GA), was a titanic battle that eventually led to Pelosi's election as the first woman floor leader and then Speaker of the House.

The Candidates

According to one study of Pelosi, "ambition . . . was in her bloodlines and character" (Peters and Rosenthal 2010, 43). The daughter of a former congressman and mayor of Baltimore, Pelosi had been active in party politics before her election to Congress in 1987. But her desire to run for party leadership had been kindled by peer recruitment: "My colleagues have been coming to me over the years saying I should run," she said in one interview. Pelosi hesitated as long as the leadership team included another Californian, Caucus Chair Vic Fazio, but when Fazio announced in 1998 that he would retire from Congress, her state was without representation in the top leadership. As Pelosi put it, "people looked around and said I had no excuse" (*The Hill* 2000). Rather than run for a lower-ranked post or challenge an incumbent leader, she let her intimates know in July that she was mounting a bid for party whip, informing her likely rival, Hoyer, the following month (Bresnahan and VandeHei 1998; Peters and Rosenthal 2010). With the large California delegation behind her and backing from the Appropriations Committee on which she served, along with her fundraising prowess and liberal credentials, Pelosi was a formidable candidate.[1]

Hoyer, her principal opponent, was formidable too. His experience in legislative leadership dated back to the mid-1970s, when he served as the youngest-ever president of the Maryland State Senate. In 1989 he was selected vice chair of the Democratic Caucus, then won a contested election for Caucus chair just six months later, serving in that position until 1994. Though not a part of elected leadership after that, he served as a chief recruiter for the Democratic Congressional Campaign Committee (DCCC) and chairman of the Steering and Policy Committee, which made decisions about committee assignments. He was also the top Democrat on the House Administration Committee, responsible for providing office benefits and other perks to colleagues. He had resisted entreaties of moderate Democrats to challenge Bonior for whip—Bonior had beaten him for the post when it was vacant in mid-1991—but he kept his eye on the position should it become open (VandeHei 1998a). Pelosi's surprise bid thus threatened Hoyer's hope to get back into elective leadership.

The third Democrat to run for the post, Chief Deputy Whip John Lewis, was first elected to the House in 1986. Lewis had tremendous prestige as an icon of the civil rights movement and was a long-time member of the sizeable Congressional Black Caucus (CBC), suggesting he could draw upon important reservoirs of support in a leadership race. In addition, Lewis offered the caucus an opportunity to elevate the first African American to a top leadership position since Bill Gray (D-PA) had stepped down as whip in 1991. As one of four chief deputy whips, Lewis could claim valuable and relevant experience, and he reportedly had long had his eye on moving up the leadership ladder. But while his rivals were securing voting commitments,

Lewis had "real reservations" about entering the race too soon and admitted he was not going to campaign "every waking moment" (Wallison 1999a, 1999b). His relative lack of eagerness gave Pelosi and Hoyer a chance to win vote commitments from minority lawmakers who might have otherwise voted for Lewis, and the Georgian was soon seen as the weakest of the three candidates (Rice 1999a; VandeHei 1998a).

Pelosi and Hoyer shared some similarities—both were about the same age, and both began their careers as staffers working together in the office of Senator Daniel Brewster (D-MD)—but the differences between them were more noteworthy. First, unlike Hoyer, Pelosi could appeal to Democrats wanting to make history by selecting a woman for a major leadership post. Second, Pelosi was relatively liberal, whereas Hoyer portrayed himself as bringing ideological balance to the leadership team and serving as a pipeline for more moderate and conservative lawmakers, such as Blue Dogs Democrats and members of the New Democrat Coalition.[2] Arguably, a third difference was that Pelosi was more of an insurgent-type candidate, having never been an elected party leader, whereas Hoyer had extensive leadership experience. However, this last difference was somewhat less clearcut, since Pelosi had worked in party organizations before (including a stint as chair of the California Democratic Party) and had helped connect elected Democrats to financial backers, such that many owed Pelosi for help she had provided them over the years (Montgomery and Eilperin 2000; Peters and Rosenthal 2010; Wallison 2000a).

The Campaign

On August 13, Pelosi sent Democratic colleagues a letter soliciting votes and made no apologies for starting a campaign for a position that did not yet exist. "Those who snooze lose," she declared. Hoyer hurriedly met with supporters and lamented Pelosi's abrupt move but admitted that, if he wanted to be whip, he needed to join the battle. Lewis also acknowledged that he "could not afford to stand on the sidelines" while Pelosi was accumulating commitments (Carr

2000). All the candidates established organizations to help garner votes and made a public case for their respective candidacies. Pelosi scored an early and surprising coup when Pennsylvania's conservative senior appropriator John Murtha (D-PA) did not endorse Hoyer, as some thought he might, and instead agreed to run Pelosi's campaign. Hoyer's allies pressed the case that Pelosi's liberalism and image would put members from swing districts in electoral danger, though at one point Hoyer admitted that "if this race is about gender and geography, then I'm going to lose" (Montgomery and Eilperin 2000; Peters and Rosenthal 2010; Rice 1999b; Wallison 1998, 1999a).

In addition to its extended length, the race for Democratic whip was unusual for the high number of public commitments made by lawmakers. Pelosi secured the open endorsements of prominent committee heavyweights, including Murtha, Sam Gejdenson (D-CT), George Miller (D-CA), Joe Moakley (D-MA), David Obey (D-WI), and Henry Waxman (D-CA). While she could not get the open support of Marylanders, she did secure the endorsement of neighboring DC delegate Eleanor Holmes Norton. Hoyer, meanwhile, managed to garner the backing of John Dingell (D-MI), the powerful chairman of the Energy and Commerce Committee, and won the public commitment of Ellen Tauscher (D-CA), who represented the eastern suburbs of Pelosi's home city of San Francisco (Montgomery and Eilperin 2000; Pianin 2000; Wallison 2000a, 2000b).

All three candidates had formed leadership political action committees (LPACs) to dispense campaign funds to other members of Congress, and they actively campaigned for Democrats in the 1998 elections—and, as the race continued, the 2000 elections. Pelosi proved the better fundraiser. In the 2000 election cycle, for instance, she raised $1.3 million, while Hoyer raised less than $1 million for Democratic candidates. Lewis was also an important fundraiser and a sought-out stump speaker for colleagues around the country, but the scale of his efforts was far smaller than that of his competitors. In fact, Lewis's tepid interest in the race at the start, his comparatively low-key campaign, and his anemic fundraising did not escape his colleagues' notice. In October 1999, more than a year after the race had started, he felt compelled to write a letter insisting that "I am in it and in it to win" (*Roll Call* 1999). Nonetheless, his natural base of fellow African Americans was being eroded by his opponents. Two Maryland members of the CBC, Elijah Cummings and Al Wynn, came out in favor of Hoyer, and Pelosi was able to secure a public commitment from Lewis's fellow Georgian and CBC member Cynthia McKinney (D-GA) (Carr 2000; Clymer 2001; Pianin 2000; Rothstein 1999).

The campaign stretched through the rest of the 105th Congress and into the next, after the party failed to win a majority in the House in November 1998 and neither Bonior nor Gephardt left their leadership positions. (A fourth potential candidate, Caucus Chair Martin Frost (D-TX), considered entering the race in 1999, but declined on the grounds that, if he won, it would result in another competitive election for his vacated post [Wallison 1999a].) Pelosi and Hoyer regularly dueled in the press, offering competing claims of high vote counts and advertising new public endorsements.

By April 2000, insiders saw the race as essentially down to Pelosi and Hoyer, with Pelosi having a slender lead in the vote count. The dual nature of the competition was confirmed in July when John Lewis, whose devotion to the interminable race had been flagging, dropped out, having "concluded that the votes are simply not there for me" (Eversley 2000). At first, it appeared this would benefit Hoyer, whom Lewis pledged to vote for after Hoyer promised to give women and minority members of the caucus prominent committee positions. Yet Pelosi claimed that she had enough second ballot commitments from many of Lewis's supporters to win. Hoyer dismissed her claim: "Every time I get somebody endorsing me," he said, "she says she's won." And both candidates continued to campaign. When lawmakers gathered in Los Angeles for the Democratic National Convention, Pelosi put together a "tech tour" of Silicon Valley technology companies for congressional candidates, while Hoyer chartered a bus to transport lawmakers to the convention (*Contra Costa Times* 2000; Eilperin 2002; Shaffrey 2000a; *The Hill* 2000; Wallison 2000c, 2000d, 2000e).

The Democratic Party was unable to capture control of the House in the 2000 elections, and Gephardt announced that he would stay on as leader. Pelosi and Hoyer faced a decision of whether or not to continue the campaign, now entering its third year, for a nonexistent vacancy in leadership. Claiming that she had the votes to win and that an opening in the whip job would occur "sooner or later," Pelosi resolutely determined to keep running (Wallison 2000f). Hoyer held a conference call with his allies, who encouraged him to continue but "take on a more 'visible' role for the Democrats." A couple of his colleagues suggested he seek the position of DCCC chair instead, to burnish his credentials and raise more money for fellow Democrats, but Hoyer opted to continue campaigning for whip (Foerstel 2000; Wallison 2000f).

Finally, in May 2001, David Bonior announced that he would leave the House to pursue the Michigan governorship. Hoyer and Pelosi were no longer campaigning for a hypothetical post, and the race took on renewed urgency. Said one undecided Democrat, "I feel like I'm in the middle of a beehive when I go to the floor, between Pelosi's people and Hoyer's people" (Foerstel 2001). Though Bonior was coy at first about when he might abdicate the whip position—leading Pelosi backers, believing they were ahead in the vote, to urge he retire sooner rather than later—he finally set a date for departure, and the election to replace him was scheduled for early autumn (Eilperin 2001a, 2001b; Wallison 2001a).

Throughout the summer and early fall of 2001, Pelosi and Hoyer offered dueling counts and tried to recruit any remaining undecided Democrats. Observers believed that Pelosi led Hoyer in commitments, and she did gain ground by winning over a number of freshmen. Hoyer made a fundraising trip in August for the CBC, but discovered that most members he talked to had made up their minds whom to vote for. In an ominous sign, he heard a repeated refrain from colleagues—male as well as female—that the party needed a fresh face in leadership, especially a woman (Cassidy 2001a; Eilperin 2001b, 2002).

Pelosi topped a hundred public commitments by early September and claimed "another 20 quiet supporters," though Hoyer refused to give up and reached out to over forty colleagues in a single day. The pair also did not hesitate to leverage contacts outside the House to pressure their uncommitted colleagues. Pelosi relied on lobbying by California venture capitalists and members of the United Farm Workers; Cal Dooley (D-CA), for instance, was urged by the prominent vintner Ernest Gallo to stand with his fellow Californian. In response, Hoyer asked erstwhile party leaders, including some lobbyists, to reach out to the rank-and-file on his behalf (Eilperin 2001b, 2002).

The terrorist attacks of September 11, 2001 delayed the vote for whip until the second week of October. After briefly suspending their campaigns, Hoyer and Pelosi made final efforts to shore up and reaffirm commitments and try to persuade the tiny pool of undecided Democrats. Pelosi surrogate Tom Udall (D-NM) attempted to sway ambivalent legislators with the argument that Pelosi had momentum, while Hoyer booster Ben Cardin (D-MD), who complained that Pelosi was trying "to convince people to go with a winner," insisted that "we have will have enough [votes] to win" (Cohen 2001). Then, a week before the election—in what was perhaps the biggest endorsement of the race—Bonior announced his support for Pelosi. She now was just a handful of public commitments shy of a majority. Hoyer could claim only seventy-seven endorsements, but he insisted that he had enough private commitments from Democrats to bring his total to over a hundred. Campaigning to the very end, he gave instructions to his campaign team for election day and faxed a final pitch to legislators the Friday before the election (Cassidy 2001b; Cohen 2001; Eilperin 2001c).

To ensure vote commitments were kept, Pelosi and Hoyer organized teams of allies to monitor lawmakers' ballots and dissuade defectors. Some Democrats even pledged to show their completed ballots to their favored candidate, ostensibly to avoid any accusation of double-crossing them. Perhaps fearing Pelosi would be more aggressive at this tactic, or that she would punish those who voted against her, Hoyer's supporters successfully lobbied the party to establish separate places for picking up and depositing ballots and to provide secluded spots for people to privately write down their selection. "There is no question," said one Hoyer staffer, "that Hoyer benefits from a secret ballot" (Cassidy 2001b; Wallison 2001b).

Finally, the day of the election arrived: October 10, 2001, over three years after the campaign had begun. Pelosi gathered her supporters together at a breakfast meeting, and her aides made early morning phone calls to lawmakers who had pledged to her, offering to transport them to the Capitol to ensure they did not miss the vote. John Murtha delivered the nominating speech for Pelosi, while Hoyer spoke on his own behalf and, to demonstrate breadth of support, recruited Dingell, John Lewis, and conservative Texan Charles Stenholm to give seconding speeches (Eilperin 2001c, 2001d, 2002; Wallison 2001b). When the votes were tallied, the conventional wisdom was proven correct. Pelosi had bested Hoyer, 118 to 95.

Not only was the race of epic length, but it had significant long-term consequences, producing bad blood between the Pelosi and Hoyer camps that would endure for many congresses. Fifteen years later, one Democratic leadership aide remarked that "those tensions always lingered. They were always there and will never go away."[3] Recalled a former Democratic congressman who had retired not long before the election, "I was glad not to be in the middle of my two friends."[4] The fault line created by the election reemerged periodically, pitting Hoyer and Pelosi supporters against each other in future races for leadership posts and committee chairmanships, most notably in an unexpected 2006 challenge to Hoyer by Murtha for the position of majority leader (see chapter 5). The election was also consequential because it put the winner on a flight path toward the speakership. Pelosi easily won the position of minority leader in November 2002 against Harold Ford (D-TN) after Dick Gephardt opted to retire and pursue a second presidential bid. Four years later, Democrats won a majority in the House, and Pelosi became the first Democratic Speaker in a dozen years and the first woman Speaker in American history. She would go on to lead the House on a number of high-profile initiatives, most notably the passage of the landmark Affordable Care Act in the 111th Congress (2009–10).

Explaining Vote Choice

To test what factors influenced the vote choice of lawmakers in the election for whip, we use probit regression for the 134 Democrats whose public preferences we could identify.[5] We test the professional connection hypothesis by looking at the effect on vote choice of serving in Maryland or California and whether a lawmaker who served with Pelosi on the Intelligence Committee was more likely to vote for her. (We do not expect membership on Appropriations to have an effect, since both Pelosi and Hoyer served on that committee, and we cannot test for membership on the House Administration Committee because none of its committee Democrats, apart from Hoyer, publicly committed to either candidate.) Several goals were also salient in the race. Both candidates gave large sums to lawmakers, suggesting their attention to electoral goals, so we test the effect of receiving funding from either candidate in the 2000 election cycle. The race was widely framed as liberals versus moderates, and Pelosi was ideologically somewhat further to the left than Hoyer, so we test the influence of ideology with the DW-NOMINATE scores of individual lawmakers, a commonly-used measurement of revealed legislator preferences. In terms of influence goals, since gender was an obvious difference between the candidates, and an important campaign theme was that women lacked representation in leadership (and that the party brand would be improved with a high-profile woman in leadership), we include legislator gender as an explanatory variable. Finally, we control for lawmakers' electoral security, age, seniority, and service as chair or leader, though we do not expect these to matter, as none were salient in the race or markedly differentiated the two candidates.

The results of the probit model are shown in table 3.1. Model 1 uses just the professional connection variables, since, as noted in chapter 1, their effect may wash out when other variables are included, while Model 2 includes the full set of explanatory variables.

The results comport well with the mixed-motive model. Note first that professional connections are an important explanation of how lawmakers voted. The California variable is statistically significant in explaining a vote for Pelosi, and the Maryland variable must be excluded because of complete separation by the dependent variable (see chapter 1), strongly suggesting that representation of Hoyer's state was an important determinant of vote choice. Service on Pelosi's Intelligence Committee is also positively associated with support for Pelosi in Model 2, though the coefficient is just shy of statistical significance (p = 0.103).[6] As predicted, members of the Appropriations Committee, their allegiances torn between Pelosi and Hoyer, were no more likely to commit to one over the other. Electoral and policy goals also determined vote choice. Campaign contributions from each candidate proved statistically significant, and lawmakers with larger (i.e. more conservative) DW-NOMINATE scores were less likely to support Pelosi, as expected. Gender was unexpectedly insignificant as a predictor of the vote, but so too were all of the variables not predicted to matter.[7]

The last column of table 3.1 shows the substantive effect of each coefficient, using an observed-value, discrete differences method wherein the average probability of voting for Pelosi is calculated before and after increasing each independent variable from 0 to 1 (for dichotomous variables) or by one standard deviation (for continuous variables) (Hanmer and Ozan 2013). The effect of professional connections was substantively quite significant: Democrats from California were 40 percent more likely to vote for Pelosi than those who were not, and legislators on the Intelligence Committee were 34 percent more likely to do so. Ideological differences had a substantial effect, with a one standard deviation increase in DW-NOMINATE score (i.e., becoming a more conservative Democrat) reducing the probability of voting for Pelosi by 17 percent. Electoral concerns were substantively significant too. A one standard deviation increase in Pelosi donations (equivalent to a $4,400 increase in contributions) improved the average probability of a Pelosi vote by 15 percent, and a one standard deviation increase in Hoyer donations (about $3,900

Table 3.1. Analysis of Estimated Vote for Pelosi as Minority Whip (2001)

Hypothesis	Independent Variable	Model 1	Model 2	Change in Probability (Model 2)
Professional Connection	From California	1.72*** (0.46)	1.98*** (0.42)	.56, .96 [+.40]
	On Intelligence	0.00 (0.75)	2.14 (1.32)	.62, .96 [+.34]
Goal Salience	$ from Pelosi (logged)	—	0.08* (0.04)	.63, .78 [+.15]
	$ from Hoyer (logged)	—	−0.06^ (0.03)	.63, .51 [−.13]
	DW-NOMINATE (1st dimension)	—	−4.37*** (1.18)	.63, .46 [−.17]
	Female	—	0.05 (0.36)	.63, .64 [+.01]
Other Variables	On Appropriations	−0.10 (0.33)	0.08 (0.44)	.63, .65 [+.02]
	% 2-party vote (logged)	—	0.12 (1.04)	.63, .64 [+.01]

	Model 1	Model 2	
In leadership	—	0.11	.63, .66
		(0.73)	[+.03]
Committee ranking member	—	−0.32	.64, .56
		(0.52)	[−.08]
Term	—	−0.04	.63, .59
		(0.05)	[−.04]
Age	—	0.02	.63, .68
		(0.02)	[+.05]
Constant	0.12	−2.43**	
	(0.14)	(0.91)	
N	130	128	
Log L	−73.34	−57.78	
McFadden's R^2	0.14	0.31	
PRE	0.0%	34.0%	

Note: Table entries for each model are probit coefficients with robust standard errors in parentheses. The final column shows the average predicted probabilities of supporting Pelosi when each variable in Model 2 is changed from 0 to 1 (for dichotomous variables) or increased by one standard deviation (for continuous variables) with the difference in brackets.

^ $p < .1$; * $p < .05$; ** $p < .01$; *** $p < .001$ (2-tailed test).

more) reduced it by 13 percent. The effect of contributions is further underscored by how they correspond to the vote choice of freshmen Democrats, most of whom received contributions from both Pelosi and Hoyer and had few, if any, other ties to the candidates. Nine received larger contributions from Pelosi, and seven of those nine endorsed her; only two received more from Hoyer, and both went with the Marylander.[8]

Immediately after the election, Hoyer told a reporter that "gender and geography in this case were overwhelming. C'est la guerre" (Hosler 2001). An analysis of the evidence provides only partial support for Hoyer's claim. All else being equal, California's large size was a major boon to Pelosi, but her gender was less so, at least among fellow women in the House. What mattered more was Pelosi's ability to bring liberal Democrats (and possibly Intelligence Committee colleagues) to her camp, Hoyer's inability to unite the Appropriations Committee behind him, and Pelosi's more generous and widespread distribution of campaign contributions. In short, Pelosi successfully leveraged key connections and salient lawmaker objectives to win over her colleagues.

A Five-Way Contest: The 1970–71 Race for Majority Leader

The journalist John Farrell rightly described the campaign for majority leader in 1970–71 as "one of the great contested leadership races of the Democratic Party's forty-year reign of the House" (J. Farrell 2001, 277–78). A major event in the public sphere at the time, it was the first seriously competitive race in the party in over thirty years (Mayhew 2000, *Washington Post* 1971). Unlike the Pelosi-Hoyer contest, in which southerners and moderates were few in number, the 1971 race for majority leader took place when liberals, though ascendant, were struggling for power against a powerful and sizeable southern conservative contingent.[9]

The race began in May 1970 when then-Speaker John McCormack (D-MA) announced his retirement from Congress at the end of the year, and Majority Leader Carl Albert (D-OK) declared that he would run for Speaker. The end of McCormack's more than three-decades-long leadership career, and Albert's almost-certain elevation to the speakership, created a long-awaited opening for ambitious Democrats seeking entrée into the party leadership, and according to one reporter, "a half-dozen or more possible candidates . . . immediately started taking soundings to assess their political support" for majority leader (N. Miller 1970a). The stakes were high, not only because the winner would be heir apparent to the Speaker, but because, as one lawmaker bluntly put it, "Carl's weak" and "anyone who has his ear last can influence him" (N. Miller 1970a, 1970b).

At least ten Democrats with nascent ambition were considered possible contenders for the post; five would eventually throw their hats in the ring.[10] Morris Udall (D-AZ), a liberal lawmaker who had had his eye on party leadership since not long after his first election to the House and who had lost a challenge against McCormack in 1969, was the first to declare his candidacy, on the very day that McCormack announced his retirement (Carson and Johnson 2001; Peabody 1976; see also chapter 6). Udall's ambitions were matched by those of Majority Whip Hale Boggs (D-LA), the most senior candidate in the race (entering his fourteenth term) and a protégé of Speaker Sam Rayburn (D-TX). As early as the 1940s, Boggs "left no doubts that he aspired to a position of leadership," and by 1955 "it was generally acknowledged . . . that Boggs had ambitions to one day become Speaker of the House" (Maney 1998, 225; Kirn 1980, 41; King 1971).[11] A southerner who was more moderate than Udall,[12] Boggs was formidable in a party in which conservatives still held sway and a third of its members were from former confederate states.

If Udall and Boggs had long-range ambitions for leadership, the remaining three contenders were more hesitant. James O'Hara (D-MI), also a liberal member of the caucus, was less a part of the House's social scene and, by one account, was an "ambivalent" candidate who "could not quite persuade himself to drop out" (Peabody 1976, 166). The twelfth-term Ohioan Wayne Hays, a member of the influential House Administration Committee, was an acerbic right-leaning Democrat[13] who decided to run because he was "unimpressed" with the field and proclaimed that no one wanted to vote for Boggs or for "Udall and his bunch of clowns" (King 1971; Peabody 1976, 167). Another conservative member of the caucus who decided to run, B. F. "Bernie" Sisk (D-CA), was starting his ninth term in the chamber; he would enter the race belatedly when the candidacy of fellow Californian John Moss failed to materialize (N. Miller 1970a; Peabody 1976).

Each candidate possessed important assets and liabilities. O'Hara and Udall were potentially looking to the same pool of Democrats for support: both were reformers, members of the liberal Democratic Study Group (DSG), the most junior of the five (Udall was forty-eight years of age and starting his sixth term, O'Hara forty-five and beginning his seventh), and appealing to "those who were liberal, black, young, or otherwise disaffected" (Hunter 1970b; Weaver 1970).[14] O'Hara, known as an intelligent and dogged legislator, had one advantage over Udall: better relations with organized labor, and especially the powerful AFL-CIO, which had "never forgiven Mr. Udall for supporting 'right to work' legislation" in the mid-1960s (J. Farrell 2001, 280; Hunter 1970d). Generally speaking, Udall was considered somewhat less liberal than O'Hara,[15] whose outspoken advocacy on issues like civil rights, labor, and education jibed with the views of left-leaning Democrats but were off-putting to the party's conservative southerners. On the other hand, Udall's early criticism of the Vietnam War made him potentially more attractive to strong opponents of the war.[16] O'Hara also "rub[bed] some of his colleagues the wrong way in personal dealings," and he himself admitted that "if they decide it on charisma, I'm afraid I won't make it." Udall, by contrast, was funny, friendly, and a polished public speaker (Hunter 1970b; King 1971; N. Miller 1970b; Peabody 1976, 164–66).[17]

Boggs potentially had strong allies on which to build a majority coalition, including fellow senior lawmakers, other leaders, and the party's large bloc of southerners. In addition, as whip he could claim that he was the "natural" successor to the post, though such a norm of succession was not yet clearly established.[18] Boggs had policy expertise, could be forceful and well-spoken, and was a high-ranking member of the Ways and Means Committee, which was responsible for tax and trade legislation and, at the time, committee assignments as well. The Louisianan also possessed some progressive, reformist bona fides. He had been one of the strongest southern defenders of the Kennedy and Johnson administrations, pushed for the expansion of the Rules Committee in 1961 to help pass liberal legislation, advocated greater accountability for committee chairmen, and had given a bold, unexpected floor speech on behalf of the Voting Rights Act in 1965. But Boggs was still seen by liberals as too close to conservative party leaders, and he often came across as arrogant and distant. Even worse, in the late 1960s his demeanor began to change, and he started demonstrating "erratic and sometimes haughty behavior," including odd, sometimes indecipherable public speeches (Hunter 1970b; King 1971; Maney 1998; N. Miller 1970b; Peabody 1976).[19]

Wayne Hays commanded a position of power as next in line to chair the House Administration Committee, which controlled the disbursement of parking spaces and other treasured resources. He could make a plausible play for southerners and other like-minded Democrats, but he gave people little reason to vote for him other than to block Boggs and Udall, and few thought he had much of a chance of winning. Worse, as Tip O'Neill (D-MA) recalled, Hays "had a mean streak and was often abusive to people he didn't agree with" (N. Miller 1970b; *New Republic* 1970; O'Neill 1987, 257; Peabody 1976).

Sisk, the fifth candidate, had some useful assets. He came from the sizeable California delegation, most of whose members quickly endorsed him, and the Texas-born lawmaker had close connections to many Democratic southerners, some of whom had persuaded him to run in the first place.[20] As a member of the Rules Committee, Sisk had been well placed to help lawmakers secure desired amendments or block unwanted legislation, and he even had some reform credentials as the successful advocate for a major congressional reorganization bill. Over time, however, Sisk had shifted further to the right ideologically, and he gave liberals pause after voting against some civil rights bills.[21] He was also less charismatic and more unassuming than other candidates, and his late entry—two weeks following the November election—put him behind his rivals in securing commitments (Hunter 1970d; King 1971; N. Miller 1970b; *New Republic* 1970; Peabody 1976; *Washington Post* 1970).

Each candidate pursued his own campaign strategies and tactics. Udall was a conscientious student of past leadership races and kept on good terms with older colleagues, provided campaign help to first-time congressional candidates, and offered to give more junior lawmakers greater influence if elected.[22] His campaign operation included at least ten Democrats who helped with lobbying and tallying commitments. Udall tried to win over the sizeable, "organization-oriented" delegations of Illinois, Massachusetts, New York, and Pennsylvania by reaching out to influential legislators from those states, such as Eddie Boland (D-MA) and Hugh Carey (D-NY).[23] Near the end of the campaign, he lobbied over ninety Democrats he identified as either uncommitted or potentially persuadable.[24] Udall's efforts to reach out beyond his base of younger, progressive, reform-minded colleagues yielded little fruit, however. He was too liberal for most southerners, while senior Democrats thought he was jumping the queue by running for a major leadership post while lacking seniority and were deeply dismayed by his prior challenge against McCormack.[25] Udall was also tainted by the reputation of his more outspoken supporters, whom Boggs aide Gary Hymel described as "fifteen or twenty of the most anti-establishmentarian and antagonistic members running full steam ahead." As Sisk noted, "a number of the members like Udall personally, but they're afraid of his people" (Hunter 1970c; King 1971; N. Miller 1970a; Peabody 1976, 179).

Boggs had begun quietly gaining commitments well before his official declaration of candidacy in early December. He focused first on influential senior colleagues and, in response to resistance from some southerners who preferred Sisk as the more reliable conservative candidate, argued that ballots cast for the Californian would divide the anti-Udall vote. At the same time, Boggs did not hesitate to point out to northern Democrats that his record was relatively liberal and that he had been attentive to the needs of northern urban areas.

He also reached an informal arrangement with Dan Rostenkowski (D-IL) to secure his help with Illinoisans in exchange for appointing Rostenkowski whip, and he may have gained the backing of Hugh Carey by supporting his bid to be the next Caucus chairman.[26] To shore up his diminished reputation, Boggs resurrected his tradition of entertaining lawmakers at garden parties, and he became a more frequent public advocate of Democratic Party policy and a critic of President Nixon. With the blessing of Speaker McCormack, who was lobbying against Udall, he presided over the House during major floor debates to heighten his profile (Evans and Novak 1970a; Hunter 1971a; J. Farrell 2001, 281; King 1971; N. Miller 1970b; O'Neill 1987, 147; Peabody 1976).[27]

The other three candidates campaigned less vigorously. O'Hara's operation remained low-key until near the end of the race, by which time Udall had garnered commitments from many of the party's younger, reform-oriented lawmakers. O'Hara petitioned his state delegation and colleagues from the Education and Labor Committee, but he relied heavily on labor lobbyists to help him win votes and did not bother seeking pledges from the party's southern bloc. His allies also began quietly negotiating with Udall's campaign team to give their second-round ballot votes to Udall (and vice versa) to ensure a reformer was elected.[28] Hays, meanwhile, hosted luncheons for potential supporters, but said, "I'm not asking commitments from any members," and he later admitted that "I didn't put on much of a campaign. I felt pretty relaxed about it. I knew I'd end up majority leader or Chairman of House Administration—either way I couldn't lose."[29] As for Sisk, he was hampered by his belated candidacy and lack of broad appeal in the caucus (Beckler 1970; N. C. Miller 1970b; Peabody 1976).

Some candidates followed tactics and strategies common to leadership races. Udall and Boggs offered campaign help to first-time candidates, and they, along with O'Hara, reached out to freshmen after the election. While Udall was wary of bringing too much external pressure on colleagues, fearing it would backfire, Boggs and O'Hara had no qualms about securing endorsements and lobbying help from interest groups.[30] Boggs sought out the support of the AFL-CIO and other unions and asked lobbyists from sympathetic industries to advocate for him, while he and Udall tried to score endorsements from newspaper columnists and garner positive news stories.[31] "Bandwagon propaganda," as Udall termed it, was also evident.[32] In September, Boggs insisted that the race was "all sewed up" in his favor, while Udall urged his supporters to participate in a *Congressional Quarterly* survey so that the Arizonan would appear to be ahead. By the eve of the election, the total number of commitments claimed publicly by each candidate totaled up to more Democrats than were serving in the House (Hunter 1970c; King 1971; Maney 1998; Peabody 1976; *Washington Post* 1971).

There were a few key developments over the course of the campaign. The biggest was Sisk's late entry, which initially meant Boggs needed to canvass harder for southern support, even if it risked making him look too conservative to party moderates and liberals. Udall received a valuable late pledge from Eddie Boland (D-MA), an influential northeastern progressive, to help with his campaign,[33] while Boggs won the aid of O'Neill, another popular Massachusetts Democrat, to nail down additional votes (Clancy and Elder 1980; Evans and Novak 1970b; J. Farrell 2001, 284; O'Neill 1987, 259–260; Peabody 1976, 184–85). Any hopes that Sisk might have had of backing from liberals dimmed when the left-leaning group Americans for Democratic Action (ADA) distributed a document highlighting his quiet opposition to progressive legislation, including civil rights.[34] Sisk's campaign was further wounded when supporter Glenn Anderson (D-CA) accidentally sent to all Democrats—including antilabor southerners—a memo emphasizing Sisk's prounion positions. Another mistake proved damaging to Udall: when one of his allies brandished a whip sheet at a press conference, a reporter caught a glimpse of some names on the sheet and called one of them, Frank Brasco (D-NY), who had made his commitment privately, leading an infuriated Brasco to rescind his support.[35] As rumors swirled of latecomers jumping into the race, all five candidates agreed in late December that no last-minute entrants would be permitted.[36] Finally, on the eve of the election, Hays reached a secret deal with Boggs to throw their votes to the other should one of their candidacies falter (Evans and Novak 1970c; Graham 1970; King 1971; Peabody 1976; Shannon 1971).

Democrats gathered to select their next majority leader on January 19, 1971. After the nominating and seconding speeches were delivered, lawmakers cast their votes in the first round of balloting. The result: Boggs had 95 votes, followed by Udall with 69, Sisk with 31, Hays with 28, and O'Hara 25. Though caucus rules allowed all the candidates to stay in for the next round of voting, Hays dropped out, seemingly satisfied that he had not come in last place,[37] and he urged his supporters to vote for Boggs. O'Hara also withdrew but, to Udall's dismay, did not endorse him. Given the vote totals, Udall nevertheless realized that it would not make a difference. Sure enough, on the next ballot, Boggs won with 140 votes, an absolute majority, while Udall received 88 and Sisk's vote total dropped to 17. Visibly disappointed House reformers departed the House floor, while Udall, in typical self-deprecating wit, took the "Mo" button he was wearing and turned it upside down to read "Ow." As in his quixotic 1969 race for Speaker, Udall had, in the words of journalist Larry L. King, "been guilty of soft counts and wishful thinking," sometimes mistaking kindness for a vote commitment (King 1971; see chapter 6). On one occasion, he had told O'Hara that Sonny Montgomery (D-MS) would "vote for me" because "he continues to be open and friendly," to which O'Hara replied sarcastically that James Whitten (D-MS), another conservative from Mississippi, "said 'Hello' to me in the corridor today" (Hunter 1971b; King 1971; Peabody 1976).

Though the liberal reformist wing of the party had lost this particular battle, the election underscored its growing influence. Udall had garnered more votes than in his race for Speaker two years before, and two of Boggs's colleagues who gave endorsement speeches touted the Louisianan's liberal positions on civil rights and energy policy (Kraft 1971). The election also had a significant impact on the future composition of congressional leadership. After Udall failed to convince Albert to make the whip position elected, and Albert refused

Boggs's request to appoint Rostenkowski to the post,[38] the whip job was given to Tip O'Neill (Jacobs 1995). Less than two years later, Boggs's plane disappeared during a campaign trip in Alaska; O'Neill replaced him as majority leader and, in 1976, became Speaker—one of the more influential liberal Speakers of the modern House.

We test our mixed-motive model of vote choice with data drawn primarily from Udall's postelection analysis, which gives vote totals that are fairly close to the final outcome.[39] The first round of the election is tested with multinomial logit regression, which allows us to estimate the effects of multiple explanatory variables when there are more than two possible values of the dependent variable (in this case, three or more candidates running for office). Multinomial logit, it should be noted, cannot determine the coefficients of variables that correlate nearly perfectly with vote choice without generating unreliable standard errors, meaning those variables must be dropped. It also assumes that legislators who chose one candidate would be equally likely to support any of the other candidates, known as the Independence of Irrelevant Alternatives (IIA) assumption. A test of this assumption suggests that O'Hara voters were not ambivalent about their remaining choices—which makes sense, if we assume they preferred another liberal, reformist candidate—so the results of the analysis for the first round of voting should be treated with caution.

Since the model predicts that professional connections will be significant, we include variables measuring whether a lawmaker shared the same state as a candidate (except for Udall, since he was the party's only Arizonan); was on the same committee as Boggs, Sisk, and Hays; or served on the Post Office Committee (on which Udall served). (Since both O'Hara and Udall were members of the Interior Committee, we do not expect membership on that committee to be statistically significant in explaining support for either.) Several goals were also likely salient. Because the candidates and campaigns differed along ideological lines, we include a measure of left-right ideology (first-dimension DW-NOMINATE scores), with the expectation that more liberal Democrats would vote for Udall or O'Hara and more conservative lawmakers would favor their opponents.[40] We also include a proximate measure of lawmakers' attitudes towards civil rights—whether they had voted against the Voting Rights Act of 1965—which the campaigns tried to make salient for Sisk (whose reputation was less pro-civil rights) and Boggs and O'Hara (who supported expanding civil rights protections). In addition, we include measures of whether a lawmaker served as a committee chair or leader, as well as their age and terms in office, since a major theme of the race was the division between younger reformers (including Udall and O'Hara) and more senior establishment Democrats (Peabody 1976; Reston 1970).[41] We also control for electoral security (as measured by two-party vote received in 1970), though it was not salient in the race. Also included is a control for membership in the large northern delegations heavily lobbied by Udall and Boggs (Illinois, Massachusetts, New York, and Pennsylvania). However, we do not expect that variable to be statistically significant, because it is unclear that either candidate successfully won those delegations (and their individual efforts may have canceled each other out).

Table 3.2 shows the results of the regression analysis for the first round of balloting. Each coefficient must be interpreted relative to the base outcome, which in this case is a vote for Boggs. It reveals that both professional connections and salient goals were statistically significant in explaining vote choice. Lawmakers were positively associated with a vote for their "home" candidate compared to Boggs, with the exception of O'Hara's fellow Michiganders (who were nonetheless negatively associated with support for Udall, Sisk, or Hays over Boggs). The substantive effect of home state on the relative probability of supporting each candidate (not shown) was also sizeable: Sisk was 54 percent more likely to be supported by Californians relative to Boggs, while Hays was 47 percent more likely to receive votes from Ohioans relative to Boggs. Multinomial logit was unable to estimate coefficients for a variable measuring Louisiana delegation membership, but all Louisianans voted for Boggs, suggesting that it was an important professional connection for the candidate. Interestingly, committee assignment is a less clear explanation of vote choice: though Boggs's colleagues were positively associated with a

Table 3.2. Analysis of Estimated Vote for Majority Leader, 1st Ballot (1971)

Hypothesis	Independent Variable	Udall	Sisk	Hays	O'Hara
Professional Connection	From California	0.34 (0.95)	5.83*** (1.52)	−14.82*** (1.03)	−0.69 (1.07)
	From Ohio	−1.13 (1.05)	−13.33*** (1.22)	2.86* (1.15)	−17.47*** (0.81)
	From Michigan	−19.60*** (1.17)	−16.98*** (1.29)	−18.11*** (1.30)	2.17 (1.59)
	On Boggs committee	−0.23 (0.85)	−0.39 (0.91)	−15.24*** (0.86)	1.03 (0.85)
	On Udall committee	0.99 (1.23)	−12.99*** (1.24)	0.16 (1.45)	−0.90 (1.32)
	On Sisk committee	−1.16 (0.85)	−17.38*** (1.26)	−1.53 (0.97)	0.35 (1.18)
	On Hays committee	0.16 (0.67)	1.95* (0.93)	2.11** (0.69)	−0.03 (0.83)
Goal Salience	DW-NOMINATE (1st dimension)	−2.49^ (1.48)	7.32* (2.82)	2.48 (1.74)	−10.24*** (2.66)
	Anti–civil rights	0.37 (0.77)	−0.47 (1.21)	0.36 (0.84)	−12.77*** (1.31)

In leadership	−16.38***	0.41	−15.19***	−16.36***
	(0.75)	(0.94)	(1.22)	(0.80)
Committee chair	−0.33	−1.05	0.77	1.16
	(1.26)	(1.65)	(0.87)	(1.44)
Terms	−0.15*	0.13	−0.13^	−0.08
	(0.06)	(0.13)	(0.08)	(0.11)
Age	−0.00	0.05	0.03	−0.00
	(0.02)	(0.05)	(0.03)	(0.03)
Other Variables On Interior	1.17	0.27	1.80	−15.31***
	(0.85)	(1.00)	(1.12)	(0.86)
% 2-party vote (Logged)	−1.97*	0.56	−0.33	−2.54
	(0.96)	(1.63)	(1.18)	(1.55)
Large northern state	−0.26	0.17	1.09	−1.20
	(0.53)	(1.20)	(0.70)	(0.76)
Constant	−0.48	−4.51^	−2.56^	−5.00*
	(1.11)	(2.34)	(1.33)	(2.18)
N			223	
Log L			−224.11	
McFadden's R²			0.30	
PRE			21.2%	

Note: Table entries are multinomial logit coefficients (compared to the base outcome, a vote for Boggs) with robust standard errors in parentheses.

^ p < .1; * p < .05; ** p < .01; *** p < .001 (2-tailed test).

vote for him over Hays, and Hays's committee colleagues appear to have preferred Hays over Boggs (by a relative increase in probability of 20 percent), members of a Hays committee were also positively related to a vote for Sisk versus Boggs. Also, Democrats from the Post Office Committee were no more likely to support fellow committee member Udall than Boggs (though they were negatively associated with a vote for Sisk over Boggs), and Sisk's committee colleagues were actually associated positively with a vote for Boggs compared to him.[42] In terms of policy-related goals, more left-leaning lawmakers (who had smaller scores) were positively associated with support for liberal candidates Udall and O'Hara over Boggs as predicted, while more conservative Democrats appear to have preferred Sisk over Boggs.[43] Civil rights also proved statistically significant in explaining support for O'Hara versus Boggs, suggesting that O'Hara was able to make the case that he, not Boggs, was the stronger advocate for civil rights protections.[44] Finally, salient influence goals help explain vote choice: serving in party leadership is negatively associated with a vote for Udall, Hays, or O'Hara compared to Boggs (by a relative decrease in probability of 31 percent, 11 percent, and 11 percent, respectively), and seniority is negatively associated with a vote for Udall or Hays compared to Boggs and is at least moderately statistically significant.[45] Other variables prove statistically insignificant, with two exceptions: electorally safer Democrats were positively associated with a vote for Boggs over Udall, and Interior Committee members were negatively associated with a vote for O'Hara over Boggs.

To determine what factors influenced the second round of voting, we employed probit regression using Udall's estimate of how fellow Democrats cast their ballots in that round. Because Udall identified very few votes for Sisk, we considered only lawmakers who voted for either Boggs or Udall on the second ballot; the dependent variable is coded as 1 if a Democrat is estimated to have voted for Boggs. The results, shown in table 3.3, also support the mixed-motive model, albeit less so than for the first round of voting. Service on Udall's committee is weakly significant and negatively associated with a vote for Boggs in Model 1, which includes only professional connection variables, but neither the Louisiana delegation nor the Boggs committee variables are statistically significant in that model or the second (full) model. In Model 2, we find that more conservative and senior lawmakers preferred Boggs, as expected; a one standard deviation increase in DW-NOMINATE score (from the 59th to 81st percentile in conservatism) increases the mean probability of voting for Boggs by 11 percent, and doing the same for terms in office (an increase of about 4.5 terms) increases the probability by 13 percent. Also, the leadership variable must be excluded because all leaders voted for Boggs, a sign that influence goals were important (though committee chairs were no more or less likely to support Boggs). Support for civil rights is not a statistically significant factor, but we would not expect it to be, since both Udall and Boggs had the same position on the issue.[46]

Our analyses of both rounds of voting show that professional connections and salient goals were important influences on Democrats' votes in the election for majority leader. They also suggest what led to Udall's loss: not only was he from a state delegation too small to serve as a base for votes, but he could not get the ballots of party leaders or more conservative Democrats—a fatal weakness when conservatives constituted a strong presence within the party.[47] More generally, professional connections and salient goals were important influences on Democrats' votes in the election for majority leader.

Opportunity amid Turmoil: The 1989 Race for Majority Leader

House Democrats were in a state of tumult in mid-1989. Speaker Jim Wright (D-TX) was under an ethics cloud and facing increasing pressure to resign, setting off speculation about a successor (Barry 1989; Harris 2014). If Wright did leave, Majority Leader Tom Foley (D-WA) was expected to take his place without opposition, leaving Foley's position vacant. That potential vacancy caught the interest of two Democrats, Ed Jenkins (D-GA) and Majority Whip Tony Coelho (D-CA). Then Coelho, confronting questions about a potentially unethical financial deal, abruptly announced that he would resign from Congress, and Wright did the same four days later.

Table 3.3. Analysis of Estimated Vote for Boggs as
Majority Leader, 2nd Ballot (1971)

Hypothesis	Independent Variable	Model 1	Model 2	Change in Probability (Model 2)
Professional	From Louisiana	0.28	−0.65	.61, .40
Connection		(0.51)	(0.68)	[−.21]
	On Boggs	0.56	0.44	.60, .73
	committee	(0.46)	(0.48)	[+.13]
	On Udall	−0.51^	−0.36	.62, .50
	committee	(0.29)	(0.32)	[−.12]
Goal	DW-NOMINATE	—	1.78**	.60, .71
Salience	(1st dimension)		(0.62)	[+.11]
	Committee chair	—	−0.22	.60, .53
			(0.51)	[−.07]
	Terms	—	0.10**	.60, .73
			(0.03)	[+.13]
	Age	—	0.00	.60, .61
			(0.01)	[+.01]
Other	% 2-party vote	—	0.65	.60, .65
Variables	(logged)		(0.52)	[+.04]
	Large northern	—	0.03	.61, .60
	state		(0.24)	[−.01]
	Anti–civil rights	—	0.10	.60, .63
			(0.43)	[+.03]
	Constant	0.28**	0.29	
		(0.10)	(0.60)	
	N	201	201	
	Log L	−132.33	−112.93	
	McFadden's R²	.02	.16	
	PRE	5.0%	26.3%	

Note: Table entries for each model are probit coefficients with robust standard errors in parentheses. The final column shows the average predicted probabilities of supporting Boggs when each variable in Model 2 is changed from 0 to 1 (for dichotomous variables) or increased by one standard deviation (for continuous variables) with the difference in brackets.
^ significant at p < .1; * significant at p < .05; ** significant at p < .01; *** significant at p < .001 (2-tailed test).

It was against this backdrop that an open competition for majority leader quickly emerged, pitting Jenkins against former Democratic Caucus Chair Dick Gephardt (D-MO).[48] Both Gephardt and Jenkins were serving their seventh term in the House and were members of the influential Ways and Means Committee. But there were also differences between the two. Gephardt had been tapped early in his career as a rising star, in part because he was a protégé of Richard Bolling, the perennial leadership aspirant who had gotten him an early appointment to Ways and Means (Brown and Peabody 1992). Elected to the Caucus chairmanship without opposition in 1984 and serving until 1988, Gephardt had more experience in party leadership than Jenkins and had developed a much higher public profile as a candidate for the Democratic nomination for president in 1988. Gephardt wanted "a way to get back in leadership" but, at the same time, was resisting "heavy pressure" from colleagues to challenge Coelho, the incumbent whip (Kenworthy 1989b, 1989c). With Coelho's departure, Gephardt had the opening he was waiting for.

Jenkins lacked Gephardt's experience and exposure, but he was a well-regarded establishment candidate and had "repeatedly . . . been mentioned as a possible leadership candidate in the past." Moreover, being from the Deep South, Jenkins had a plausible advantage among those subscribing to the long-standing tradition of having at least one southerner on the Democratic leadership team (Hook 1989c; see also Champagne et al. 2009). Jenkins was also more conservative than Gephardt,[49] though it was unclear how helpful that would be in an increasingly left-leaning party.

Though Gephardt had been reluctant to challenge Coelho, he appears to have anticipated the opportunity to run for a leadership post and the need to preclude others from getting a head start in campaigning. Gephardt's staff—including seasoned campaign staffer Tom O'Donnell, originally hired to help plan another presidential run—began sketching out a campaign plan, which included recruiting colleagues to whip for votes and send letters to other Democrats "to show momentum," coding lawmakers by the strength of their support or opposition, and doing "a continious [sic] check on absences, rumors, etc."[50] Gephardt had also established an LPAC and been giving campaign donations to other legislators in the previous Congress.

As soon as he decided to run for leader, Gephardt, along with O'Donnell and other aides, managed to contact nearly two hundred colleagues in just a few days. His campaign sought to demonstrate that the Missourian was the best to lead a relatively diverse party, distributing favorable letters from a variety of lawmakers and sending talking points with words to that effect to House allies and, in the words of one staffer, "our downtown friends."[51] In case his past ambitions were seen as a liability, Gephardt promised that he would not run for president in 1992 (Brown and Peabody 1992).

In contrast to Gephardt, Jenkins focused his attention on courting ideological and regional allies. He repeatedly cited the fact that one-third of the Democratic Caucus was from the South and that their voices should be represented in leadership. For example, in a letter to southern members he emphasized his Georgian roots, a track record of "dedication to keep America strong militarily, economically, socially, and morally," and his commitment to "traditional values," and he warned that "if the party leadership is not broadened to include all of us, we shall disappear from the House and the Democratic Party shall become the minority party."[52] Jenkins also enjoyed the support of Dan Rostenkowski, the powerful chairman of Ways and Means, though it is unclear whether Rostenkowski's opposition to Gephardt—in part personal and in part because Gephardt was less deferential to committees than he wished—was shared by other chairmen (Cohen 1999).[53] Jenkins's principal tactics included making individual visits with lawmakers, participating in meetings with small subsets of Democrats, and asking colleagues to circulate so-called "theme letters."[54] Some letters would be sent to select groups of sympathetic lawmakers, including fellow committee members, "Conservatives/Southerners," and colleagues who, like Jenkins, had voted to fund the Nicaraguan Contras fighting a guerilla war against the communist government of that country. Others, like Rostenkowski and members of the Georgia delegation, were asked to send letters to key committees, lawmakers, and state delegations.[55]

Though the need for ideological and regional balance in leadership was the core theme of Jenkins's campaign, it was unclear how well this claim would work with Gephardt as his opponent. Gephardt, along with Foley and (future) whip Bill Gray, was well known within the Caucus as a figure who could negotiate with competing groups to build legislative coalitions. The Missourian was considered less combatively partisan than outgoing Speaker Wright and Whip Coelho, making him less threatening to conservatives (Eaton 1989). Moreover, southerners and right-leaning lawmakers were increasingly outnumbered in the caucus, a fact Jenkins himself acknowledged by insisting that a southerner needed to be chosen and not taking such a selection for granted. It also meant Jenkins's candidacy was greeted with suspicion by the more progressive elements of the party. On one occasion, Jenkins felt compelled to write to Don Edwards (D-CA) after Edwards mistakenly told his California delegation colleagues that Jenkins had voted against a civil rights bill the year before.[56]

Both candidates employed other common campaign tactics, including donating to peers, leveraging help from outsiders, and employing a public media strategy. Though neither candidate had given campaign funds to more than a handful of caucus members since the 1988 elections, Jenkins, like Gephardt, had been fairly generous in donating to other incumbents—perhaps anticipating a future vacancy in leadership—and he hoped that past contributions could serve as an additional incentive for lawmakers to vote for him.[57] To counter Gephardt's advantages in media politics, Jenkins sought out a DC-based media consultant to help him polish his public persona, and he reached out to reporters from major networks and newspapers, noting that "when talking to reporter, you are talking to colleagues."[58] The Jenkins campaign also recruited supporters in Georgia to ask veterans groups in D.C. to talk up Jenkins's candidacy with other House Democrats, and it urged Coca-Cola's lobbying office to touch base with nine members of the California delegation on Jenkins' behalf.[59]

The election did not turn out to be especially close. Jenkins did receive a nomination speech from liberal Democrat and civil rights leader John Lewis, a gesture that suggested Jenkins had broader appeal within the caucus.[60] Nonetheless, it was not enough to save him, and he lost to Gephardt in a lopsided, 181–76 victory. For the first time in decades, the South was left without any top leadership posts in the House Democratic Party. The election would also be an important victory for Gephardt. He served as majority leader until 1994, when he became minority leader after Foley's stunning reelection defeat, part of the electoral wave that brought Republicans control of the chamber for the first time in forty years. Gephardt stayed on the front lines in Congress's increasingly partisan environment in the years that followed, but Democrats remained the minority party throughout his tenure, and he decided to leave the House in 2002 to make one more (failed) presidential run. As for Jenkins, he remained a representative until retiring in 1992. Though he had lost the majority leader race, his candidacy represented a high-water mark: Jenkins was one of the last white southern Democrats to run for a contested leadership post in the House, and he won more votes in the election than any Democratic southerner has since, apart from Martin Frost (D-TX), who was elected Caucus chair in 1998.

Can the mixed-motive model shed light on the question of why some Democrats supported Gephardt, while others voted for Jenkins? We test the model's two central hypotheses—that professional connections and salient goals influence vote choice—using probit regression, with vote estimates derived from three whip tallies kept by Gephardt and one gathered by Jenkins.[61] If correct, professional connections forged by a shared state, and by Jenkins via his assignment to the Budget Committee, should help explain some Democrats' votes. Yet because both candidates served on Ways and Means, we expect that members of that committee split their allegiance between them. Jenkins was not only more conservative than Gephardt, but policy preferences were a notable theme of the race, so we include a measure of ideology (via DW-NOMINATE scores), even though Gephardt tried to negate that difference by emphasizing his

coalition-building skills.[62] We also expect southerners to dispropor-
tionally oppose Gephardt, given that southern representation was a
core theme of Jenkins's campaign. Neither electoral goals nor other
influence-related objectives are expected to be significant, but since
both candidates were unusually generous with campaign contributions in the previous electoral cycle, we do test for the effect of donations from that cycle (plus whatever money they had donated by
early 1989).

The results, shown in table 3.4, lend only limited support to the
mixed-motive model. Model 1, which tests the effect of the professional connection variables alone, reveals that the Budget Committee
variable, while having a substantive effect (increasing the probability
of voting for Jenkins by 14 percent), is not statistically significant,
contrary to expectation. However, the state delegation variables must
be dropped because all Georgians supported Jenkins and all Missou-
rians voted for Gephardt, a strong indication that delegation influenced vote choice. In terms of goals, contributions from Jenkins are
not statistically significant, but those from Gephardt must be omitted
because they are perfectly separated by the dependent variable, suggesting they did matter for his candidacy.[63] The southern representation variable is unexpectedly insignificant,[64] and while the ideology
variable is statistically significant, its coefficient is positive, meaning
conservatives were more, not less, likely to support Gephardt (by
11 percent, with a shift from the 50th to 82nd percentile in ideological
conservatism). This may signify that Gephardt, as a border state representative widely regarded as an inclusive leader, was able to counter
Jenkins's presumed ideological advantages. Finally, term and age are
statistically significant, contrary to expectation, though that finding
is not entirely robust.[65]

Conclusion

Open competition races for leadership posts present an opportunity to uncover the choices for leader that party members make
when unconstrained by incumbency or patterns of succession. When

Table 3.4. Analysis of Estimated Vote for Gephardt as Majority Leader (1989)

Hypothesis	Independent Variable	Model 1	Model 2	Change in Probability (Model 2)
Professional	On Budget	0.43	0.43	.59, .73
Connection	Committee	(0.32)	(0.32)	[+.14]
Goal	$ from Jenkins	—	−0.01	.60, .60
Salience	(logged)		(0.03)	[−.01]
	DW-NOMINATE	—	2.15**	.60, .72
	(1st dimension)		(0.57)	[+.11]
	From South	—	0.23	.58, .66
			(0.22)	[+.08]
Other	On Ways and	0.06	0.01	.60, .61
Variables	Means Committee	(0.30)	(0.30)	[+.00]
	% 2-party vote	—	−0.12	.60, .60
	(logged)		(0.43)	[−.01]
	In leadership	—	0.34	.60, .71
			(0.53)	[+.11]
	Committee chair	—	−0.01	.60, .60
			(0.32)	[−.00]
	Term	—	0.06^	.60, .68
			(0.03)	[+.08]
	Age	—	−0.03*	.60, .50
			(0.01)	[−.10]
	Constant	0.19	1.81**	
		(0.08)	(0.64)	
	N	263	253	
	Log L	−177.08	−155.94	
	McFadden's R²	.01	.08	
	PRE	0.0%	12.0%	

Note: Table entries for each model are probit coefficients with robust standard errors in parentheses. The final column shows the average predicted probabilities of supporting Gephardt when each variable in Model 2 is changed from 0 to 1 (for dichotomous variables) or increased by one standard deviation (for continuous variables) with the difference in brackets.

^ significant at p < .1; * significant at p < .05; ** significant at p < .01; *** significant at p < .001 (2-tailed test).

considered in historical sequence, the three races examined in this chapter highlight how the House Democratic Party transitioned from a period of solid conservative internal influence (i.e., Udall and O'Hara failing to defeat Boggs, the more moderate establishment candidate, for majority leader in 1971) to liberal dominance (with Pelosi beating Hoyer for minority whip in 2001). This is seen not only in the nature of the campaigns in each race but also in statistical analyses of vote choice, which demonstrate that ideology played a role in influencing how lawmakers selected among candidates in all three races.

However, our analyses reveal that there is much more to understanding these leadership elections than ideology. Professional connections also influenced vote choice, forged both within state and committee delegations. Salient electoral and influence goals mattered too, as shown by the varying effects of campaign contributions, institutional position, age, and seniority. Our findings, in other words, are consistent with the mixed-motive model, albeit less so for the 1989 majority leader election.

In the next chapter we continue our analysis of open competition races for party leadership posts, looking at several noteworthy races within the House Republican Party over the past several decades. We find that the mixed-motive model explains these races as well, though the common intraparty cleavage they reveal is strategic, not ideological.

The GOP, like the Democratic Party, has seen its share of open competition races for party leadership posts in the House of Representatives. In fact, it has had far more: Democrats experienced twenty-two open competition races between 1961 and 2016, while Republicans saw fifty-two during the same time period. This is largely due to Republicans having more elected positions, and thus more opportunities for open races, as well as lacking a clear ladder of succession (Nelson 1977; Peabody 1976).[1]

Another important difference between the parties has been the nature of the division that often characterized these open races. While the Democrats' leadership selection was colored by intraparty ideological balancing, as noted in the previous chapter, Republican leadership selection focused more on party strategy, tactics, and style. In particular—and especially before 1995, when Republicans became a majority party—lawmakers often had a choice between at least one confrontational insurgent candidate who eschewed accommodation with Democrats and at least one establishment candidate more willing to compromise with the majority (Connelly and Pitney 1994; Harris 2006; Lee 2016). This divide was present to some degree in each of the four cases we analyze in this chapter.

We begin with a detailed discussion of perhaps the most consequential GOP leadership election in the past three decades: the 1989 race for whip, in which Newt Gingrich (R-GA) narrowly bested Ed Madigan (R-IL) and positioned himself to become the first Republican Speaker of the House in forty years. We then consider three additional cases of open competition for GOP posts: the minority leader and whip races in 1980 and the majority whip contest in 1994. As in the previous chapter, our findings are consistent with the mixed-motive model of vote choice.

A Party Changes Direction: The 1989 Race for Minority Whip

On March 10, 1989, President George H. W. Bush nominated House Republican Whip Dick Cheney (R-WY) to be his secretary of defense,[2] provoking a hotly contested race between Newt Gingrich and Ed Madigan to replace him as whip. The stakes would be high: the minority leader at the time, Robert Michel (R-IL), was in his mid-sixties, so the next whip would be the odds-on favorite to lead the party in the near future. As two reporters presciently wrote, "Republicans will effectively be voting on their style of leadership for the 1990s" (Kenworthy and Phillips 1989).

The Candidates

Gingrich, a sixth-term member of Congress, had been entertaining ambitions for a leadership post, though accounts vary of exactly how long. He was often coy in public about seeking a position of power in his party, extolling the virtues of being a backbencher. However, intimates of Gingrich, according to his biographer Mel Steely, believed he had been "positioning himself within the Republican caucus to have influence over the long haul," and perhaps even hoping to become Speaker (Gimpel 1996; Steely 2000, 110). Gingrich himself claimed that he had decided to run the moment he heard about Cheney's appointment, but there is also evidence that Gingrich's decision to run for whip was a result of peer recruitment (Garrett 2005, Z. Smith 2012, Steely 2000).[3]

By the time of Cheney's imminent exit from Congress, Gingrich had made a name for himself as a combative, political firebrand eager to confront the Democrats' tight control of the House. He had helped create a group of backbenchers, the Conservative Opportunity Society (COS), that employed aggressive procedural tactics and media events to attack Democrats; repeatedly challenged the authority and ethics of the majority party's leaders, most notably House Speaker Jim Wright; and recruited and trained numerous Republican congressional candidates (Barry 1989; Harris 2010, 2014; Hook

1989a). For Republicans who had tired of decades of minority status and chafed under the increasingly partisan and exclusionary tactics of the Democratic majority, Gingrich's candidacy promised a way forward. The contextual environment also meant that he was attractive to the growing number of southerners in the party, since the GOP's top leadership lacked southern representation after Trent Lott departed to the Senate the previous year.

Gingrich's opponent, Ed Madigan, was serving in his ninth term in the House. If Gingrich was an insurgent, Madigan was, in many ways, the quintessential establishment candidate. A skilled and accomplished legislator with prominent assignments on the Energy and Commerce Committee and the Agriculture Committee, Madigan had been chair of the Republican Research Committee in the 97th Congress (1981–82). He then put aside his ambitions for elective leadership to become ranking member of Agriculture, but returned to the fold as the appointed chief deputy whip to Minority Whip Lott. When the whip position opened up, he "was thinking seriously" about running, as minority leader and fellow Illinois lawmaker Bob Michel encouraged him to do.[4] Madigan's closeness to Michel was a double-edged sword: though the minority leader was a potent ally, colleagues might frown on two Illinoisans occupying both top spots in the leadership.

Other possible candidates ultimately did not run. Henry Hyde (R-IL), a favorite among many Republicans, declined, as did Bill McCollum (R-FL) (Hook 1989a).[5] Jerry Lewis (R-CA) announced that he would make a bid for the position, but he was persuaded by Michel to withdraw less than week later.[6] Michel was no fan of Gingrich's confrontational approach and saw him as a potentially dangerous rival; by keeping the race to two candidates, Michel could ensure Madigan consolidated the anti-Gingrich vote, while also forestalling a wave of disruptive leadership races if Lewis vacated his post of Conference chair (Toner 1989a).[7]

The GOP faced a stark choice along a number of dimensions. Madigan was older (aged fifty-three, versus the forty-five-year-old Gingrich) and more senior, and he represented the traditional

Midwestern wing of the party, whereas the younger and more junior Gingrich was of the new breed of southern Republicans. Madigan was also ideologically more moderate than Gingrich.[8] The Gingrich-Madigan race offered stylistic differences as well. Gingrich was practiced in public confrontation, using press appearances, one-minute and special order speeches, and guerilla-style political tactics to embarrass the majority party. Madigan, like Michel, was more likely to seek out Democratic partners to craft legislation and cooperate where it could yield legislative benefits. Though the contest was widely seen as a Newt versus anti-Newt contest, the two contenders' differing styles underscored a more fundamental strategic choice facing the party: should House Republicans focus on securing legislative benefits via compromises with majority party, or should they seek to challenge Democrats in hopes of building a Republican majority?[9]

The Campaign

Though he did not make a formal announcement of candidacy until March 13, Gingrich began campaigning almost immediately after Cheney was nominated, quickly calling fellow Republicans over the next two days. In terms of campaign strategy, Madigan flew under the media radar and largely steered clear of television appearances, opting instead for member-to-member lobbying and intraparty communication. Conversely, Gingrich sought the aid of outside groups and individuals, particularly conservative journalists and activists. But he was also playing an inside game, lining up dozens of promised votes even before Madigan entered the race. Gingrich ally Bob Walker later recounted making "fifty or sixty calls" to lawmakers shortly after Cheney's nomination was announced (Clift and Brazaitis 1996; Hook 1989b; Phillips 1989a; Steely 2000; Toner 1989b).

Both sides downplayed ideology and focused more on leadership style (Koopman 1996). Madigan decried "verbally abusing people in an acrimonious way" because it imposed obstacles to coalition-building (Toner 1989b). Gingrich's campaign manager, Vin Weber (R-MN), argued that "generation" rather than ideology was the primary fault line for the House GOP. Senior Republicans, usually well placed on committees, would likely favor Madigan's approach to make minority status work for them, while junior lawmakers could afford to wait for Gingrich's majority-building efforts to bear fruit (Phillips and Kenworthy 1989; Z. Smith 2012). Unsurprisingly, Gingrich was likely to be supported, and even actively helped in his campaign, by members of the COS. Yet he was also endorsed by some moderate Republicans, including members of the 92 Group, a collection of centrists who hoped to create a GOP majority by 1992 in a quiet alliance with the more conservative COS (Steely 2000, 201–2). As Weber put it, "Newt's candidacy is propelled by a good many frustrations" built up over the years of minority status that crossed ideological lines (Toner 1989a). Interestingly, "frustration" was the word Michel used to describe the motivation of four women in the conference who, to his dismay, "jump[ed] on the Gingrich bandwagon so early in the game."[10]

If activist Republicans were pro-Gingrich, much of the party establishment and many moderates were against him. Gingrich's allies sought ways to mitigate their opposition. In a key move, several of his supporters showed up unexpectedly in Michel's office and demanded he not use the power of his office to lobby on behalf of Madigan.[11] Gingrich's campaign may have also reached an agreement with Republican moderates to give them more influence in exchange for their votes. In addition, Gingrich publicly claimed large numbers of commitments in an effort to convince others that he had an insurmountable lead. On March 15, only two days after formally admitting his candidacy, he insisted he had over 70 votes, less than 20 from a majority, though his internal count was probably closer to 65, if not lower.[12] Madigan exaggerated his vote count too: on March 20 he claimed to have 93 commitments, enough to win but likely fewer than he actually had (Kenworthy 1989a; Oreskes 1989; Z. Smith 2012).[13]

As the election approached, both candidates realized how close the outcome was likely to be, and there were last-minute efforts to squeeze out every last possible vote from the conference.[14] For instance, when it seemed likely that Madigan supporter Jim Courter (R-NJ) would miss the election while campaigning for the New Jersey governorship, Michel offered to charter a flight to bring him back to the capital. Still trying to build support beyond conservatives, Gingrich openly touted the endorsements of key moderates like Steve Gunderson (R-WI), Nancy Johnson (R-CT), and Claudine Schneider (R-RI). On the day of balloting, two other moderates, Bill Frenzel (R-MN) and Olympia Snowe (R-ME), delivered his nominating and seconding speeches respectively (McGrory 1989; Phillips and Kenworthy 1989).[15]

The election was as close as predicted: by a mere two-vote margin, 87–85, Gingrich was elected whip. The results would bring dramatic changes to the GOP and eventually the House itself. Gingrich and Michel had never gotten along well, and though Michel realized he would have to "make do with Newt as my whip," tension between the two continued through the remainder of the minority leader's tenure—especially since Gingrich, in the words of political scientist Douglas Koopman, "barely hid his ambition to succeed Michel as Leader" (Koopman 1996, 13).[16] The Georgian undertook several durable reforms of the whip's office to expand its responsibilities in crafting policy, strategy, and partisan communication (Green 2015; Meinke 2016). The election was also widely heralded as vindication for the more confrontational wing of the party, exacerbating partisan conflict in the chamber in the years ahead. When Republicans took control of the House in 1994, Michel had already decided to retire from Congress, meaning Gingrich, who had cleared the field of would-be contenders for Michel's vacant post, would become the first Republican Speaker since Joe Martin in 1954. His speakership transformed the institution in far-reaching ways and further propelled polarization in Congress (Sinclair 2006; Strahan 2007).

Explaining Vote Choice

To test whether the mixed-motive model can explain how Republicans voted in this close race, we use probit regression. The preferences of lawmakers are estimated using a tally sheet kept by Gingrich during the campaign (Harris 2006).[17] We measure professional connections with variables equal to one if a lawmaker was a member of the Illinois delegation, the Public Works or House Administration committees (on which Gingrich sat), or the Agriculture or Energy and Commerce committees (on which Madigan served). (Membership in the Georgia delegation is not included because Gingrich was its only Republican member at the time.) Regional concerns about influence are expected to be statistically significant: in particular, southern representatives should be more likely to support Gingrich since, if Madigan were elected, the GOP's growing southern wing would continue to suffer from the absence of a fellow southerner in top leadership. We also expect lawmakers with less influence—younger, more junior, nonleadership Republicans—to lean toward Gingrich's insurgent candidacy and his emphasis on doing political battle with Democrats. In addition, members of the COS are expected to support his candidacy, both because of the group's connection with him and from its shared view of the best collective strategy for the conference. We include one other measure of support for Gingrich's confrontational leadership style: whether a lawmaker cosigned a May 1988 letter urging the House Ethics Committee to take action on Gingrich's formal ethics charges against Speaker Wright, thereby endorsing his provocative and aggressive strategy against the majority party.[18] Concerns about electoral security were not especially salient, and the candidates gave little (if any) money to their colleagues' reelection campaigns in 1989 (nor in the previous electoral cycle), likely because neither Gingrich nor Madigan had expected a vacancy in the minority whip position. Ideology was not salient either, insofar as both candidates downplayed their policy differences.

The results of the regression analysis, shown in table 4.1, show that some professional connections and salient goals do help explain vote choice.[19] To be sure, neither the Illinois delegation variable nor the Gingrich committee variable is statistically significant. But service on a Madigan Committee is significant, and those from the South were more likely to vote for Gingrich (by a sizeable 17 percent). While leadership position, committee ranking status, and seniority are not statistically significant, age is moderately significant ($p < .10$), with an increase in age by one standard deviation (9.5 years) decreasing the probability of voting for Gingrich by 8 percent. Two other variables capturing views of party strategy are also at least modestly statistically significant: COS membership, which increases the chances of voting for Gingrich by a whopping 42 percent (and which could also measure a professional connection with Gingrich), and signing the Wright ethics letter, which increases the chances of supporting the Georgian by 13 percent.[20] Neither electoral security nor ideology are statistically significant, as expected.[21]

Our analysis cannot explain definitely why Gingrich won, especially since the outcome could have been reversed by just two Republicans. Nonetheless, the Gingrich-Madigan race is a good example of how ideology is unlikely to be the basis for vote choice if it is not salient to a leadership election. Madigan chose not to emphasize it, while Gingrich neutralized its relevance by appealing to moderates' common concern about minority party status, and perhaps by assuring them a seat at the leadership table as well. Gingrich also successfully appealed to the interests of southerners and younger colleagues. More generally, just enough members of the conference were willing to support confrontation as a means of winning power to give Gingrich a narrow edge over his opponent.[22] The firebrand Republican would subsequently help move his party—and the House—into a new, more combative political era.

Orator versus Legislator: The 1980 Race for Minority Leader

John Rhodes (R-AZ), Republican leader since his predecessor Gerald Ford (R-MI) became vice president in 1973, announced in December 1979 that he would stay in the House but not run again for leader. Though Rhodes claimed he would seek the speakership if his party gained the majority in the 1980 elections, he almost certainly would have faced resistance had he tried. Rhodes had recently

Table 4.1. Analysis of Estimated Vote for Gingrich as Minority Whip (1989)

Hypothesis	Independent Variable	Model 1	Model 2	Change in Probability (Model 2)
Professional Connection	From Illinois	-0.68 (0.51)	-0.47 (0.54)	.51, .35 [-.21]
	On Madigan committee	-0.46^ (0.26)	-0.59* (0.28)	.54, .34 [-.19]
	On Gingrich committee	-0.06 (0.27)	-0.03 (0.30)	.50, .49 [-.01]
Goal Salience	From South	—	0.51^ (0.27)	.46, .63 [+.17]
	In leadership	—	-1.03 (0.77)	.51, .21 [-.30]
	Committee ranking member	—	0.21 (0.42)	.49, .56 [+.07]
	Term	—	-0.03 (0.05)	.50, .47 [-.04]
	Age	—	-0.02^ (0.01)	.50, .43 [-.08]

COS member	—	1.49** (0.53)	.47, .89 [+.42]
Cosigned Wright ethics letter	—	0.38^ (0.22)	.45, .58 [+.13]
% 2-party vote (logged)	—	-0.86 (0.60)	.50, .45 [-.05]
DW-NOMINATE (1st dimension)	—	0.96 (0.69)	.50, .55 [+.05]
Constant	0.12 (0.12)	0.52 (0.69)	
N	171	171	
Log L	-116.22	-100.63	
McFadden's R^2	.02	.15	
PRE	12.9%	28.2%	

Other Variables

Note: Table entries for each model are probit coefficients with robust standard errors in parentheses. The final column shows the average predicted probabilities of supporting Gingrich when each variable in Model 2 is changed from 0 to 1 (for dichotomous variables) or increased by one standard deviation (for continuous variables) with the difference in brackets.

^ significant at $p < .1$; * significant at $p < .05$; ** significant at $p < .01$;
*** significant at $p < .001$ (2-tailed test).

quieted a potential uprising of younger members who thought him too complacent, and he had been warned by then-Minority Whip Bob Michel and others that he would likely face an intraparty challenge (Russell 1979b).[23] By August 1979, a consultant who had surveyed numerous House Republicans found "a lot of competition and positioning in preparation for the upcoming leadership fight should Mr. Rhodes retire."[24]

Rhodes's retirement announcement set off a race between Michel and Guy Vander Jagt (R-MI), chairman of the National Republican Campaign Committee (NRCC). Michel had been on a glide path to leadership since entering Congress. A former staff aide to Illinois Congressman Harold Velde, whom he succeeded in 1956, Michel was elected president of his freshman class and was the only first-year member to join the Republican Policy Committee (Mackaman, forthcoming).[25] Michel eventually became a member of the GOP whip team, chaired the NRCC for the 1973–74 election cycle, and won a contested race for whip in 1974. Though moving from GOP whip to leader was not an established pattern of succession in 1980, Michel did not see it that way: "when you're No. 2," he said at the time, "you aspire to be No. 1. For me, it's a natural step of progression" (Mackay 1980).

Vander Jagt took a different path into leadership. He had succeeded Michel as NRCC chairman and was credited with revitalizing and professionalizing the organization, getting more Republicans elected, and increasing the NRCC's fundraising totals more than ten-fold (Kolodny 1998; Russell 1979b). With that success came praise from colleagues and ties to the younger members he had helped elect. He was also encouraged by peers to seek higher office. In a 1979 letter to Gene Snyder (R-KY), Vander Jagt wrote, "when you started me thinking about a higher leadership post last year, I never dreamed I'd be running for Minority Leader in less than a year. You really started something, Gene."[26] He also credited freshmen with convincing him to run. To two of them, Bill Thomas (R-CA) and Newt Gingrich (R-GA), he insisted that "without the enthusiasm of the freshman class and encouragement of leaders in it like yourself, I might not have become a candidate for Minority Leader."[27]

In some ways, the two candidates were similar: Michel and Vander Jagt were Midwestern conservatives, both served on prominent committees (Michel on Appropriations, Vander Jagt on Ways and Means), and some saw them as ideologically indistinguishable.[28] However, Michel was considerably older (fifty-seven) and more senior (serving his twelfth term in the 96th Congress) versus Vander Jagt (aged forty-nine and serving his seventh term). More fundamentally, the race pitted the House Republicans' top external campaigner against their top internal vote counter, leading observers to characterize the choice as "Mr. Outside vs. Mr. Inside" or "a show horse against a work horse" (Russell 1979b; Tolchin 1980a).

These terms were shorthand for several fundamental differences between the candidates. First, Vander Jagt was viewed as more effective than Michel in electioneering and messaging. He had been lauded for his innovations in the NRCC and was hard at work helping Republican candidates in 1980, raising money and flying over half a million miles in campaign trips.[29] He argued that "the fellow writing the checks and making the contacts has something of an advantage" in a leadership race, but his efforts also evinced a willingness to take the party out of its seemingly permanent minority status (Tolchin 1980a). Vander Jagt even penned a piece in the summer of 1980 for a conservative magazine titled "Planning for a Republican Majority" (Vander Jagt 1980). Michel, on the other hand, had preceded Vander Jagt as NRCC chair, serving just one term during the 1973–74 election cycle—one of the worst for House Republicans, though the Watergate scandal, not Michel's stewardship of the NRCC, was largely to blame.

Second, while Vander Jagt was a compelling speaker with a commanding media presence, Michel was considered more of a legislator who could work effectively with Democrats and manage an effective whip operation (Russell 1979b). In the words of one former Hill aide (and Michel supporter), "day in and day out, [Michel] would be there [in committee], asking questions . . . Michel was a very substantive congressman" who "knew how the game was played; he knew how to make deals." But Vander Jagt, he said, "I personally thought was a lightweight . . . a blowhard."[30]

Third, as a "movement conservative," Vander Jagt was seen as possibly a better fit with the GOP's presidential nominee, Ronald Reagan. There were rumors that Vander Jagt was on Reagan's vice presidential short list, and he delivered an inspirational performance as keynote speaker at the 1980 Republican Convention. Reagan's lieutenants were quick to offer Michel an important role at the convention as well—floor leader—but this further illustrated Michel's procedural strengths versus Vander Jagt's oratorical abilities (J. Miller 1980).

Michel announced for the minority leader position quickly, and archival data indicate that he had been canvassing members for votes as early as the summer of 1979.[31] He assembled a diverse team of colleagues, including senior appropriator Silvio Conte (R-MA) and then-freshman Dick Cheney, to strategize and win commitments. Vander Jagt, who did not enter the race until December of that year, also built a campaign operation, creating an "Executive Committee" of intimate advisors and staff, as well as a "Campaign Leadership Committee" composed of a number of lawmakers, including freshman class president Ed Bethune (R-AR), Mickey Edwards (R-OK), Newt Gingrich, and David Stockman (R-MI).[32]

Vander Jagt's campaign sought multiple opportunities to remind fellow Republicans of his innovative and successful work at the NRCC. He circulated a set of talking points to allies that referenced the huge increase in campaign contributions under his watch, his creation of training seminars for GOP candidates and staff, and his 1980 media campaign "Vote Republican—For a Change," which would be followed by big seat gains for the party. Vander Jagt pointedly contrasted these accomplishments with the huge seat losses of 1974, when Michel headed the NRCC. "Bottom line," he wrote in one set of talking points, "1975 House Republican Membership 144; 1981 House Republican Membership 192." In the same document, the Michigan lawmaker highlighted his rhetorical abilities, frequent presence on television, and willingness to debate Democratic leaders.[33]

Michel's allies saw the choice differently. Once the election was over, they believed, it was time to govern, and that was Michel's forte. A speech drafted by Michel aides to be delivered by a supporter pointedly described the Illinoisan as a "producer" who had won major victories on the House floor, blocking or nearly blocking liberal legislation because "he was the one on the floor hustling the votes, twisting arms and generating the swell of opposition."[34]

Each candidate more or less acknowledged the relative advantages of the other and instead worked to define the role of the minority leader to fit their individual skills. For Michel, the job was best filled by a member of the party establishment who could work with, and exact concessions from, Democrats. He argued that his primary role would be moving legislation and advancing Republican policy goals. For Vander Jagt, the real question was, as he put it, "who can best transform our minority into a majority" (Russell 1979b). For his supporters, this meant the party should change its tactics. As Ed Bethune said, "The issue implicit in this race . . . is whether Republicans will increasingly engage in the politics of confrontation that younger members favor or the politics of compromise" (J. Miller 1980).

These appeals held different prospects for lawmakers depending on their age, seniority, and position of influence. Though all Republicans would gain if their party won a majority in 1980, more senior, establishment Republicans stood to benefit most from legislative concessions the GOP might win by compromising with the Democratic majority. They also had less time to wait for control of the House, whereas members who were new to the chamber could more realistically wait to win majority status at some point in their overall congressional career. Moreover, junior Republicans had greater interest in electing leaders who, like them, were more media-oriented than focused on internal House procedure.[35]

Vander Jagt and Michel worked to solidify support during the 97th Congress and, after the November 1980 elections, make inroads with newly elected lawmakers. None of these freshmen had congressional experience enough to judge Michel's qualities as an establishment candidate, but all had likely seen Vander Jagt's performance at the 1980 convention and benefited from the help of the NRCC. Vander Jagt pressed that advantage, using "tremendous telephone and personal contact work," hosting them at a reception in his home, and giving them a private tour of the Capitol. His aide Jim Sparling outlined a postelection plan, which involved immediately calling "*all* newly-elected*" party members, sending letters to every Republican elected to the House, offering to "help retire any campaign debts," and directing allies to send additional letters on his behalf.[36] On November 14, Gingrich wrote the freshmen a letter endorsing Vander Jagt, asserting that he was "a fighter who will press energetically Republican initiatives that come from a Republican White House and Senate; a man who will listen carefully to the requests of the House's junior Members; and someone who is accessible."[37]

Seeking to stall Vander Jagt's momentum with freshmen, Michel wrote them a letter of his own, suggesting that they defer to the senior members of their state delegations in choosing a candidate and noting that he was a member of the party's executive committee responsible for determining committee assignments.[38] Two weeks later, Michel surrogates from the 1978 freshman class—Carroll Campbell (R-SC), Dick Cheney, James Courter (R-NJ), Thomas Loeffler (R-TX), Jim Sensenbrenner (R-WI), and Thomas Tauke (R-IA)—sent a joint missive to the incoming freshmen endorsing Michel as "a legislative craftsman who will be able to build the coalitions necessary to pass as much of our new President's program as we can, as well as to lead a floor fight to stake out our position on the parts of our program where the votes aren't there."[39] The Vander Jagt team countered by accusing Michel of "intimidating the freshmen and others on committee assignments" and assuring the junior-most Republicans that Vander Jagt was "keenly interested," "supportive," and "as Campaign Chairman . . . more sympathetic to the political importance of their committee assignments."[40] If victorious, he said he would consider changing the timing of committee assignments in an effort to "protect and expand [the] interests" of new members.[41] In response, Michel charged that Vander Jagt was doling out NRCC funds to promote his candidacy (J. Miller 1980).

Despite efforts to burnish his own legislative credentials,[42] Vander Jagt could not seem to overcome the lead that Michel, an experienced vote counter, had built with sitting members, nor could he shake the perception that the floor leader's job was essentially legislative. In addition to trying to leverage help from conservative groups outside the chamber and, atypically, enlist staff to obtain vote commitments, Vander Jagt also sought one last "Hail Mary" play: breaking with party tradition, he proposed that the two candidates, rather than just their supporters, should address the conference on the day of the vote. That proposal was nixed by GOP leadership and staff, but he sought other ways to emphasize that he was the better orator. Supporter Bob Whittaker (R-KS) implored his colleagues in a letter "to take just a few minutes to read over the enclosures [a CBS radio interview and Vander Jagt's *Commonsense* article] in which Guy Vander Jagt is featured. . . . We all know that our new Minority Leader assumes a role as national spokesman for all House Republicans. No one can deny that Guy is well prepared for that great responsibility."[43]

On the eve of the election, both candidates claimed that they had commitments from a majority of the conference. Vander Jagt posited that he had a "hard count" of more than 100 expected votes, while Michel quipped that "I'm better at counting on this sort of thing than he is. And I guess no one is lying to me" (Raum 1980). Vander Jagt also sought to keep his election team inspired by exaggerating his vote count. In a strategy memo dated November 17, 1980, one of his staffers proposed writing to their campaign team that they could count on 82 votes, versus 61 for Michel.[44]

As it turned out, Vander Jagt's claims were less realistic than Michel's. Though the race appeared closer than Michel had wanted or anticipated, media accounts depicting Michel as having an unassailable lead proved correct. In the December 8 vote he defeated Vander Jagt, 103–87. Interestingly, both candidates had overestimated the number of votes they would receive—Michel counting 115 votes in his favor, Vander Jagt 95—hampered by the fact that 27 lawmakers were counted as supporters by both.[45]

In a sense, Vander Jagt's challenge to the establishment had come too soon. Though he would never make another run for GOP leader, remaining chair of the NRCC until he was defeated in a primary in 1992, his candidacy was an augur for the Republican Conference's shift toward confrontational and communications-oriented leaders later in the decade (Lee 2016). As the House GOP became increasingly populated with lawmakers who emphasized majority status and employed partisan tactics to achieve it, candidates similar to Vander Jagt would fare better in leadership races, culminating in Newt Gingrich's election as whip in 1989.

As with other two-candidate races, we test the mixed-motive model of vote choice in the 1980 leader election with probit regression. We use two estimates of how lawmakers voted, both based on whip counts taken by Michel and Vander Jagt, with the dependent variable coded 1 if a lawmaker is believed to have voted for Michel.[46] The more restrictive estimate (Models 1 and 2) only counts a lawmaker as voting for a candidate if that lawmaker's preference is noted on both candidates' tallies. The second, more liberal estimate (Models 3 and 4) counts a vote in favor of a candidate if noted as such on either candidate's tally.[47]

To determine whether professional connections explain vote choice, we include variables equal to one if a lawmaker shared a state delegation or committee with either leadership candidate. We also operationalize several salient lawmaker goals. Electoral goals were an important theme of Vander Jagt's campaign, and he had helped many legislators as chair of the NRCC, so we expect lawmakers who received a smaller percentage of the two-party vote in 1980, and thus more sensitive to electoral concerns, to have a greater probability of voting against Michel. We also include measures of campaign contributions made by both candidates as well as by Vander Jagt's NRCC. Since Vander Jagt was more junior than Michel, ran on a theme of being the insurgent, and focused on reelection to a greater extent than on legislative prowess, we would expect lawmakers in leadership, ranking on committees, or with greater seniority more likely to vote for Michel. Finally, as control variables we include a standard measure of ideology (DW-NOMINATE scores) and lawmaker age, though neither candidate emphasized ideological or age differences in his campaign, so we do not expect either to be salient in the race.

The results of the analysis appear in table 4.2. We find, first, that professional connections do help explain vote choice. Shared committee with Michel is statistically significant in the reduced models (Model 1 and 3), as is membership in the Michigan delegation, and the former increases the probability of voting for Michel in Model 4 by 13 percent.[48] The effect of the Illinois delegation variable cannot be determined because all lawmakers from that state voted for Michel, an indication that it was an important explanation of vote choice. Vander Jagt, however, was no more or less likely to get votes from fellow committee members. Second, we find evidence for goal salience. Two-party vote, as expected, helps explain vote choice,[49] and it also has a fairly substantial effect: a one standard deviation increase in the vote share (which translates to a growth in mean vote share from 67 percent to 81 percent) increases the probability of voting for Michel by 14 percent. Campaign contributions from Vander Jagt or the NRCC are not statistically significant in either Model 2 or 4, but contributions from Michel are significant in Model 4 and must be omitted from the reduced model (Model 2) because all recipients of Michel funding voted for him, a strong sign that his contributions mattered. (On one tally sheet, Michel made note of the amounts he gave to some colleagues, further suggesting that campaign contributions were tied to vote choice.)[50] Though the ranking member variable is not statistically significant in Model 4, it had to be dropped from Model 2 because all ranking members supported Michel, and the leadership variable had to be omitted from both Model 2 and 4 because every party leader voted for Michel.[51] More senior lawmakers were more likely to vote for Michel, and substantially so: an increase in seniority by one standard deviation (nearly four terms) increased the average probability of voting for Michel by 20 percent.

Table 4.2. Analysis of Estimated Vote for Michel as Minority Leader (1980)

Hypothesis	Independent Variable	Stringent Vote Estimate		Relaxed Vote Estimate		Change in Probability (Model 4)
		Model 1	Model 2	Model 3	Model 4	
Professional Connection	From Michigan	-1.37* (0.54)	-0.12 (0.74)	-1.30* (0.53)	0.17 (0.72)	.56, .61 [+.05]
	On Michel committee	1.34* (0.62)	0.56 (0.70)	1.50* (0.60)	0.50 (0.70)	.56, .69 [+.13]
	On Vander Jagt committee	0.32 (0.44)	-0.39 (0.50)	0.45 (0.43)	-0.35 (0.51)	.57, .47 [-.09]
Goal Salience	% 2-party vote (logged)	—	2.07* (0.88)	—	2.78** (0.84)	.56, .70 [+.14]
	$ from Michel (logged)	—	—	—	0.07** (0.02)	.56, .66 [+.10]
	$ from Vander Jagt (logged)	—	-0.03 (0.03)	—	-0.02 (0.02)	.56, .54 [-.02]
	$ from NRCC (logged)	—	-0.01 (0.02)	—	-0.00 (0.01)	.56, .56 [-.00]

Committee ranking member	—	—	—	-0.22 (0.74)	.56, .51 [-.06]
Terms	—	0.20** (0.07)	—	0.26** (0.08)	.56, .76 [+.20]
Other Variables					
DW-NOMINATE (1st dimension)	—	0.21 (0.78)	—	-0.20 (0.66)	.56, .55 [-.01]
Age	—	-0.01 (0.02)	—	-0.01 (0.02)	.56, .54 [-.03]
Constant	0.20 (0.13)	0.55 (0.87)	0.07 (0.11)	1.34^ (0.79)	
N	114	113	154	153	
Log L	-70.91	-58.87	-98.94	-73.62	
McFadden's R^2	.07	.22	.06	.30	
PRE	6.8%	34.9%	4.5%	40.9%	

Note: Table entries for each model are probit coefficients with robust standard errors in parentheses. Models 1 and 2 use a more restrictive estimate of vote choice; models 3 and 4 use a more relaxed estimate. The final column shows the average predicted probabilities of supporting Michel when each variable in Model 4 is changed from 0 to 1 (for dichotomous variables) or increased by one standard deviation (for continuous variables) with the difference in brackets.

^ significant at $p < .1$; * significant at $p < .05$; ** significant at $p < .01$; *** significant at $p < .001$ (2-tailed test).

Finally, there is no evidence that either age or ideological preferences influenced vote choice, as expected.

Both candidates gave campaign contributions to many freshmen, and looking at the vote choice of those lawmakers, who were unlikely to know the candidates as well as their incumbent colleagues, serves as a further test of the power of contributions to sway votes independent of other factors.[52] Of the five who received a contribution from Vander Jagt but not Michel, four endorsed Vander Jagt, but of the eleven who were given funds by Michel but not Vander Jagt, only six committed to Michel. Indeed, eighteen of the nineteen freshmen who got funding from neither opted to vote for Vander Jagt. This suggests that while Michel's campaign contributions had a positive effect on the likelihood of voting for Michel within the party at large, campaign donations were not a definitive factor in swaying the vote choice of freshmen, since Vander Jagt had a decided advantage among newly elected Republicans whether he gave them money or not.[53]

In short, the results are consistent with the predictions of the mixed-motive model. The 1980 race was one in which Michel, the establishment candidate, was victorious, taking advantage of his professional connections, adroitly exploiting his advantages with senior and more influential partisans, and making strategic use of campaign donations. The insurgent candidate endeared himself to freshmen and more marginal members, as expected, but failed to win over enough colleagues in his state delegation or committee, nor secure enough votes from nonfreshmen to whom he contributed financially.[54]

Two Rising Stars: The 1980 Race for Minority Whip

When GOP Whip Bob Michel announced his candidacy for minority leader, Bud Shuster (R-PA) quickly announced that he would run for Michel's job. Shuster was a rising star: after first entering the House in 1972, he was chosen president of his freshman class, subsequently served as a ranking subcommittee member on the Committee on Public Works, defeated Bill Frenzel 80–55 in an election for

Republican Policy Committee (RPC) chairman in 1978, and racked up some significant accomplishments combating Democrats as RPC chair (Meinke 2016).[55] However, there was no established pattern of succession from the RPC to whip, and rumors circulated that several other House Republicans might run for the post, including Henry Hyde and Robert Bauman (R-MD), the party's watchdog over floor proceedings. Shuster was eventually joined in the race by Mississippi Republican Trent Lott, who admittedly "hesitated at first" because, as he put it, he "wasn't sure I could win" (*Congressional Quarterly Weekly Report* 1979; Lott 2005). Lott, a former Hill aide, also first joined Congress in 1972 and was relatively young as well (thirty-nine years old, nine years younger than Shuster). He was the first Republican to represent his district since Reconstruction, and Lott's candidacy had appeal in a party that was slowly gaining adherents in the South. Lott was also in leadership, having won a three-way race for chairman of the Republican Research Committee in 1978. Though perhaps unsure whether he could beat Shuster, Lott was "tickled" by the opportunity to whip votes, and Bob Michel observed in retrospect that Lott "always had eyes on becoming leader" (*Congressional Quarterly Weekly Report* 1978; Lott 2005, 78).[56]

There were a couple of potentially salient differences between the pair. One was regional: Shuster was a northerner, while Lott, if elected, would be the first Republican southerner to hold such a highly ranked party position. The other difference was stylistic. Though both were in leadership, Lott was seen as more a member of the establishment, a "popular party figure" credited with having "maintained a lower profile," according to one media account (Arieff 1980a). Shuster, by contrast, was a practitioner of firebrand politics, more practiced in the art of building unified Republican opposition to Democratic legislation than in making bipartisan deals. For example, as RPC chair Shuster had pressed House Democrats to swiftly punish Charles Diggs (D-MI) following his conviction for taking kickbacks from his staff, at one point threatening to "take an expulsion motion directly to the floor" (Arieff 1980a; "Censure of Rep. Diggs" 1980, 561–63).[57] Ideologically, the difference between

Shuster and Lott was murky. Southern Republicans often tended toward being socially conservative, but DW-NOMINATE scores of the pair suggest that Lott was, if anything, slightly more liberal than Shuster.[58] Also, when he and Shuster won their respective leadership races in 1978, reporters characterized them both as examples of "conservatives" gaining entry into leadership (*Congressional Quarterly Weekly Report* 1978).

That both Shuster and Lott had recently been elected to leadership posts meant they had some experience in campaigning and vote counting, and both could conceivably rekindle commitments of support from their past races. A number of Lott allies signed a "Dear Colleague" letter touting Lott's "strong sense of teamwork" as well as his "knowledge and ability to spearhead our battles on the House floor." Meanwhile, several Shuster supporters cited his performance as RPC chair as evidence that he was ready to be whip and "help us all fight the battles aimed at achieving a Republican Majority in the 1980s." "The proof of the pudding," they wrote, "lies in the fact that under Bud's leadership, the Republican Policy Committee staked out Republican positions on more key votes than in the previous Congress while achieving an incredible 92.3 percent support among Republicans."[59] When the 1980 elections resulted in a large freshman class of Republicans, both candidates courted their votes assiduously. Shuster, for instance, wrote each of them letters of congratulation and invited them to a welcoming reception.[60] Shuster believed his attention to freshmen was yielding results, and he estimated that he would win them by a 3 to 2 margin.[61]

The whip election followed Michel's victory over Guy Vander Jagt as minority leader (see above). Perhaps Shuster hoped that the election of Michel would help him, under the assumption that colleagues would want a brash partisan as a counterweight to the more conciliatory Michel. But it was not to be. Lott narrowly triumphed over Shuster, 96–90, the closest of the five GOP leadership elections held that day (Arieff 1980b; Tolchin 1980b). Surprised and embittered by the outcome, Shuster pondered where his campaign had failed. He speculated that allies Joseph McDade (R-PA) and Clair Burgener

(R-CA) had focused more on helping Bob Michel win and "didn't work" their regions enough on his behalf. He also regretted not visiting Republican districts personally, and he wondered whether having someone from his home state nominate him for whip had implied a lack of broad support in the conference.[62] Shuster even suspected treachery: he believed Michel and Lott had struck a secret deal in which southerners cast their ballots for Michel in exchange for Illinois Republicans voting for Lott.[63] He was also obsessed by the notion that some colleagues had lied to him about their voting intentions. In his final postelection tally, he wrote that the conference had eight "liars" and six "misleaders," and one former Republican member recalled that "Shuster . . . literally spent months [after the race] trying to track down the people who had lied to him." Though deception was a possibility, another, less sinister explanation is that Shuster simply overcounted commitments. For instance, in one early whip count, Shuster tallied both "yes" and "probable" votes as supporters.[64]

The outcome of the election would resonate for many years. Shuster shifted his focus to committee and policy work, becoming a powerful chairman of the Transportation Committee in the mid-1990s. Despite being in the minority, Lott had several successes in leading "commando raids for votes" to pass Reagan-endorsed bills (Arieff 1980b). He left the House for the Senate in 1988, became the only lawmaker in history to serve as whip in both chambers of Congress, and eventually rose to the position of Senate majority leader.

If the mixed-motive model of leadership selection is correct, we should expect to see both professional connections and salient goals explain vote choice in the 1980 election for whip. To estimate how Republicans voted, we use a postelection whip sheet tabulated by Shuster, which included 67 "definite" supporters and another 26 freshmen he believed voted for him—a total of 93, just 3 more than he received—and, as before, employ probit to test the independent effect of various explanatory variables.[65] Professional connections are estimated with variables measuring if a lawmaker shared a committee with either candidate, plus a variable measuring whether a Republican was from Shuster's state of Pennsylvania. (We do not control for membership in Lott's state delegation, since the only other Republican representing Mississippi supported Lott.) Salient goals in the election were principally influence-related, insofar as Lott was considered the establishment candidate. We therefore test the effect of tenure and serving in party leadership or as a committee chair—though it is unclear which of these, if any, would be statistically significant, since both candidates were elected at the same time, both were in leadership, and neither made an explicit reference to influence goals in their campaigns. We also test whether a lawmaker was from the South and thus especially eager to see one of their own (Lott) finally elected to leadership (and if, as Shuster believed, southern Republicans voted against him in the race). We also test for the effect of electoral concerns. Electoral vulnerability is not hypothesized to have an effect, but campaign contributions are: though Lott gave no such contributions, Shuster did donate to a handful of colleagues. Also included is a measure of lawmakers' DW-NOMINATE scores to capture policy-related goals, though they are not expected to matter, since the pair's ideological differences were opaque.[66]

The results of our test of the mixed-motive model are shown in table 4.3. One kind of professional connection—notably, serving with Shuster in the Pennsylvania delegation—proves statistically significant in explaining vote choice in Model 1, which tests the effect of just the professional connection variables, and is nearly so in Model 2 (p = 0.10), and membership in that delegation reduces the probability of voting for Lott by a sizeable 23 percent. Committee assignments also appear to have translated into votes for both Lott and Shuster; for the former, it is perfectly separated by the dependent variable (and so must be omitted from the model), while for the latter, it is just shy of statistical significance (p = 0.10). The coefficients of two influence-related variables prove statistically significant and in the predicted direction: seniority, with a one standard deviation increase in service (3.2 terms) raising the likelihood of voting for the establishment candidate (Lott) by 12 percent, and region, with southerners nearly 40 percent more likely to back Lott. Campaign

Table 4.3. Analysis of Estimated Vote for Lott as Minority Whip (1980)

Hypothesis	Independent Variable	Model 1	Model 2	Change in Probability (Model 2)
Professional Connection	From Pennsylvania	−1.47*	−0.72	.53, .30
		(0.73)	(0.44)	[−.23]
	On Shuster committee	−0.53	−0.53	.53, .36
		(0.50)	(0.32)	[−.17]
Goal Salience	Terms	—	0.11*	.51, .63
			(0.05)	[+.12]
	In leadership	—	−0.20	.52, .45
			(0.60)	[−.07]
	Committee ranking member	—	−0.30	.52, .43
			(0.40)	[−.10]
	South	—	1.22***	.45, .84
			(0.32)	[+.39]
Other Variables	% 2-party vote (logged)	—	0.42	.51, .54
			(.63)	[+.03]
	DW-NOMINATE (1st dimension)	—	1.73**	.51, .61
			(0.63)	[+.10]
	Age	—	−0.01	.51, .47
			(0.01)	[−.04]
	Constant	0.11	−0.13	
		(0.10)	(0.69)	
	N	190	187	
	Log L	−128.40	−107.90	
	McFadden's R^2	.02	.17	
	PRE	9.8%	39.6%	

Note: Table entries for each model are probit coefficients with robust standard errors in parentheses. The final column shows the average predicted probabilities of supporting Lott when each variable in Model 2 is changed from 0 to 1 (for dichotomous variables) or increased by one standard deviation (for continuous variables) with the difference in brackets.

^ significant at $p < .1$; * significant at $p < .05$; ** significant at $p < .01$; *** significant at $p < .001$ (2-tailed test).

contributions are also important, as indicated by the fact that Shuster donations must be excluded from the analysis because every candidate who received money from Shuster voted for him. While these results support the mixed-motive model, they also unexpectedly provide support for the ideology hypothesis: DW-NOMINATE scores have a statistically significant effect, and the coefficient's sign indicates that more conservative lawmakers preferred Lott over Shuster. In short, some professional connections and salient goals—but also ideology—influenced the vote choice of Republicans in the 1980 whip race.[67] Lott, it seems, overcame Shuster's connections with Pennsylvania colleagues and support from donation recipients in part by earning the votes of southerners, conservatives, and more senior colleagues.

From Minority to Majority: The 1994 Race for Majority Whip

Following the historic Republican takeover of the House of Representatives after the 1994 midterm elections, the GOP selected a new slate of leaders that would include the first Republican Speaker of the House since 1954. Bob Michel was retiring, and GOP whip Newt Gingrich, widely credited with having led the party's long march to majority status, would ascend to the speakership unopposed.[68] Conference Chairman Dick Armey, a Gingrich collaborator, would also move to a new leadership post (majority leader) without opposition. There was open and intense competition for several lower-level leadership offices, however. Perhaps the most important was majority whip, the post Gingrich was vacating, which carried with it the responsibility of marshaling votes for the GOP's agenda. Chief deputy whip and close Gingrich ally Bob Walker mounted a campaign for the position against two other leaders, Conference Secretary Tom DeLay and Conference Vice Chairman Bill McCollum (R-FL).[69]

Of the three candidates, Walker, a fifty-one-year old congressman in his fifth term, had the most seniority and leadership experience. He had run for elective leadership earlier in his career, losing a Research Committee chairmanship race to Ed Madigan in 1980, then was appointed chief deputy whip by Gingrich in 1989. He was also a founding member of Gingrich's Conservative Opportunity Society, the group of activist backbenchers who had made life difficult for Democrats. In addition to his close ties with Gingrich, Walker had three other advantages: he was from a decent-sized state delegation, could offer regional diversity to a southern-dominated leadership team, and as deputy whip had "at least a titular claim on moving up," though there was no clear tradition of Republican deputy whips being heirs apparent to the office.[70]

Walker's primary rival was DeLay, a forty-seven-year-old former exterminator from Texas finishing his ninth term in the House. DeLay would have to overcome resentment that the Lone Star State already claimed one top leadership spot and that southerners occupied two of the top three offices. He also had a cooler relationship with Gingrich, dating at least as far back as 1989, when he served as campaign manager for Ed Madigan, Gingrich's opponent for whip (see above). DeLay had nonetheless worked diligently to fulfill his aspirations for influence, reportedly having desired a leadership spot since his first election to the House in 1984 (Burger 1993a; Camia 1994b; B. Donovan 1993). The Texan was a stalwart social and economic conservative and served on the influential Appropriations Committee.[71]

The third candidate, McCollum, was an experienced television spokesperson for Republican causes. Aged fifty and completing his seventh term in Congress, he was next in line to chair the Financial Institutions subcommittee of the House Committee on Banking, a spot that afforded him access to many potential donors (Garsson 1994). McCollum was ambitious, but he wavered between moving up within the conference and seeking elected office outside the chamber.[72] He had distinguished himself on the Judiciary Committee as a partisan on gun control, crime, and abortion issues, though he was somewhat less conservative than his rivals and, as a southerner, he could not offer the regional diversity that Walker did.[73]

The campaign for whip began unofficially in mid-1993, before it was clear that the Republicans would be in the majority, as rumors spread that Michel would retire and Gingrich was his likely successor. Interestingly, despite his strengths Walker "had no intention of running for whip" until he was "talked into it by David Dreier [a Republican from California] and Bob Michel." Michel in particular feared the absence of a "real institutionalist" in the party leadership, and believed Walker best fit that profile. Walker began meeting with staff and close allies in the conference in August, and after that month's congressional recess he started sounding out colleagues about his candidacy while successfully persuading two possible contenders, Duncan Hunter (R-CA) and Henry Hyde, to support him. But Walker had no such luck with DeLay, who told the Pennsylvanian that he thought he "had more supporters than Bob, and that he didn't believe that 'Southern' top three leaders was a problem for Members."[74] As DeLay later recalled, "I knew I could do a better job at whip than Walker because I was simply better at counting and working votes than he was." He also argued that "I was better known among the incoming freshman class because of my work in their campaigns. . . . I had travelled to twenty-five states in support of candidates, and had developed fund-raising networks that covered every state in the nation" (DeLay 2007). DeLay was also the first to officially throw his hat in the ring, announcing his candidacy three days after Michel declared he would retire, and he chose Dennis Hastert (R-IL) to manage his campaign. Walker hurriedly circulated his own declaration of candidacy the next day, as did McCollum (Burger 1993b).

Walker's campaign emphasized his parliamentary expertise and experience asserting Republican viewpoints and amendments and slowing down the Democrats' legislative agenda. In his announcement letter, Walker argued that the next whip should "have a regular presence on the House floor," "provide the leadership with accurate vote counts," "build coalitions within our Party and with the opposition," and be "tactically competent" and a "firm party loyalist" who can "win legislative victories." Walker circulated a list of those committed to voting for him that contained not only Gingrich's name but also the ranking members of nearly a dozen committees.[75] His campaign made as its substantive "centerpiece" the periodic release of "Dear Colleague" endorsements by colleagues, almost all of them citing his parliamentary knowledge and dedication to floor proceedings, and some including personal anecdotes about his successful attempts at bipartisan coalition building.[76]

DeLay pointedly dismissed these letter writers' claims that, in his words, "because a person is a fine parliamentarian he would make a good Whip." Offering a "different vision of what constitutes an effective whip," DeLay wrote to his colleagues that it "needs to fill a number of roles: vote counter, vote worker, strategist, coalition builder inside and outside the House, facilitator, negotiator, salesman and perhaps most importantly, good listener." More than just "framing issues," he wrote, the position entails "maximizing Republican support" by "not only counting votes but by working long before to structure the vote in a way that takes into consideration the views and needs of all Republican members."[77] DeLay's view of the whip was thus less about procedure than about partisan agenda setting and policy making.

McCollum's vision of the whip's job placed greater emphasis on media outreach and fundraising. His campaign manager Jim Hansen (R-UT) wrote to colleagues in March 1994 that "if we are going to win control of the House and run it, we must choose . . . a person who can articulate the Republican positions on key issues, build consensus within the Conference, and reach out to House Democrats to win votes." He also added that McCollum "is a motivational speaker and fund-raiser; he is exceptionally good on television and is highly respected by key players all over Washington."[78]

Regional politics emerged as an important theme of the race. Walker argued that, as a Pennsylvanian, he could provide nonsouthern Democrats with needed representation in the party's leadership. His campaign circulated a document which noted that, since 1919, House majority parties had had a Speaker, majority leader, whip, and Ways and Means chairman from different areas of the country, but if his party took back the House in 1994, all four leadership posts would be occupied by southerners, three from Texas alone.[79] McCollum struck the same theme, though as a southerner he was limited to complaining about Texas dominance (Cooper 1994). Yet DeLay did not cede the North to Walker. As Hastert later recounted, "one of the things we should do was surround Walker, I thought. He'd be able to carry Pennsylvania, his home state, but we ought to get New York, New Jersey, Delaware, Maryland, and Ohio—neutralize him with easterners and isolate him in his base" (Hastert 2004, 110). In late July 1994, five New York freshmen all announced that they would vote for DeLay over Walker, and Hastert made a deal with Dean Gallo (R-NJ) to secure the New Jersey delegation for DeLay, perhaps in exchange for helping Dick Zimmer (R-NJ) secure a spot on the coveted Ways and Means Committee (Burger 1994a, 1994e; Hastert 2004).

All three candidates offered services to colleagues and employed the novel tactic of hiring outside consultants to advise them on strategy. One of DeLay's advantages was that he had been what one critic called "a House 'concierge' who arranged golf tee-off times for members and got them free concert tickets" and connected incumbent Republicans with campaign money from lobbyists and conservative interest groups (Reid 2014, 62). The candidates also provided colleagues with campaign funds, but to different degrees. By late 1994, DeLay and McCollum had created LPACs and donated hundreds of thousands of dollars to incumbents and first-time House candidates. By contrast, Walker—who did not "believe in leadership PACs" and, furthermore, "just didn't have access to that kind of money" that his opponents did—did not create an LPAC, and he lagged significantly behind in campaign contributions (Burger 1994b; Cooper 1994; Simpson 1994; Winneker 1994).[80]

McCollum and DeLay were especially generous to potential Republican freshmen. McCollum bet heavily on defeating key incumbent Democrats, including Speaker Tom Foley of Washington, investing $30,000 in anti-Foley ads. DeLay created what he termed a "candidate school" for Republicans running against Democratic incumbents and in open House seats and even endorsed candidates in Republican primaries, a risky bet that paid off when thirty-seven of his thirty-eight favored candidates won. Walker believed that at least some Republican candidates would be "turned off" by what appeared to be a quid pro quo of money for votes, and he hoped instead to win their votes by "providing technical support to all candidates regardless of the races' prospects for victory."[81] By early August 1994, Walker was aware that he was behind in lobbying potential freshmen, but he reasoned that, if history was any guide, the new Republican freshman class would consist of "between 50 and 55 Members." He estimated he would only need about half of those freshmen's votes to survive the first ballot, whereas his strongest competitor, Tom DeLay, would need between 80 and 90 percent of the freshmen to win, a feat "almost beyond imagination" (Burger 1994b, 1994d, 1994f; DeLay 2007).[82]

Each candidate exaggerated his level of vote commitments to buoy the morale of allies and convince wavering Republicans to cast their ballots for the winning side. In mid-August, a DeLay staffer showed one journalist a list of seventy-one supporters, and Walker privately expressed frustration that DeLay was engaged in a "disinformation campaign," "attempt[ing] . . . to create a bandwagon effect" by over-stating his support.[83] McCollum, too, was sharing optimistic vote counts. By early October, the capitol newspaper *Roll Call* reported that the total count of votes claimed by all three candidates were twenty-three more than the actual size of the party. Nevertheless, as the campaign progressed in the fall of 1994, it appeared increasingly likely that, despite his public optimism, McCollum would run a distant third. If true, then McCollum's supporters would be free agents if there were a second round of voting, and both DeLay and Walker tried to garner second ballot commitments from them (Burger 1994b, 1994c; Goldstein 1994).

On the evening of November 8, 1994, Republicans joyfully discovered that their long stint in the minority was about to end. This was not good news for the leadership campaigns of either McCollum or Walker, however. Having a skilled spokesperson for whip, as McCollum insisted he would be, was now less important with Gingrich's promise to be a high-profile public Speaker (Harris 1998).

Meanwhile, Walker's emphasis on having procedural skills to outwit majority Democrats had become moot,[84] and because the Pennsylvanian had underestimated the size of the freshmen Republican class, he was put at a grave disadvantage against his rivals who had been aggressively courting and funding new GOP candidates. Nonetheless, Walker and McCollum as well as DeLay continued to fight for votes, hosting receptions for new members, sending out checks, and publicizing endorsements—and, in Walker's case, emphasizing his close ties to Gingrich (Burger 1994f; Burger and Jacoby 1994; Sheffner 1994).

The first Republican Conference to elect majority leadership in forty years met in December 1994. Though two DeLay supporters told the Texan they would no longer vote for him, it was not enough to eliminate DeLay's lead over his rivals, and he won on the first ballot, with 119 votes to Walker's 80 and McCollum's 28 (Burger 1994g).

The election brought into the top GOP leadership one of the most influential figures of the modern House. DeLay would help his party win many close votes over the years, and while Gingrich became a highly visible Speaker, DeLay leveraged K Street ties and used other techniques to build up an independent foundation of support within the conference. Gingrich's star began to fade in 1996 and early 1997, and DeLay played at least a secondary role in a failed coup attempt against Gingrich in July 1997, weakening the Speaker's stature still further. When Gingrich announced his resignation in late 1998, DeLay ushered his former campaign manager and current deputy whip Dennis Hastert into the speakership, and he eventually became second-in-command as majority leader.

We test the impact of salient goals and professional connections for the 1994 whip election with an estimate of vote choice derived from two preelection counts tabulated by Walker.[85] Though the number of lawmakers who positively committed to Walker (82) is just two more than the number of votes he actually received,[86] Walker did not record those who committed specifically to DeLay or McCollum, so we can only test whether lawmakers voted for or against the Penn-sylvanian. We therefore use probit to test what factors influenced the votes of lawmakers. To estimate the role of professional connections, we include dichotomous variables capturing whether lawmakers were from the same states as Walker, DeLay, or McCollum, or served on the same committee as one of the candidates (Appropriations for De-Lay, Science for Walker, and Banking or Judiciary for McCollum). In terms of lawmaker goals, though reelection concerns were not es-pecially salient in the race, all three candidates did donate campaign funds to Republicans running for office, so we include a logged mea-sure of all monies donated by each candidate's LPAC to a lawmaker in the 1994 election cycle.[87] Policy goals were not salient in any of the campaigns, so we do not expect ideology to explain vote choice. Influence goals, by contrast, were more salient. Walker was the most senior candidate, next in line to be a committee chairman, and seen as more of an institutionalist, and he also sought out the commit-ments of senior and higher-ranking Republicans, so we include mea-sures of term in office and ranking committee status. While serving in leadership could explain a vote for Walker, who was close to Newt Gingrich, the other candidates were also in leadership, likely negat-ing the effect of that variable. We also control for membership in a mid-Atlantic state delegation, though we are doubtful that regional influence played a role. Two of the three candidates were from the South, likely splitting southerners' allegiance, and though Walker sought to appeal to nonsoutherners seeking a place at the leadership table, DeLay also targeted large northern delegations.

The results of the analysis, which appear in table 4.4, provide solid evidence for the mixed-motive model. Note that all state delegation variables are perfectly separated by vote choice and must be omitted, and though only one committee variable (shared Walker committee) is statistically significant (in Model 1), in Model 2 it increases the probability of voting for Walker by 18 percent.[88] Several variables measuring salient goals are also statistically significant. The Walker contribution variable is not significant, but the DeLay variable is; a

Table 4.4. Analysis of Estimated Vote for Walker as Majority Whip (1994)

Hypothesis	Independent Variable	Model 1	Model 2	Change in Probability (Model 2)
Professional Connections	On Walker committee	0.63* (0.32)	0.54 (0.36)	.34, .52 [+.18]
	On DeLay committee	0.28 (0.31)	−0.34 (0.34)	.37, .27 [−.10]
	On McCollum committee	0.28 (0.27)	0.12 (0.30)	.35, .39 [+.04]
Goal Salience	$ from Walker (logged)	—	0.02 (0.02)	.36, .40 [+.05]
	$ from DeLay (logged)	—	−0.05* (0.02)	.36, .25 [−.11]
	$ from McCollum (logged)	—	0.03* (0.01)	.36, .44 [+.08]
	Committee ranking member	—	−0.33 (0.39)	.37, .27 [−.10]
	Term	—	0.09* (0.04)	.36, .46 [+.11]
	Age	—	0.03* (0.01)	.21, .22 [+.02]

Other Variables			
% 2-party vote (logged)	—	−0.19 (0.57)	.36, .34 [−.01]
DW-NOMINATE (1st dimension)	—	−0.15 (0.56)	.36, .35 [−.01]
In leadership	—	0.26 (0.44)	.35, .44 [+.08]
From Mid-Atlantic	—	0.23 (0.27)	.35, .42 [+.07]
Constant	−0.47*** (0.10)	−2.44** (0.73)	
N	227	227	
Log L	−145.01	−125.41	
McFadden's R^2	.02	.15	
PRE	3.7%	18.5%	

Note: Table entries for each model are probit coefficients with robust standard errors in parentheses. The final column shows the average predicted probabilities of supporting Walker when each variable in Model 2 is changed from 0 to 1 (for dichotomous variables) or increased by one standard deviation (for continuous variables) with the difference in brackets.

^ significant at $p < .1$; * significant at $p < .05$; ** significant at $p < .01$; *** significant at $p < .001$ (2-tailed test).

one standard deviation increase in contributions (about $3,600) above the mean decreases the probability of a Walker vote by 11 percent. Interestingly, the coefficient of the McCollum contribution variable, while significant, is in an unexpectedly positive direction; this is perhaps because McCollum hoped to "buy back" the support of legislators already committed to the Pennsylvanian. Age and seniority are also both statistically significant and in the expected direction. In addition, seniority has a fairly substantial effect, with a one standard increase in terms served (3.5 terms) raising the likelihood of a vote for Walker by 11 percent. As expected, the variables measuring two-party vote, ideology, leadership position, and region are not statistically significant.[89]

The effectiveness of campaign contributions can also be estimated by looking at the relationship between donations and vote choice of freshmen, who presumably had no personal or professional relationships with the candidates. The results suggest that money, particularly the size of contributions, mattered. Of the forty-four Republican freshmen to whom Walker gave money, sixteen (36 percent) voted for the Pennsylvanian, but of the twenty-seven freshmen to whom he gave nothing, only six (or 22 percent) did so. Walker's opponents also had two advantages with respect to campaign donations: they gave much larger contributions—Walker donated a median $500 contribution to freshmen, whereas McCollum gave $2,500 on average and DeLay gave an average of $3,500—and they did so earlier. This may explain why over 60 percent (twenty-five) of the forty who received money from Walker and at least one opponent opted to side with the opponent. DeLay and McCollum apparently had other ways of winning over freshmen as well, for all five who got no funding from Walker's opponents still voted for one of them over Walker.

In sum, each of the candidates in the 1994 race for Republican whip possessed certain advantages going into the election. McCollum had the fewest of the three, however, and while Walker was able to draw votes from older, more senior colleagues and from fellow committee members, DeLay was not only able to win the votes of his large Texas delegation but earned additional support by outspending his rivals. The net result is that professional connections and salient goals were significant factors in explaining vote choice in the election.

Conclusion

As noted in the previous chapter, open competition races represent opportunities for ambitious lawmakers to gain a desired leadership post without the risks of challenging incumbents or the heir apparent—and, as a result, are the most common type of party leadership election in the House. Just as it helps explain vote choice in open races in the Democratic Party, the mixed-motive model provides insight into the selection of Republicans in their party's open leadership races. Professional connections and salient lawmaker goals are statistically significant factors in all four races discussed in this chapter.

One important difference from the Democrats' open races is the limited importance of legislator ideology. Whereas DW-NOMINATE scores are statistically significant in all three races analyzed in chapter 3, they are only significant in one of the four analyzed in this chapter. This finding underscores the fact that the GOP often selected leaders in the 1980s and 1990s based on whether they were establishment candidates with an accommodating style or insurgents with a more confrontational approach to the opposite party (Harris 2006; Lee 2016). But we also show that other factors, like campaign donations, mattered in these races as well.

In the next chapter, we turn to a different kind of election: when a party leader is the heir apparent to a vacant leadership office but is challenged in her bid to move into that office. Though the dynamics of those races differ from the ones examined here, we provide evidence that the mixed-motive model applies to these leadership elections, too.

Congressional parties often establish informal patterns of succession in which the occupant of one leadership post is expected to fill a vacancy in another. This leadership ladder serves at least two purposes: it gives would-be leaders a chance to prove themselves in subordinate positions of authority, and it reduces intraparty conflict and competition for the most consequential leadership offices (Nelson 1977; Peabody 1976). But the ladder is a norm, not a rule. It cannot prevent an ambitious or attention-seeking individual from running for a post "out of turn," nor is it enforced against party members who, unhappy with the heir apparent, vote against him. Such leadership races are the subject of this chapter.

When Robert Peabody suggested this category of elections, he introduced a tricky definitional problem: how do we know that an "established pattern of succession," as he put it, exists (Peabody 1976, 267)? There are at least two ways of identifying one. The first is lawmakers and observers widely recognizing the existence of a leadership ladder. The second, which we employ because it is easier to measure and less prone to subjectivity, is the presence of a documented pattern of succession. Specifically, if at least two of the past three vacancies for a leadership post (including the most recent vacancy) were filled by someone from the same "lower" leadership position, we consider the occupant of the latter position to be the heir apparent to the former. We also buttress this claim with anecdotal evidence, when available, that a nontrivial number of lawmakers believed a norm of succession existed.

Such elections are rare. Only five times between 1961 and 2016 could a contested House leadership election be described as a challenge to the heir apparent, based on our definition.[1] Their paucity is due in part to the formidable skills and resources most heirs apparent have, which deter potential challengers; in part to lawmakers' conformity with the leadership hierarchy, particularly by Democrats during this period; and in part to the large number of leadership positions that have not been considered part of an established ladder of succession (Nelson 1977). As a result, even though Peabody argued that insurgent challenges to existing leaders tend to follow disappointing elections, they do not take the form of challenges to heirs apparent, as none of the five occurred after negative election returns for the party (Peabody 1976). If they are rare, they are nonetheless still important, for they can reveal deeper intraparty fissures and have major long-term effects. The winner of the 1976 majority leader race, for instance, went on to become a polarizing Speaker of the House who expanded the power of the office in new ways, and the victor of the 2006 Republican majority leader race would eventually become Speaker as well.

What kind of politics characterizes these sorts of leadership races? Unsurprisingly, heirs apparent tend to campaign with an emphasis on their experience and place in the leadership ladder. The assumption is that they win support from those more accustomed to, and more likely to uphold, established patterns of succession—namely, older lawmakers and those in positions of leadership in the party or on a committee. If they have won a leadership election before, their prior campaign experience may help them secure votes. "When you have staff who are experienced in whipping votes," as one Republican aide put it, you have "an enormous advantage."[2] In addition, heirs apparent may possess a slight edge in winning the support of ambivalent lawmakers since, all else being equal, those legislators are likely to succumb to tradition and vote for the "status quo" choice. Their victory is by no means guaranteed, however: in two of the five races between 1961 and 2016, the heir apparent lost.

In this chapter, we analyze three challenges to the heir apparent. The first was probably the most famous example of this type of race in the contemporary House—the 1976 race for Democratic majority leader—and the other two were races for Republican majority leader in early 2006 and, after that year's congressional elections,

Democratic majority leader. In all three instances, one of the candidates running for majority leader was serving as whip, a position that at the time was the "natural" precursor to becoming leader. In 1976, the last three Democratic majority leaders had previously been whip, and in 2006, five of the last seven Democratic leaders, and two of the last three Republican leaders, had been party whips.[3]

By One Vote: The 1976 Race for Majority Leader

For political impact and sheer drama, few leadership contests from the last fifty years surpass the 1976 election for House majority leader. A four-candidate race that involved some of the biggest personalities ever elected to the chamber, it underlined how an heir apparent cannot take victory for granted, especially when running against strong rivals. Not only was the outcome decided by a single vote, but the victor, Jim Wright of Texas, would later become a powerful Speaker who inadvertently boosted the career of Republican gadfly Newt Gingrich.[4]

The Candidates

The opportunity for a new House majority leader emerged when Speaker Carl Albert announced his retirement in June 1976. Majority Leader Tip O'Neill, heir apparent for Albert's job, ran unopposed, leaving his own leadership job vacant. The traditional successor was the majority whip, a post held by John McFall of California.[5] A relatively long-serving lawmaker (fifty-nine years old and finishing his tenth term) with a clear claim to the position, McFall was expected to earn the votes of more senior Democrats and, as the most conservative candidate, was a natural choice of the rightmost wing of the party.[6] He could also hope to draw support from two large voting blocs, fellow Californians and colleagues on the Appropriations Committee. Furthermore, McFall was generally seen as loyal and friendly, appreciated for his efforts to improve the Democrats' whip operation, and would in all probability garner the endorsement of O'Neill, who had originally appointed him whip. Unfortunately, McFall was relatively unassuming and, more problematic, unskilled at the art of asking for votes. He himself later admitted that "I didn't go about campaigning with the aggressiveness that it required," and while other candidates were rounding up support, he waited patiently until Albert officially announced his retirement. As a result, according to the political scientists Bruce Oppenheimer and Robert Peabody, McFall "was never perceived as the frontrunner" (Jacobs 1995, 305; Oppenheimer and Peabody 1977, 18–19, 39).

The actual frontrunner was another Californian, Phil Burton. In contrast to McFall, the highly ambitious Burton was what one observer described as an "indefatigable" campaigner who would "go wherever the votes are," and he had demonstrated his skills by winning two elected positions in the party: chair of the liberal activist Democratic Study Group (DSG) in 1971 and chair of the House Democratic Caucus in 1974 (Jacobs 1995). Burton challenged McFall's ability to call on fellow Californians for support, and he had done favors for many legislators in the past, including nonvoting delegates and those from coal-mining and cotton districts.[7] But what made Burton truly formidable was his unabashed liberalism coupled with a mastery of policy and politics.[8] By 1976 he could take credit for an impressive array of legislative achievements, ranging from a major expansion of minimum wage eligibility to the creation of the Supplemental Security Income program, thus earning the respect of the party's growing cadre of liberals. Also, Burton was not only the youngest candidate running (aged fifty in January 1977) but had earned the gratitude of more junior progressives by supporting rules changes that helped them at the expense of older, more conservative members and chairmen (Oppenheimer and Peabody 1977).[9]

Burton also had some substantial flaws. The reforms he undertook threatened the long-standing authority of senior Democrats, whose votes he might need in a close race. His relentless desire for influence rubbed many the wrong way, and some even called him "power-mad" and "ruthless."[10] The aggressive parliamentary tactics he sometimes employed as chair of the Democratic Caucus were off-putting to several lawmakers, and a number of Democrats found Burton's coarseness repellent. When he wanted his way, Burton could be "his typical overpowering self, screaming, bullying, [and] manipulating" others, and he was even worse when drinking, "spewing saliva as he screamed vulgarities or berated colleagues in front of staff or peers," according to Burton biographer John Jacobs. Even supporters admitted that Burton had, as Morris Udall (D-AZ) put it, "the personality of a brillo pad." Jacobs identified a baker's dozen Democrats who were either Burton's personal rivals or had been offended by him for some reason (Jacobs 1995; Oppenheimer and Peabody 1977).[11]

The third Democrat to make a go for the office was Richard Bolling (D-MO). Groomed by Speaker Sam Rayburn early in his career, Bolling became a regular attendee at Rayburn's informal gatherings of top Democrats and was appointed to the prestigious Committee on Rules. Bolling had briefly run against Carl Albert for majority leader in 1962, and Jim Wright recalled that "from early in his career, he had dreamed of someday being Speaker" (Wright 1996, 259). Perhaps just as importantly, Bolling wanted Burton—who had helped defeat Bolling's proposal for committee reform in the previous Congress—to lose. Persuaded to run by colleagues desperate for a strong competitor against Burton, Bolling had several strengths as a candidate. Because he was moderate to liberal,[12] with a track record of endorsing House reform, he could hope to tap into support from the liberal, reformist wing of the party. Bolling was also the oldest and longest-serving candidate (aged sixty-one and starting his fifteenth term in the House at the time of the election) and, given his former connections to Rayburn, had ties to senior members. Still, he was far from a perfect candidate. Bolling's past criticisms of Speaker John McCormack and the seniority system had alienated many; his state delegation and committees (Rules and Joint Economic) were relatively small; and he had a less impressive record of legislative achievement than Burton. "We support him [Bolling] for what he's thinking about doing, and how he'd like to do it," as one of his supporters put it, "not because we believe he's able to accomplish everything."[13] The Missourian was also arrogant and aloof. "He is not a politician who glad-hands," one Democrat later observed, and John Rhodes remarked that Bolling "doesn't suffer a fool gladly" (Champagne et al. 2009; Chapman 1982; J. Farrell 2001; Jacobs 1995; Oppenheimer and Peabody 1977; Struck 1976).

Such were the choices facing Democrats in early June 1976. Then, after other possible contenders like Brock Adams (D-WA) and Chief Deputy Whip John Brademas (D-IN) declined to run, a fourth candidate joined the pack. Jim Wright was a beneficiary of the Austin-Boston alliance, becoming deputy whip in part as a counterweight to the northern contingent in the Democratic leadership, and in the words of journalist John Barry, "ambition burned in him as fiercely as in anyone in Washington" (Barry 1989, 12). Nonetheless, he had deferred to the heir apparent and did not run for majority leader until, as McFall's candidacy stalled, he was encouraged by others, including Commerce Committee chairman Harley Staggers (D-WV) and Dan Rostenkowski (D-IL), to consider a run.[14] After sounding out other representatives and prospective freshmen Democrats at the Democratic National Convention that summer, he decided he had a solid chance of winning. Both likeable and an impressive public speaker, Wright could draw votes from his large Texas delegation and Public Works committee, which funded special projects in lawmakers' districts. He was uniquely positioned as the only conservative southerner in the race, and the party's southern wing still represented about one-third of the caucus.[15] He was also simultaneously the second-youngest and second-most senior candidate to run (aged fifty-five and starting his twelfth term in January 1977), suggesting an ability to appeal to both junior and senior Democrats. But Wright's competitors had had a six-week head start in gathering votes, and Wright had taken some positions on the Vietnam War and civil rights that were unpopular with liberals. "No one thought Wright could win," Burton supporter Abner Mikva (D-IL) later claimed, explaining that he was "an afterthought, put up by the power brokers who didn't want Burton or Bolling" (Barry 1989; Champagne et al. 2009; Jacobs 1995; Naughton 1976; Oppenheimer and Peabody 1977; Russell 1976a; Wright 1996).

The Campaign

Each of the four candidates used his campaign to play up his perceived strengths. Burton and his allies stressed his liberalism and support for reforming the House.[16] McFall highlighted his successful and dutiful tenure as whip, while Bolling pointed to his lengthy efforts to improve the operations of the chamber, extolled the need to improve the Democrats' whip system and organizational structure, and drew a contrast with Burton by emphasizing his fairness and good relations with O'Neill.[17] Wright advertised his ideological and regional identity, though near the end of the campaign—following an ill-advised comment by Bolling about why Wright would lose, which made its way back to Wright—his staff also brought up his support for some civil rights bills (Champagne et al. 2009; Jacobs 1995; Oppenheimer and Peabody 1977).[18]

A number of the candidates tried to strike broader themes they thought might help. Burton portrayed himself as the frontrunner to win over wavering Democrats who might want to back the victor. Bolling's campaign argued that their candidate was the most likely to beat Burton, underscored with probably the largest and most developed campaign operation of any of the candidates. Wright hoped that an early endorsement by the Texas delegation would create the same impression, and he emphasized "balance"—a reference to not being a northern liberal like O'Neill—while also insisting he was in the "mainstream of the party" and "not regional or colloquial in outlook" (Oppenheimer and Peabody 1977).[19]

With the possible exception of McFall, the candidates had started informally gathering vote commitments well before officially declaring their candidacies. Committee colleagues and state delegation members were an important target of all four. Recent and potential new members were another valuable constituency, and Burton and Wright met with them at the party's presidential convention in July, raised money for them, and visited their districts. Burton had done the same for the huge freshman class of 1974, but Bolling's campaign team worked to woo them away from Burton, lobbying them early on and recruiting some of them to his campaign team (Jacobs 1995; Leamer 1977; Mintz 1976; Oppenheimer and Peabody 1977; Russell 1976b).[20]

Some candidates sought outside endorsements and support from interest groups. For instance, after the 1976 elections, Wright tried to create the impression that president-elect Jimmy Carter supported him; he did this by wearing a gold peanut lapel pin and circulating a news report (written by a Wright ally) that speculated Wright was Carter's favored candidate (King 1999). With the encouragement of ally Dan Rostenkowski, the mayors of Chicago, New York, and Philadelphia reportedly asked their congressional delegations to support Wright, who had advocated for urban funding from his post on Public Works (Jacobs 1995; Leamer 1977; Oppenheimer and Peabody 1977).[21]

Wright's late entry altered the strategic calculations of the other three to some degree. McFall had the most to fear, since Wright could appeal to his base of conservatives. Burton reemphasized his liberalism, early support for civil rights bills (particularly the Civil Rights Act of 1964, which Wright had voted against), and steadfast opposition to the Vietnam War to distinguish himself from his more hawkish rivals.[22] Bolling criticized Wright for being too conservative and less supportive of civil rights than he, and to stem the possible tide of conservative votes to Wright, he tried to convince Burton opponents that he would be stronger than Wright in a one-on-one matchup against Burton.[23] On this last point, Burton and his allies agreed, and may have even tried to create the impression that Wright had more support than Bolling, hoping it would give Wright enough momentum to defeat Bolling in an early round of balloting (Oppenheimer and Peabody 1977).[24]

Tip O'Neill was a popular party leader, and his preference among the candidates was potentially critical. Publicly, the Speaker-elect endorsed McFall, but he also did not expect McFall to beat Burton, whose rampant ambition and erratic, vulgar personality unnerved him. Despite repeated public denials by O'Neill and his staff, as one reporter put it, "many believed . . . that he could work with 'anybody but Burton'" (Struck 1976). This might have swayed some Democrats, but more importantly, O'Neill—via his staff and through subtle hints to Wright—had helped recruit Wright to run in the first place and had blessed the well-connected Rostenkowski to help Wright's campaign (Baron 1976; J. Farrell 2001; Jacobs 1995).[25]

The election would be conducted in rounds, with the lowest vote getter forced to drop out after each round (except the first, which was considered nonbinding), until one candidate received an absolute majority. As McFall's odds of victory fell, his supporters became a coveted prize for the other contenders. Burton figured he would get them; Wright desperately needed them to survive the second round of balloting; and some of Bolling's allies, anxious that McFall would divert votes that their candidate might otherwise get, contemplated pressuring McFall to withdraw altogether (Oppenheimer and Peabody 1977).

Two unexpected developments potentially altered some lawmakers' preferences. In May 1976, it was revealed that Wayne Hays, chair of the Administration Committee, one-time candidate for majority leader (see chapter 3), and a close ally of Burton's, had hired a secretary to serve as his mistress. Hays's subsequent resignation not only cost Burton a vote but also hurt his relationship with Democrats, particularly the many freshmen who had, with Burton's urging, voted to retain Hays as chair in 1974 (Jacobs 1995; Leamer 1977). Then, shortly after the November congressional elections, it was reported that McFall had taken cash from a foreign lobbyist. Though McFall had not technically broken any laws, the scandal damaged his reputation and distracted him from campaigning (Oppenheimer and Peabody 1977). By mid-November, six McFall supporters had told Wright they would vote for him on the first ballot instead.[26]

Between the congressional elections and the election for majority leader, the candidates continued to scurry for last-minute votes. Wright hosted a luncheon for incoming freshmen the week before the election, at which he magnanimously praised his opponents and Carroll Hubbard (D-KY), the president of the class of 1974—a group presumably fully behind Burton—unexpectedly endorsed Wright.

The DSG also hosted a forum for freshmen at which all the candidates appeared. Illustrating the extent to which the race had garnered national publicity, the four candidates made a joint appearance on *Meet the Press* the Sunday before the election. Wright used the opportunity to defend a senior colleague, Robert Sikes (D-FL), who had been accused of ethical wrongdoing, possibly shoring up his support among older Democrats. Despite these moves by Wright, he was still considered an underdog. By the end of November, the conventional wisdom was that Burton was in the lead with 100 to 120 commitments—about 25 to 45 votes shy of a majority—Bolling was in second, Wright was in a close third, and McFall had the fewest (Baron 1976; Lyons 1976; Oppenheimer and Peabody 1977).

The Election

On Monday morning, December 6, the candidates and their allies lobbied lawmakers and double-checked commitments for the last time, and in the early afternoon House Democrats congregated on the floor of the chamber to vote. Each candidate was nominated and seconded by a handful of legislators, including fellow state delegation or committee members (with Wright alone being seconded by a freshman), and one-on-one campaigning continued quietly even as the speeches were being delivered. Rostenkowski gave the last speech, an "especially vehement" oration that made thinly veiled criticisms of Burton and Bolling; he pointedly declared that Wright "hasn't engaged in backbiting or petty intrigue" and "has never demagogued against this institution" ("95th Congress Elected New Leaders" 1978; Oppenheimer and Peabody 1977).[27] Then the voting began.

The results of the first ballot were relatively unsurprising. Burton came in first, with 106 votes; Bolling in second, with 81; Wright in third, with 77; and McFall fourth, with 31 votes. Though glad to be in first place, Burton was disappointed that Wright, a weaker opponent, was in danger of elimination in the next round, while Bolling was disheartened that Wright had earned so many votes. Under the rules, all four contenders were eligible for the second ballot, but

McFall withdrew, and the remaining candidates and their supporters lobbied McFall voters as the second round of voting began. When the balloting concluded, the results yielded a pair of major surprises. Wright had narrowly come in second, with 95 ballots, beating Bolling by a mere 2 votes. Furthermore, while Burton remained in first, he had garnered 107 votes, just one more than he had gotten before. This suggested a couple of troubling possibilities: either Burton was not as preferable to McFall supporters as had been believed, or some of his supporters had thrown their votes to Wright to push Bolling out (Bachrach and Radcliffe 1976; Oppenheimer and Peabody 1977).[28]

A final showdown between Burton and Wright was widely assumed to be advantageous to Burton. But as lobbying by the surviving candidates and their campaign teams began one more time, three factors were working against the Californian. First, although Burton was "twisting arms and punching chests with an eager forefinger," according to the journalist (and former Wright aide) Larry King, he had kept his campaign team small, making it harder to reach as many Bolling voters as could Wright's larger team which, in the Texan's words, "fanned out like a bunch of June bugs" on the House floor (King 1980; Oppenheimer and Peabody 1977). Second, Burton's suspicious lack of second-round support convinced some Democrats that he had "kicked back votes" to Wright, which reinforced critics' claim that he was untrustworthy. Third, the anti-Burton animus of Bolling and his supporters was so strong that they were willing to lobby against Burton no matter who his opponent was (Jacobs 1995; Leamer 1977; Rennert 1977).[29]

The last round of voting was so close that it came down to the final ballot, counted by Charlie Wilson (D-TX). "I reached out like my hand was deadweight and turned up the last card," he later recalled. "It was 'Jim Wright'" (King 1980). Wright had won, 148 to 147. He and his supporters were jubilant. Bolling was also pleased, as was O'Neill. Burton was devastated by the loss, however, and he never fully recovered from it. Burton supporters angrily, if briefly, contemplated forming a "147 Club" of Burton loyalists, and the Californian announced his interest in running for whip should it switch from being an appointed position to an elected one. Unfortunately for Burton, that change would not happen until 1985, over a year after his death. Although Wright and others remained vigilant of the possibility that the ambitious Burton would run again for majority leader, he never did (Jacobs 1995; Oppenheimer and Peabody 1977; Russell 1976c).[30]

In addition to the incredibly close outcome, the 1976 election for majority leader was important for its political consequences. The election positioned Jim Wright to become Speaker of the House of Representatives—a Speaker who, after expanding the powers of the speakership in new ways, became embroiled in an ethical controversy and resigned from office (Barry 1989; Davidson 1988; Flippen 2018). That resignation in turn bolstered the reputation of his primary antagonist, Newt Gingrich, who became one of the most influential and polarizing Speakers of the House of Representatives.

Explaining Vote Choice

The outcome of a race decided by a single ballot that involved strategic voting and strong sentiments about certain candidates can probably never be fully explained. The mixed-motive model may nonetheless shed at least some light into the general reasons that Democrats chose one particular candidate over another. To test the model in the first round of voting, we use multinomial logit regression, which calculates the likelihood of voting for three of the candidates (Burton, Bolling, or McFall) compared to the likelihood of voting for the fourth (Wright). As noted in chapter 3, multinomial logit is unable to estimate coefficients of variables that nearly perfectly correlate with vote choice, and it depends on the Independence of Irrelevant Alternatives (IIA) assumption. While an IIA test suggests that the assumption is valid, the fact that most McFall supporters appear to have cast their second-round ballots for either Wright or Bolling implies they were far from indifferent about Burton.[31] Some degree of caution in interpreting the results is therefore warranted.

To determine the effect of shared professional connections, we include dichotomous variables equal to 1 if a Democrat shared a state delegation or committee assignment with one of the candidates. In terms of legislator goals, concerns about reelection were generally not salient, so we should not expect electoral vulnerability to influence vote choice, though we still control for it in our regression analysis. Most campaign contributions and other electoral benefits distributed by the candidates went unrecorded and thus cannot be controlled for (R. Baker 1989).[32] Policy goals, on the other hand, were more salient. Burton was presumably more attractive a candidate to Democratic liberals, and Wright and McFall more appealing to conservatives, so we include DW-NOMINATE scores as a measurement of lawmakers' ideology. The Vietnam War was also a major campaign theme; we approximate support for the war with a dichotomous variable measuring if a lawmaker voted against a resolution offered by Bolling in 1972 to strip Vietnam withdrawal language from a foreign aid bill.[33] Another prominent policy issue was urban affairs. To capture whether Wright earned the votes of urban lawmakers, thanks to Rostenkowski's lobbying of city leaders and Wright's service on Public Works, we include a dichotomous variable equal to 1 if a lawmaker was from one of the three largest urban delegations in the party: New York, Chicago, or Philadelphia (Oppenheimer and Peabody 1977, 22). Influence goals were salient, too. We would expect older and more senior Democrats, plus those in leadership, to prefer McFall, but also Wright, since he held a (lower) leadership post and was understood by many to be a favorite of O'Neill. By contrast, younger and newer lawmakers should lean toward Burton, while Bolling, who could appeal to both junior and senior legislators, may well have received support from both (or neither).[34] We therefore include measures of lawmaker age, terms served, and service as a party leader or committee chair. We also test our expectation that Wright, the sole representative from the South who was running, earned the votes of southern Democrats who wanted to maintain their region's influence.[35] In addition, for the first round of balloting we add a variable measuring whether a lawmaker served on a committee targeted for elimination or loss of jurisdiction by the Bolling Committee, since those Democrats may well have seen a Bolling victory as a threat to their committee's influence in the future. Finally, we test the effect of membership in the class of 1974; we expect members of that class to oppose McFall, who did little to win their votes, but are otherwise agnostic as to their support for the other three candidates, who all made a point of cultivating them (though Burton may have well lost some of their support due to the Wayne Hays scandal).

For the first round of voting, we calculate two estimates of vote choice based on whip counts kept by Wright and Rostenkowski. The more restrictive estimate uses as a baseline a Wright preelection campaign memo listing whether lawmakers were committed to Wright, committed to another candidate, or uncommitted.[36] For uncommitted lawmakers, we consulted a pair of additional, shorter memos that identified some lawmakers' non-Wright vote preferences, with contradictory or uncertain estimates from those memos coded as "uncertain" and thus excluded from our analysis.[37] The more relaxed estimate draws from several sources to estimate uncertain or unclear vote preferences in the first count, including a whip list in the Burton Papers, a brief Bolling memo from late July 1976, books or monographs that identified individual legislator vote choices, and other miscellaneous sources.[38] Lawmakers still coded as uncertain in the relaxed estimate are assumed to have voted for a candidate identified in a shorter Wright memo as a first ballot choice but noted with a question mark.[39]

The results of the analysis of the first ballot using the restrictive vote estimate (Model 1) and the relaxed vote estimate (Model 2) appear in table 5.1, and the effect of each variable on the relative probability of voting for each candidate versus Wright (for Model 2 only) is shown in table 5.2. Note that the leadership variable correlates perfectly with a vote for McFall, and variables measuring membership in the Missouri or Texas delegations, on a Wright committee, and on a Bolling committee (in Model 1) also correlate perfectly or nearly perfectly with the dependent variable, a strong sign that these professional connections shaped vote choice. All of these variables

Table 5.1. Analysis of Estimated Vote for Majority Leader (1976), 1st Ballot

Hypothesis	Independent Variable	Model 1 (Stringent Vote Estimate)			Model 2 (Relaxed Vote Estimate)		
		Burton	Bolling	McFall	Burton	Bolling	McFall
Professional Connection	From California	2.83*	−15.65***	4.11*	2.65*	−13.13***	3.23*
		(1.20)	(1.06)	(1.59)	(1.07)	(1.02)	(1.33)
	On Burton committee	1.69^	0.62	−0.70	1.68**	0.25	−0.07
		(0.97)	(0.90)	(1.04)	(0.61)	(0.68)	(0.94)
	On Bolling committee	—	—	—	0.08	0.62	−0.54
					(1.21)	(1.25)	(0.99)
	On McFall committee	−14.31***	0.09	−0.27	−0.74	−0.11	0.63
		(0.77)	(0.70)	(1.23)	(0.95)	(0.62)	(0.82)
Goal Salience	DW-NOMINATE (1st dimension)	−10.65**	−4.32^	−0.37	−8.21***	−2.84^	−1.01
		(4.05)	(2.21)	(2.35)	(2.05)	(1.67)	(1.89)
	Vietnam War	−0.05	0.73	−0.40	0.02	0.51	−0.31
		(1.03)	(0.71)	(0.97)	(0.69)	(0.57)	(0.82)
	Urban district	−16.02***	−1.01	−0.86	−0.81	−0.45	−0.42
		(1.23)	(1.20)	(1.44)	(1.03)	(1.02)	(0.98)
	Term	−0.04	0.21^	0.34*	−0.05	0.22*	0.27*
		(0.15)	(0.11)	(0.15)	(0.11)	(0.09)	(0.12)

Age	−0.03 (0.04)	0.05 (0.03)	−0.05 (0.04)	−0.05 (0.07)	−0.07* (0.03)	−0.04 (0.04)
Committee chair	1.95 (1.56)	0.04 (0.98)	1.08 (1.16)	−16.63*** (1.02)	−0.51 (0.91)	−15.52*** (0.98)
South	−0.69 (0.97)	−0.95 (0.71)	−0.18 (0.66)	−2.88** (1.06)	−1.09^ (0.56)	−2.52** (0.83)
Opposed committee reorganization	−0.42 (0.97)	−0.76 (0.69)	0.24 (0.60)	2.49** (0.87)	−0.45 (0.56)	1.98** (0.74)
Class of 1974	0.40 (0.84)	1.56* (0.71)	0.50 (0.61)	−12.05*** (1.16)	1.22* (0.59)	0.11 (1.30)
Other Variables % 2-party vote (logged)	−1.86 (2.22)	1.03 (1.37)	−0.41 (1.39)	5.14* (2.40)	0.99 (1.06)	3.35* (1.57)
Constant	−4.08 (2.54)	−0.50 (1.64)	−1.18 (1.75)	−1.04 (3.19)	1.12 (1.37)	−0.97 (1.75)
N		155			205	
Log L		−108.24			−183.81	
McFadden's R^2		.39			.31	
PRE		8.1%			17.2%	

Note: Table entries are multinomial logit coefficients (compared to the base outcome, a vote for Wright) with robust standard errors in parentheses.

^ p < .1; * p < .05; ** p < .01; *** p < .001 (2-tailed test).

Table 5.2. Change in Probabilities in Vote for Majority Leader (1976), 1st Ballot

Hypothesis	Independent Variable	Model 2 (Relaxed Vote Estimate) Burton	Bolling	McFall
Professional Connection	From California	.21, .52 [+.32]	.25, .00 [−.25]	.11, .33 [+.22]
	On Burton committee	.20, .43 [+.23]	.24, .18 [−.06]	.13, .09 [−.04]
	On Bolling committee	.23, .22 [−.01]	.22, .33 [+.10]	.13, .08 [−.04]
	On McFall committee	.24, .15 [−.09]	.23, .23 [+.00]	.11, .18 [+.07]
Goal Salience	DW-NOMINATE (1st dimension)	.23, .10 [−.13]	.22, .20 [−.02]	.13, .15 [+.02]
	Vietnam War	.24, .22 [−.02]	.20, .28 [+.08]	.14, .11 [−.03]
	Urban district	.24, .17 [−.06]	.23, .20 [−.02]	.13, .12 [−.01]
	Term	.23, .14 [−.09]	.22, .36 [+.13]	.13, .20 [+.07]
	Age	.23, .20 [−.03]	.22, .16 [−.07]	.13, .12 [−.01]
	Committee chair	.23, .44 [+.21]	.22, .14 [−.08]	.14, .00 [−.14]
	South	.24, .30 [.06]	.42, .27 [−.15]	.08, .01 [−.07]
	Opposed committee reorganization	.24, .24 [+.01]	.27, .15 [−.12]	.05, .20 [+.15]
	Class of 1974	.23, .23 [+.00]	.18, .34 [+.16]	.13, .10 [−.03]
Other Variables	% 2-party vote (logged)	.23, .20 [−.03]	.22, .24 [+.02]	.13, .18 [+.05]

Note: The columns show the average predictive probabilities of supporting each candidate when each variable is changed from 0 to 1 (for dichotomous variables) or increased by one standard deviation (for continuous variables) with the difference in brackets.

must be excluded to avoid overinflated coefficients and uncertain standard errors. Coefficients for the remaining variables are mostly consistent with the mixed-motive model. The California delegation variable is statistically significant in both models. Members of the delegation were positively associated with a vote for Burton or Mc-Fall relative to Wright—increasing the relative probability of voting for each by 32 percent and 22 percent, respectively—but negatively associated with a vote for Bolling relative to Wright (reducing the probability of voting for Bolling to near-zero). Democrats from Burton's committees were positively associated with a vote for Burton over Wright, increasing the probability of supporting Burton by 23 percent compared to Wright. In terms of salient goals, conservative Democrats were negatively associated with a vote for Burton or Bolling compared to Wright, as expected.[40] Opposition to the Vietnam War is not statistically significant, but urban Democrats were positively associated with support for Wright compared to his rivals, as expected (and the associated variable is statistically significant for Burton in Model 1). Influence-related objectives also contributed to vote choice, though not always in the expected direction. Seniority is statistically significant and positively related to a vote for McFall (and, interestingly, Bolling) over Wright, suggesting Wright won over more junior Democrats, contrary to expectations. Age is also statistically insignificant for all three candidates opposing Wright (except for Bolling, in Model 2), though this finding may be an artifact of the correlation between term and age.[41] We expected committee chairs to vote for McFall or Wright; when forced to choose between them, they appear to have preferred the latter over the former, reducing the relative probability of supporting McFall by 14 percent. Southerners were also negatively associated with a vote for McFall or Bolling relative to Wright. The Bolling committee reorganization variable does not prove statistically significant in explaining opposition to Bolling, though it does help explain support for McFall versus Wright. In Model 1, the class of 1974 variable is statistically significant and negative in explaining a vote for McFall over Wright, as expected, and in both models, the variable is positive in explaining support for Bolling relative to Wright, increasing the probability of support for Bolling in Model 2 by 16 percent. Finally, one factor provides some unexpected explanatory leverage: election performance in 1976, which is statistically significant for McFall.[42]

Unfortunately, we were unable to locate sufficient data for analysis of the second round of balloting, but we did obtain data for the final round, for which we again used two estimates of vote choice. The first and more stringent estimate identifies voting preference when there is agreement among two tallies found in Burton's papers; if there is no agreement, the vote is considered undetermined.[43] The second, more relaxed estimate assigns vote choice for undetermined Democrats if it is identified as such by at least one of three sources: a Burton preelection count of lawmakers from California, Texas, New York, and Illinois; a postelection Burton staffer's tally of some lawmakers' vote; and addenda to one of the Burton whip counts. If there are any contradictory estimates among those three sources, the vote remains coded as undetermined.[44] Since there are only two candidates, we test the effect of professional connections and salient goals with probit regression, and the results are shown in table 5.3.

The results provide additional evidence for the mixed-motive model. All four professional connection variables are at least moderately statistically significant ($p < .10$) in at least one regression model, and their effects can be substantial: in Model 4, Californians were 18 percent less likely to vote for Wright, Texans were 20 percent more likely to do so, and Wright's fellow committee members were 22 percent more likely to support him. General ideology was also statistically significant; conservatives, as expected, were more likely to commit to Wright. Other policy-related variables show no statistical significance, but older and more senior lawmakers preferred Wright, as expected: a one standard deviation increase in seniority (3.4 terms) increased the probability of voting for Wright by 15 percent, and a one standard deviation increase in age (9.5 years) raised the probability by 7 percent. Though committee chairs were, surprisingly, less likely to support Wright, the leadership variable must be omitted because it perfectly predicts a vote for Wright, another indication that influence-related goals shaped vote choice in the expected direction. As predicted, electoral concerns are not statistically significant, nor is membership in the class of 1974 (given both Wright and Burton were campaigning for their votes).[45]

As in any leadership race, we cannot disprove the claim that other, unmeasurable factors played an important role in this election, which has earned such scrutiny that a slew of possible influences on the vote have been identified by scholars and observers. These factors include outside endorsements or interest group lobbying, scandal-related media coverage,[46] O'Neill's rumored opposition to Burton, lobbying by O'Neill and his associates, and private favors given by the candidates (J. Farrell 2001; Oppenheimer and Peabody 1977; Panetta 2014).[47] Nor can one deny the possibility that for some the choice was, as Burton put it, "personal and chemical in a way" (Champagne et al. 2009, 221). More than one Democrat shared the general sentiments of Frank Thompson (D-NJ), who quipped, "I would rather have a dose of clap than have Phil Burton in my district" (Leamer 1977, 382). One witness even alleged that Wright's team had won the second ballot in part by rousing a sleeping supporter who had nearly missed the vote (King 1980). Given how incredibly close the election was, just one or two lawmakers voting for idiosyncratic reasons could have reversed the outcome.

Nevertheless, the findings reveal that the candidates' campaigns and professional connections played an important role in determining lawmakers' voting decision. They also shed some new light on why Burton, the presumptive front-runner, lost the race. Californians were more likely to support him on the first ballot, and generally stuck with him on the third ballot, but he failed to secure support from as many members of the class of 1974 as he had hoped. Meanwhile, Wright had Texans behind him and, in the final round, senior lawmakers. As important as ideology may have been, it failed to attract enough Democrats to Burton's candidacy. Indeed, it was Burton's mistaken belief that ideology would be the principal factor in the race—and that therefore no moderate candidate could beat him on the final ballot—that contributed to his undoing. The outcome

Table 5.3. Analysis of Estimated Vote for Wright as Majority Leader (1976), 3rd Ballot

Hypothesis	Independent Variable	Stringent Vote Estimate		Relaxed Vote Estimate		Change in Probability (Model 4)
		Model 1	Model 2	Model 3	Model 4	
Professional Connection	From California	−0.54^ (0.28)	−0.38 (0.33)	−0.61* (0.27)	−0.61^ (0.32)	.53, .35 [−.18]
	From Texas	1.35** (0.39)	0.70 (0.49)	1.07** (0.35)	0.69^ (0.40)	.49, .70 [+.20]
	On Burton committee	−0.75** (0.26)	−0.58^ (0.30)	−0.56* (0.24)	−0.39 (0.27)	.53, .41 [−.12]
	On Wright committee	0.83* (0.38)	0.86* (0.37)	0.62^ (0.33)	0.76* (0.31)	.49, .72 [+.22]
Goal Salience	DW-NOMINATE (1st dimension)	—	3.48*** (0.74)	—	2.13** (0.81)	.51, .63 [+.12]
	Vietnam War	—	−0.03 (0.26)	—	−0.30 (0.26)	.54, .45 [−.08]
	Urban district	—	−0.03 (0.35)	—	0.02 (0.32)	.51, .51 [+.01]

	Model 1	Model 2	Model 3	Model 4	
Term	—	0.10* (0.04)	—	0.12** (0.04)	.51,.66 [+.15]
Age	—	0.03* (0.01)	—	0.02^ (0.01)	.51,.58 [+.07]
Committee chair	—	−0.60 (0.51)	—	−0.94^ (0.50)	.52,.27 [−.25]
South	—	0.19 (0.28)	—	−0.02 (0.26)	.51,.51 [−.01]
Other Variables					
% 2-party vote (logged)	—	0.71 (0.50)	—	0.67 (0.45)	.51,.55 [+.04]
Class of 1974	—	−0.30 (0.26)	—	−0.29 (0.23)	.53,.45 [−.09]
Constant	0.02 (0.10)	−0.38 (0.65)	0.04 (0.09)	−0.50 (0.58)	
N	255	248	275	268	
Log L	−159.31	−116.89	−177.17	−141.43	
McFadden's R²	.10	.32	.07	.24	
PRE	23.6%	54.9%	19.1%	43.5%	

Note: Table entries for each model are probit coefficients with robust standard errors in parentheses. The final column shows the average predicted probabilities of supporting Wright when each variable in Model 4 is changed from 0 to 1 (for dichotomous variables) or increased by one standard deviation (for continuous variables) with the difference in brackets.

^p < .1; *p < .05; **p < .01; ***p < .001 (2-tailed test).

also highlighted how important candidate emergence and the rules of an election can be: had Burton only faced McFall, the weakest candidate in the race, he would have likely had a lopsided victory, while the multiple-round balloting system and a requirement that the winner get a majority, not a plurality, of votes gave other candidates a chance to gain momentum against Burton.

Change versus the Status Quo: The 2006 Race for Majority Leader

In September 2005, Majority Leader Tom DeLay, facing criminal charges in his home state, temporarily stepped down from his leadership office. Whip Roy Blunt stepped in as acting leader, and when DeLay's temporary resignation became permanent, an election to fill his post was scheduled for February 2006. The election was not only a surprise defeat for heir apparent Blunt; it also propelled the victor, John Boehner, back into a leadership position that would lead to his selection as Speaker of the House five years later.

Blunt could make a solid case that he was entitled to the post. He was already serving in the position on a temporary basis, and he would be following in the footsteps of his predecessor by moving from whip to leader, just as Bob Michel had in 1980 (see chapter 4). Blunt was closely associated with DeLay, who had named him chief deputy whip in his second term in the House and who had supported Blunt's bid to succeed him as whip in 2002, helping clear the field of would-be challengers. To acknowledge his mentor, and perhaps to reinforce his heir apparent status, Blunt cited DeLay's leadership in his declaration of candidacy for majority leader (Pershing 2006a; Willis 2002). Doing so was risky, however, since it associated him with a party figure facing serious legal problems, magnified by other emerging Republican corruption scandals and low public-approval ratings for the GOP. Early missteps as acting floor leader also led some lawmakers to question Blunt's ability to serve in the position.

John Boehner shared Blunt's age, was roughly the same ideologically,[48] and also had some leadership experience. He had allegedly been "planning a return to leadership" for a while since losing reelection as Conference chair in 1998, though he had resisted pleas by some to run against DeLay when the majority leader position had last become vacant (Willis 2002).[49] Besides personal ambition, Boehner's candidacy seemed to be motivated (or at least framed) by the prospect of reforming his party and the chamber. He argued in his campaign manifesto that the GOP was "on a losing streak," "adrift," and "unsure," and it needed to move away from the "dangerous and demoralizing cycle of the status quo." He also observed that Republicans needed to "set big goals that express our vision" and "to develop mechanisms that ground these principles in the everyday work of the House." Citing his prior service as Conference chair, his chairmanship of the Education and Workforce Committee, and his reformist credentials as an outspoken critic of the House Bank and Post Office scandals in the early 1990s, Boehner pledged to solicit committee members' opinions on policy goals while also returning to the principles of the 1994 "Republican Revolution."[50]

John Shadegg (R-AZ), a late entrant into the race, could draw sharper distinctions from the other two candidates. The most conservative of the three, he had been chair of the Republican Study Committee (RSC), a large group of rightward-leaning Republicans who expressed frustration with the George W. Bush administration and House leadership for being insufficiently conservative.[51] The Arizonian had the least amount of party leadership experience of the three, having served for just one year as chairman of the Republican Policy Committee (RPC). On the other hand, like Boehner he was both ambitious and motivated to run for leader by the opportunity to implement change—specifically, change in his party's image and agenda. He urged "a clean break from the past," emphasized conservative policy goals, including tax reduction and limited government, and claimed that neither of his opponents were "idea people" like him (Bolton 2006; Hulse 2006; Weisman 2006a).

Blunt's campaign team boasted four dozen members and access to Blunt's whip resources, including a computerized vote-counting system and a database of legislators' professional and personal contact information. In 2005, Blunt's Rely on Your Beliefs (ROYB) leadership PAC contributed over $470,000 to House Republican incumbents. He soon claimed to have secured the support of enough Republicans to win, and he publicized the names of many of them, leading Boehner and Shadegg to follow suit. Blunt was also well-positioned as whip to distribute scarce goods to secure votes, and word spread that Blunt was offering to help colleagues get on desired committees in exchange for their support. In particular, to win over the large Texas and Florida delegations, he allegedly pledged to endorse Floridian Clay Shaw as chair of Ways and Means, and offered Texan Joe Barton, chair of the Energy and Commerce Committee, some of the jurisdictional turf of the Judiciary Committee. Word of these deals may have hurt Blunt with members of Judiciary, however, as well as committee chairmen sensitive to Boehner's claim that committee leadership had become subservient to party interests in recent years (O'Connor 2006b; Pershing 2006b, 2006c; VandeHei and Murray 2006).

Boehner assembled an informal campaign team that made calls on his behalf and reportedly worked "18 hours a day" (O'Connor 2006a). According to one Boehner aide, the campaign "started with the Ohio delegation, Education and Workforce [Committee], and Agriculture [Committee]," the two committees on which he served. Boehner's LPAC, Freedom Project, gave over $380,000 to Republican incumbents in 2005, and Boehner had traveled to various members' districts to help with their campaigns, favors he could bank for votes.[52] Shadegg's campaign team was also sizeable, with fifteen to twenty members, but despite endorsements from right-wing media sources as well as the conservative political action committee Club for Growth, he lacked the resources of his competitors. Not only had Shadegg given up his chairmanship of the RPC to run for majority leader, but he had no LPAC funds and had made just $9,000 in personal contributions to incumbents in the previous election cycle. He also did not declare his candidacy until five days after Boehner, missing a short but critical opportunity to earn commitments from many RSC members who had already declared support for Boehner or Blunt. When Boehner met with the RSC a week before the election, he delivered a strong speech—what one Boehner staffer called "a homerun in every conceivable way"—that may have further dissuaded the group from endorsing Shadegg (Pershing 2006b; Weisman 2006a).[53]

Shadegg's decision to run for majority leader theoretically helped Blunt, since it divided the anti-Blunt vote. But if Blunt did not win outright on the first ballot, the lowest vote getter would be eliminated, and that candidate's supporters would be free to back the second place finisher on the next ballot, denying Blunt the majority he needed. Anticipating this possibility, Boehner began an intensive and seemingly successful effort to troll for second ballot votes. Jeff Flake (R-AZ), an influential Shadegg supporter, indicated a week before the election that Boehner would be his second choice, and some alleged an implicit tactical agreement between the Boehner and Shadegg campaigns to vote against Blunt on a second round ballot. As a Boehner aide recalled, "a big component [of the communications effort] was to embrace Shadegg" to show "that they were the ones challenging the status quo," something that was not only advantageous campaign messaging but "a good second ballot strategy too" (Fagan 2006; Hulse 2006; Weisman 2006b).[54]

On February 2, after close to a month of campaigning, House Republicans gathered to elect their next majority leader. Each candidate had one or more of their allies deliver nominating speeches. Mark Souder (R-IN), who nominated Shadegg, tied Blunt to the party's shaky public reputation, while Shadegg ally Paul Ryan (R-WI) argued that "it was not enough to vote for the candidate who asked for the members' support first or was nice to them." Boehner was nominated by Ways and Means Chairman Bill Thomas (R-CA), which Boehner hoped would give him additional momentum while further suggesting that he was a closer ally of committee chairs (Weisman 2006c).

On the first round, Blunt came in first with 110 votes, Boehner was second with 79, and Shadegg came in third with 40 votes, with 2 write-in votes for Jim Ryun (R-KS).[55] With Shadegg out, Boehner surged ahead on the second ballot, beating Blunt by a vote of 122 to

109. Boehner had not only managed to convince Shadegg supporters to vote for him[56]—including, reportedly, Shadegg himself—but
had possibly won at least a few Blunt supporters as well (Dinan 2006;
Fagan 2006). Shadegg retired from Congress four years later, and
Blunt would eventually leave the House and join the U.S. Senate,
while Boehner went on to lead his party through four years in the
minority and another five tumultuous years as Speaker before resign-
ing in the fall of 2015.

To test the influence of professional connections and salient goals
for the initial round of voting, we employ multinomial logit, using
the public vote commitments made by 167 House Republicans as a
proxy for vote choice.[57] A test of the IIA assumption for multinomial
logit suggests the assumption holds, though the results should still
be viewed with some care, since one can reasonably assume that the
majority of legislators supporting Shadegg voted for Boehner on the
second ballot. We measure professional connections with dichotomous variables equal to 1 if a lawmaker shared the same state delegation or committee of any of the three candidates. Since Blunt and
Shadegg both served on Energy and Commerce, we do not expect
membership on that committee to have an effect. We also test salient
lawmaker goals. Electoral objectives were made salient by the receipt
of campaign contributions from the candidates; salient policy-related
variables include ideology (given Shadegg's distinctive conservatism
and emphasis on ideology in his campaign) and membership in the
large, reform-minded electoral class of 1994, which may have supported Shadegg (a member of that class) or Boehner (who argued he
would restore that cohort's core values). The most salient influence-
related factors are serving as committee chair or party leader, since
Boehner, himself a chairman, promised to redistribute power from
leaders to chairs, while Blunt was the only candidate with both extensive and recent experience as a party leader.[58] Blunt's rumored
machinations with respect to the Florida and Texas delegations, if
true, also had clear implications for the internal distribution of influence, so we also test membership in either state delegation or the Judiciary Committee (which would have lost jurisdiction to the Energy

and Commerce Committee under Blunt's plan). In addition, we include controls that capture other, less salient goals, such as electoral security (measured by the (logged) percent of the two-party vote in 2004),[59] legislator age, and seniority, though more senior lawmakers might generally defer to the heir apparent in a contested race.

Table 5.4 shows the results of our analysis of the first round of voting. Each coefficient must be interpreted relative to the base outcome, which in this case is a vote for Blunt. As with previous analyses, we provide some substantive meaning to the results by noting in the last two columns changes in average calculated probabilities of supporting Boehner or Shadegg, relative to Blunt, following a one-standard deviation increase in each predictive variable or, for dichotomous variables, a change from 0 to 1. State delegation perfectly (or nearly perfectly) predicts support for each delegate's candidate, a strong indication that state-related professional connections influenced vote choice, meaning those variables must be excluded to avoid inflated coefficients and less certain standard errors. As expected, members of Boehner's committee were positively associated with support for him over Blunt, with a 24 percent increase in the relative probability of voting for Boehner. Campaign contributions from all three candidates are statistically significant; the surprisingly negative effect of Shadegg donations may be due to Shadegg's strategic distribution of funds to individuals already disinclined to support him.[60] The findings support the claim that Shadegg was the preferred candidate of more conservative Republicans and fellow members of the class of 1994, at least when compared with Blunt, and lawmakers elected that year were 17 percent more likely to vote for Shadegg compared to Blunt.[61] Influence goals mattered too: although Boehner's appeal to committee chairs appeared to fall flat, party leaders uniformly supported Blunt, so the leadership variable must be omitted. The rumored deal by Blunt to give an influential post to a Texan did not seem to sway the vote of other Texans (at least in terms of statistical significance), but the variable measuring membership on the Judiciary Committee is statistically significant and positively associated with a vote for Shadegg relative to Blunt, and Floridians

Table 5.4. Analysis of Estimated Vote for Republican Majority Leader (2006), 1st Ballot

Hypothesis	Independent Variable	Coefficients		Change in Probability	
		Boehner	Shadegg	Boehner	Shadegg
Professional Connection	On Boehner committee	1.29* (0.50)	0.03 (0.84)	.25, .49 [+.24]	.10, .07 [-.03]
Goal Salience	Donation from Blunt (logged)	-0.24** (0.07)	-0.32 (0.21)	.30, .17 [-.12]	.09, .05 [-.05]
	Donation from Boehner (logged)	0.25** (0.08)	-0.02 (0.13)	.30, .48 [+.19]	.09, .06 [-.03]
	Donation from Shadegg (logged)	0.14 (0.13)	-1.20*** (0.25)	.30, .36 [+.06]	.09, .03 [-.07]
	DW-NOMINATE (1st dimension)	0.67 (1.39)	6.76* (3.10)	.30, .28 [-.02]	.09, .17 [+.08]
	Class of 1994	0.93 (0.61)	2.51** (0.89)	.29, .35 [+.07]	.07, .24 [+.17]
	Committee chair	1.31 (0.86)	0.31 (1.26)	.28, .51 [+.23]	.10, .08 [-.02]
	From Texas	-1.54 (1.04)	-0.45 (1.00)	.32, .12 [-.20]	.09, .09 [+.00]

On Judiciary Committee	0.75 (0.93)	1.63* (0.79)	.30, .37 [+.08]	.08, .18 [+.10]
On Energy and Commerce Committee	-0.04 (0.60)	-1.42 (1.26)	.29, .32 [+.02]	.11, .04 [-.07]
% 2-party vote (logged)	-2.31 (1.45)	-2.49 (1.62)	.30, .24 [-.06]	.09, .08 [-.02]
Term	0.05 (0.07)	0.21^ (0.13)	.30, .31 [+.01]	.09, .14 [+.05]
Age	0.00 (0.02)	-0.11** (0.04)	.30, .32 [+.03]	.09, .04 [-.05]
Constant	-3.00^ (1.71)	-2.55 (2.18)		
N	161			
Log L	-107.27			
McFadden's R^2	.25			
PRE	14.3%			

Other Variables (left-margin label spanning the lower rows)

Note: Coefficient table entries are multinomial logit coefficients (compared to the base outcome, a vote for Blunt) with robust standard errors in parentheses. The last two columns show the average predictive probabilities of supporting each candidate compared to support for Blunt when each variable is changed from 0 to 1 (for dichotomous variables) or increased by one standard deviation (for continuous variables) with the difference in brackets.

^ significant at p < .1; * significant at p < .05; ** significant at p < .01;
*** significant at p < .001 (2-tailed test).

endorsed Blunt to such an extent that the variable had to be excluded. Electoral security and service on Energy and Commerce both prove statistically insignificant, as expected.[62] However, both seniority and age are statistically significant when explaining support for Shadegg over Blunt, contrary to expectation. Though the sign on the seniority coefficient is unexpectedly positive, the sign on the age variable is negative, and may be a consequence of Blunt being the heir apparent candidate and thus more appealing to older, and thereby more tradition-bound, Republicans.[63]

Table 5.5 shows the results of a probit model that tests the (speculative but conceivable) possibility that Shadegg supporters uniformly cast their second-ballot votes for Boehner. Model 1 uses just professional connection variables, while Model 2 uses the full set of explanatory variables. Every member of Blunt and Boehner's state delegations that made a public vote commitment pledged to their respective home colleague, so those respective variables must be omitted. (So must the leadership variable, as it was in the analysis of the first round of balloting, because all leaders endorsed Blunt.) Membership on a Boehner committee is both statistically and substantively significant—those who served on such a committee are 19 percent more likely to support him over Blunt in Model 2—as are campaign donations: a one standard deviation increase in funding from Boehner (about $700) increases the probability of supporting the Ohioan from 38 percent to 53 percent. Also statistically significant are ideology (more conservative Republicans preferring Boehner), members of the class of 1994 (who are 21 percent more likely to support Boehner than those not in the class), lawmakers from Texas (who are 23 percent less likely to support Boehner), and, contrary to expectation, two-party vote (with lawmakers from safer districts less likely to commit to Boehner).

In short, the analysis reveals that a mix of professional connections and salient electoral, policy, and influence goals shaped vote choice for Republican majority leader. Boehner's unexpected victory was attributable in part to his appeal to committee and state colleagues, his distribution of campaign contributions, and his skill in winning over

Shadegg supporters in the second round of balloting. In this context, Blunt's position as heir apparent proved not an asset but a liability—the consequence of a "national mood to move away from DeLay, Inc.," as one GOP aide close to the Boehner campaign put it.[64]

Hoyer versus Pelosi, Redux: The 2006 Race for Majority Leader

When the Democratic Party won control of the House in November 2006, it held elections for six different leadership positions. The campaign for one office in particular, majority leader, gained the most attention—not only for its prominence, but because the expected occupant, Minority Whip Steny Hoyer, was challenged by a fellow moderate Democrat with the backing of the incoming Speaker of the House, Nancy Pelosi. It would, in some ways, be a replay of their marathon race for whip four years before, discussed in chapter 3.

Though Democrats were still in the minority in mid-2006, the ascension of Hoyer to the post of majority leader—if and when it became open—seemed a fait accompli. The ambitious Marylander had extensive leadership experience, was the clear heir apparent as whip (an office he had held since 2003), and had a sizeable LPAC and network of contributors he could call upon to distribute campaign money to others. Yet his many advantages did not deter John Murtha (D-PA) from declaring his intent in June to run for the post. Murtha seemed an unlikely challenger. A ranking member of an Appropriations subcommittee, Murtha had never held or even run for a party leadership office before, and he was slightly more conservative than Hoyer, a liability in the liberal-leaning caucus.[65] However, the Pennsylvanian had become more prominent when, seven months earlier, he unexpectedly called for the withdrawal of U.S. troops from Iraq, garnering him multiple press appearances and praise from liberals and antiwar Democrats. Murtha was also close to Pelosi, having managed her campaign for whip against Hoyer, and there was speculation that Pelosi had encouraged, if not recruited, Murtha out of lingering animosity toward Hoyer. Others suspected that Murtha

Table 5-5. Analysis of Estimated Vote for Republican Majority Leader (2006), 2nd Ballot

Hypothesis	Independent Variable	Model 1	Model 2	Change in Probability (Model 2)
Professional Connection	On Boehner committee	0.56* (0.25)	0.61* (0.28)	.34, .53 [+.19]
Goal Salience	Donation from Blunt (logged)	—	-0.14*** (0.04)	.38, .23 [-.15]
	Donation from Boehner (logged)	—	0.12** (0.04)	.38, .53 [+.14]
	DW-NOMINATE (1st dimension)	—	1.31^ (0.79)	.38, .45 [+.06]
	Class of 1994	—	0.70* (0.33)	.35, .57 [+.21]
	Committee chair	—	0.39 (0.48)	.38, .49 [+.12]
	From Texas	—	-0.87* (0.43)	.41, .18 [-.23]
	From Florida	—	-0.47 (0.44)	.39, .26 [-.13]

	Other Variables		
On Judiciary Committee	—	0.70 (0.47)	.37, .59 [+.22]
On Energy and Commerce Committee	-0.25 (0.31)	-0.25 (0.34)	.39, .32 [-.07]
% 2-party vote (logged)	—	-1.65* (0.79)	.38, .30 [-.09]
Term	—	0.04 (0.04)	.38, .43 [+.04]
Age	—	-0.01 (0.01)	.38, .35 [-.03]
Constant	-0.38** (0.12)	-1.41 (0.91)	
N	162	160	
Log L	-104.85	-84.78	
McFadden's R^2	.03	.21	
PRE	9.5%	30.6%	

Note: Table entries for each model are probit coefficients with robust standard errors in parentheses. The final column shows the average predicted probabilities of supporting Boehner when each variable in Model 2 is changed from 0 to 1 (for dichotomous variables) or increased by one standard deviation (for continuous variables) with the difference in brackets.

^ significant at $p < .1$; * significant at $p < .05$; ** significant at $p < .01$;
*** significant at $p < .001$ (2-tailed test).

was settling an old score with Hoyer, who had been part of a coterie of Democrats plotting to challenge Speaker Tip O'Neill, a friend of Murtha's, decades before (Drew 2007; Green 2008; Kornacki 2006; Ota 2006).

The contest between Hoyer and Murtha began unofficially the moment Murtha entered the race. Murtha agreed to suspend his campaign until after the November elections, following criticism for creating a potentially divisive and distracting leadership contest. Nonetheless, by announcing his plans, he had potentially given Hoyer extra time to win legislator commitments, and according to one Democratic chief of staff, "Murtha was still talking to people" about his candidacy.[66] After the elections, both campaigns communicated themes that reflected a stark choice between the pair. In a note sent shortly after midnight of election day, Hoyer referenced his prior experience as whip, his intent as leader to regularly seek opinions of both chairmen and rank-and-file Democrats, and his support for "core Democratic principles."[67] Murtha, by contrast, emphasized his early criticism of the Iraq War (Bresnahan and Yachnin 2006; Hearn and Allen 2006; Kornacki 2006; Yachnin and Bresnahan 2006).

The candidates and their supporters sent an abundance of letters, faxes, and "Dear Colleague" missives throughout the campaign; as one Democratic staffer put it, "we had letters walked into our office daily."[68] Pro-Hoyer letters came from would-be committee chairmen, moderate legislators, and, perhaps to counter Murtha's position on Iraq, six members of the liberal Progressive Caucus (Hearn 2006c). The letters most commonly cited Hoyer's extensive campaign and legislative experience, claimed he had good working relations with other party leaders, and argued he could build consensus within a diverse party. Letters in favor of Murtha differed sharply from Hoyer's, almost uniformly citing the lawmaker's opposition to the war in Iraq and hinting at his closer relationship with Pelosi. One such letter, signed by four Californians, insisted that Murtha's "courage to speak truth to power" is why "we are in the majority today" and explicitly extolled Murtha's loyalty "to our next Speaker, Nancy Pelosi."[69] Both candidates also made campaign contributions to fellow legislators. Hoyer gave over $700,000 to seventy-one Democrats, while Murtha provided over $200,000 to fifty-eight party members. Interviews with congressional staffers suggest that the candidates used more personal tactics as well, making phone calls to undeclared legislators and keeping tabs on the legislative requests of their colleagues.[70]

The wildcard in the race was Nancy Pelosi. She remained officially neutral until the Sunday before the election, when she wrote in a widely circulated letter addressed to Murtha, "I salute your courageous leadership" on Iraq (Weisman 2006d). Pelosi's move was greeted with skepticism, if not bewilderment, because Hoyer's win seemed to be a foregone conclusion at that point. Yet within two days she was reportedly applying pressure on undecided Democrats and suggesting to incoming freshmen that their committee assignments would be contingent on their vote. Pelosi allies also lobbied on behalf of Murtha, sometimes quite aggressively. Anna Eshoo (D-CA) and George Miller (D-CA), according to one Democrat, were "really beating up on people to back Jack or else" (Yachnin and Bresnahan 2006). Whether these efforts helped or hurt Murtha, it reinforced the fact that, according to the chief of staff quoted previously, "people saw this as a Pelosi-Hoyer thing."[71] Perhaps in response, an anonymous group called YouDon'tKnowJack.org sent a series of e-mails to legislator offices criticizing Murtha's ethics problems, including a famous videotape from the 1970s that featured Murtha debating whether to take a cash bribe from an undercover federal agent (Bresnahan and Yachnin 2006; Hearn 2006a, 2006b; Weisman and Romano 2006).

In the end, despite Pelosi's help, Hoyer decisively beat Murtha, 149–86. Contrary to fears at the time, the race did not deepen any rifts in the party. Murtha gained an unofficial leadership role as advisor to the caucus on legislative strategy regarding Iraq. Perhaps more importantly, the campaign opened a wider window onto Pelosi's emphasis on loyalty (Green 2008). That emphasis would help keep her party unified in challenging times, especially during passage of the Affordable Care Act in the 111th Congress (2009–10), but it would also maintain the Pelosi-Hoyer division within the party, and it eventually bred resentment and frustration that led many Democrats to vote against her for leader after the 2010 elections and fueled calls to distribute power more widely.

Newly uncovered whip data kept by Murtha are used to test the influence of salient goals and professional connections on vote choice.[72] Unfortunately, the data—a count of lawmaker commitments updated the day before the election—badly overstates Murtha's support, estimating the Pennsylvanian would get 114 votes, nearly a third more than he actually did. (The total increases to 120 if one counts the six Democrats recorded as leaning toward Murtha.)[73] We therefore modify that estimate by excluding from Murtha's count six Democrats who publicly committed to Hoyer, assuming these were counted by Murtha in error;[74] eleven lawmakers who refused to state their vote choice publicly; and six others who were publicly undecided, under the reasonable assumption that Democrats would be more wary of stating their preference if they planned to vote against an ally of Pelosi.[75] We also do not count the six "leaners" whose support for Murtha was probably too tepid to be dependable. That leaves 90 estimated votes for Murtha (excluding Murtha himself), just 5 more than he received. This serves as our more relaxed vote estimate, but we also use a more stringent estimate of vote choice, counting only the votes of lawmakers who openly committed to Murtha or Hoyer and were similarly recorded in Murtha's tally (52 for Murtha and 91 for Hoyer).[76]

As in previous analyses, shared state and committee assignment variables are used to capture the professional connection hypothesis. Hoyer and Murtha were both on the Appropriations Committee, but Murtha was a ranking subcommittee member (and Pelosi was also a former appropriator), so we expect Murtha to profit more from his membership on that committee. Given the weight of Pelosi's endorsement of Murtha and lobbying for Murtha by her allies, it seems reasonable to expect that the Democratic leader's strong connections with the California delegation led lawmakers from her state to support Murtha, so we test this "second degree" professional connection with Murtha.[77] In terms of electoral goals, both candidates gave substantial amounts to other legislators, so we include logged measures of total campaign contributions made by each candidate. Ideologically, the two candidates were fairly similar, but since the race was seen as a proxy battle between the more liberal Pelosi and more conservative Hoyer, we include DW-NOMINATE scores to capture the likely effect of ideological differences. We also add controls measuring less salient goals and concerns, including electoral security, seniority, age, and whether a Democrat occupied a leadership position in the party or on a committee. (Though Hoyer claimed he would solicit the views of committee chairs, he was not ranking on any committee, and nothing about the context of the race pointed to this being a significant issue.) It is nevertheless possible that more senior Democrats, older party members, and Democrats in leadership leaned toward Hoyer because he was the traditional successor to the post.

The results of a probit analysis are shown in table 5.6.[78] Models 1 and 2 use the more stringent estimate of vote choice, while Models 3 and 4 use the more relaxed estimate. The findings are consistent with the predictions of the mixed-motive model. The Pennsylvania delegation variable must be excluded because it is separated perfectly by the vote for Murtha, a good sign that his state delegation mattered. So too must the Maryland variable for the more stringent estimate of vote choice, and in the relaxed estimate, though it is not statistically significant, Maryland representation increases the probability of a Hoyer vote substantially (20 percent). The indirect California connection fostered by Pelosi's support for Murtha also helps explain support for the Pennsylvanian, and Appropriations membership reduces the likelihood of support for Hoyer by a substantial 25 percent, suggesting that Murtha, perhaps with Pelosi's help, was better able to leverage his professional connections on the committee. In terms of electoral goals, campaign contributions from both candidates are both statistically and substantively significant and in the expected direction. Their effect is further revealed when looking at donations to freshmen, lawmakers least likely to have professional or personal connections to the candidates. Of the thirty-two freshmen whose

Table 5.6. Analysis of Estimated Vote for Hoyer as Democratic Majority Leader (2006)

Hypothesis	Independent Variable	Stringent Vote Estimate		Relaxed Vote Estimate		Change in Probability (Model 4)
		Model 1	Model 2	Model 3	Model 4	
Professional Connection	From Maryland	—	—	0.76 (0.65)	0.69 (0.65)	.46, .66 [+.20]
	From California	-0.56^ (0.31)	-0.62^ (0.36)	-0.57* (0.25)	-0.34 (0.28)	.48, .38 [-.10]
	On Appropriations Committee	-0.93* (0.37)	-0.56 (0.52)	-0.90** (0.31)	-0.91* (0.39)	.50, .24 [-.25]
Goal Salience	Donation from Hoyer (logged)	—	0.18** (0.06)	—	0.15*** (.04)	.47, .66 [+.19]
	Donation from Murtha (logged)	—	-0.21** (0.07)	—	-0.16*** (.04)	.47, .31 [-.16]
	DW-NOMINATE (1st dimension)	—	3.27* (1.28)	—	4.04*** (0.94)	.47, .63 [+.16]

Other Variables					
% 2-party vote (logged)	—	0.24 (0.76)	—	0.25 (0.56)	.47, .48 [+.02]
Term	—	-0.10 (0.07)	—	-0.01 (0.04)	.47, .45 [-.02]
Age	—	0.04* (0.02)	—	0.02^ (.01)	.47, .53 [+.07]
In leadership	—	1.11* (0.52)	—	0.65^ (0.39)	.45, .65 [+.19]
Committee ranking member	—	1.78* (0.82)	—	0.07 (0.41)	.46, .48 [+.02]
Constant	0.55*** (0.13)	-0.36 (0.78)	0.08 (0.10)	0.18 (0.65)	
N	141	140	234	229	
Log L	-87.28	-63.43	-153.15	-119.23	
McFadden's R^2	.05	.31	.05	.25	
PRE	13.7%	47.1%	14.5%	46.2%	

Note: Table entries for each model are probit coefficients with robust standard errors in parentheses. The final column shows the average predicted probabilities of supporting Hoyer when each variable in Model 4 is changed from 0 to 1 (for dichotomous variables) or increased by one standard deviation (for continuous variables) with the difference in brackets.

^ significant at p < .1; * significant at p < .05; ** significant at p < .01; *** significant at p < .001 (2-tailed test).

vote preferences were recorded by Murtha, Murtha won the votes of all four who received contributions from Murtha that were equal to, or greater than, funding from Hoyer. Of the remaining twenty-eight, Hoyer won the votes of twenty-two of them, and eleven of thirteen who received $10,000 or more from Hoyer compared to Murtha. Finally, there is evidence that general policy preferences shaped vote choice—a one standard deviation increase in DW-NOMINATE increases the likelihood of a Hoyer vote by 16 percent—suggesting that the race was indeed an extension of the ideological division that had emerged when Pelosi and Hoyer competed for the whip post.[79] Neither electoral vulnerability nor term in office are statistically significant, as expected, though three other variables are, contrary to expectation: age (older lawmakers preferring Hoyer, the heir apparent), leadership post (increasing the probability of voting for Hoyer by a sizeable 19 percent), and, for the stringent vote estimate, committee ranking status (perhaps because Hoyer was the heir apparent, or because of Hoyer's promise to give more authority to committee chairs).[80]

These findings support the professional connections and salient goal hypotheses. They also suggest what went wrong with Murtha's campaign. Though he distributed campaign funds to other Democrats and successfully drew support from more liberal legislators, he failed to overcome Hoyer's more generous campaign contributions and senior lawmakers' preference to support the heir apparent. Pelosi's help was not enough to overcome Hoyer's other advantages.

Conclusion

The three heir apparent races examined here show that, as with open competition races, members of Congress consider an array of professional connections and individual goals when choosing whom to support for party leader. Our analyses also support the claim that heirs apparent benefit from the votes of older, more senior, and more influential party members, even if their particular goals are not made explicitly salient by the candidates, their campaigns, or the political context. As a result, there are some discernible advantages to being heir to a leadership post that probably dissuade most would-be challengers. That the heir lost in two of our three cases, however, indicates that those advantages are not insurmountable. The very fact that a race emerges might be an indicator of not just sharp intraparty divisions but major weaknesses of the heir apparent as well.

In the next chapter, we study a third category of leadership races which can produce, or be a sign of, even greater intraparty turmoil: when an incumbent is challenged for reelection by one or more party members. Like heir apparent races, they are relatively uncommon, and when they do occur they tend to result in lopsided victories for the incumbent. Nonetheless, as will be seen, even an election that ends in a one-sided victory can be politically consequential.

Incumbent party leaders are never free from the possibility of a challenge by lawmakers who wish to replace them. These kinds of races, known as revolts, are seldom successful, but they serve as periodic reminders that elected leaders of congressional parties must not only win office but regularly nurture their bases of support to protect themselves. A successful revolt can be highly consequential, with "individual careers . . . made and broken" and a party's "organization and policy orientation" shifting dramatically (Peabody 1967, 675).[1] Even a failed revolt may leave the incumbent leader exposed and weakened, hastening his or her departure.

We discuss two types of revolts in this chapter. The first and more traditional type is when a leader is challenged for reelection within his or her party. Between 1961 and 2016 there have been twenty-four such leadership elections in the House of Representatives, of which six resulted in the ouster of the incumbent leader. The second type is a significant intraparty challenge against a nominee for Speaker of the House on the floor of the chamber, of which there have been five during that same fifty-five-year time span; four happened within the majority party, and none of those four resulted in the defeat of the majority party's official nominee for Speaker.[2]

Revolts against incumbent leaders were the kind of race Robert Peabody probably had in mind when he argued that leadership change is more likely after a party loses seats in elections, since nineteen of the twenty-nine followed net partisan seat losses. However, more important is if an election loss is sizeable or unexpected, which by our estimate accounts for fourteen of the twenty-nine revolts.[3] Republicans have historically been more prone to revolt elections than Democrats—three-quarters occurred within the GOP—thanks to the party's relative lack of established succession patterns, larger number of elective leadership posts, and greater willingness by congressional Republicans to retaliate against their leaders after suffering big election losses or other challenging political conditions, including their long stint in the minority (Bibby and Davidson 1967; Nelson 1977; Peabody 1976). Nominees for Speaker from both parties have also been increasingly subject to floor revolts in recent years.

Though revolts are the second most common type of leadership election in the House, they still make up just 27 percent of all contested leadership races between 1961 and 2016. Their relative scarcity makes intuitive sense. For one thing, revolts are risky. Failure to remove the incumbent leader may result in retaliation, such as denial of desirable committee assignments. Incumbent leaders also have informational advantages that allow them to identify potential challenges before they emerge. They may be able to squelch threats by offering side-payments to wavering lawmakers, like campaign contributions or better committee positions. Furthermore, leaders who cannot prevent a revolt and have reason to believe it may be successful are likely to choose a more dignified exit by stepping down from office altogether, which means revolts that do occur are usually against incumbents who are politically strong.

Members of Congress who openly support revolts tend to be younger, more junior legislators who are less invested in the existing leadership structure and more impatient with the status quo (Hinckley 1970; Peabody 1976). However, freshmen lawmakers are seldom supportive of challengers, for they have not experienced the negative aspects of the incumbent leader firsthand and are loath to risk angering him before starting their congressional career. Lawmakers in positions of influence are similarly reluctant to back revolts, since they threaten the existing intraparty distribution of power.

We begin this chapter with an important revolt that stresses the difficulties challengers face when trying to remove an incumbent leader: the 1998 race for Republican majority leader, in which Dick Armey fought off a challenge from two other lawmakers and a third, last-minute opponent. We then briefly examine two other revolts, the 1965 race for Republican leader and the 1969 challenge against incumbent Speaker John McCormack. As in previous chapters, we draw upon whip count data to estimate vote choice, using regression analysis to test the ability of the mixed-motive model to explain that choice. Finally, we conclude with a brief discussion of intraparty floor challenges against a party's nominee for Speaker, looking at one example from 2013 to glean whether our mixed model might explain those kinds of revolts too.

Two against One: The 1998 Race for Majority Leader

In late 1998 the House Republican Conference was in turmoil. In the midst of pursuing unpopular impeachment proceedings against President Bill Clinton, the GOP lost seats in the November midterm elections, a rare outcome with an opposite-party president in the White House. It was but the latest in a series of setbacks for Republican leaders, coming on the heels of intraparty squabbling and unhappiness with the leadership of Speaker Newt Gingrich that had persisted throughout the 105th Congress (1997–98). A group of younger Republicans had even attempted a coup against Gingrich in July 1997, and although the attempt failed, insurgents remained disillusioned with not only the Speaker but also Majority Leader Armey, an early confidant of the coup plotters who, many believed, had leaked their plan to Gingrich (Seelye 1998c).

The environment was ripe for intraparty revolts against the leadership, and the last two months of 1998 would prove to be one of the most tumultuous periods for a congressional party in decades. Appropriations Committee Chairman Bob Livingston (R-LA), who had been mounting a potential challenge to Gingrich for most of 1998, announced just days after the election that he was an official candidate for Speaker. Facing likely defeat, Gingrich opted to resign (P. Baker 2000; Gugliotta and Eilperin 1998a; Hastert 2004). Meanwhile, Congressman Tom Davis (R-VA) challenged the incumbent chair of the National Republican Campaign Committee (NRCC), John Linder (R-GA), and J. C. Watts (R-OK) declared that he would run against Conference Chairman John Boehner, whom Republican dissidents also accused of betraying their planned coup against Gingrich (VandeHei 1997). The leader who attracted the most opponents, however, was Armey. Two lawmakers initially sought to oust him, Steve Largent of Oklahoma and Conference Vice Chairwoman Jennifer Dunn of Washington State, and a third, Dennis Hastert of Illinois, would be put up to challenge Armey late in the campaign.

The Candidates

Armey had first entered the House of Representatives in 1984. An economist by training, he was a reliable conservative who focused on fiscal policy, advocating for a flat tax and urging reductions in federal spending.[4] Armey joined the elected leadership by defeating the incumbent Conference chairman, Jerry Lewis (R-CA), in a December 1992 revolt, and soon distinguished himself as a potent critic of the Clinton administration, particularly its doomed health care initiative. Alongside Gingrich, Armey and conference staff spearheaded the creation and marketing of the "Contract with America" election-year agenda in 1994. Armey made it clear that he would seek to become majority leader if Gingrich became Speaker, and after the GOP won a majority of House seats that year, he ascended to the position unopposed. Armey became an important legislative agenda-setter and day-to-day manager of the House floor. By 1998, he was to some degree untainted by the problems that beset his fellow leaders, but he still had reason to worry about a general "blame the leadership" mentality that was spreading through the party. Furthermore, his ambivalent role in the attempt to overthrow Gingrich angered many coup participants, including Steve Largent, and exacerbated tensions between Armey and Majority Whip Tom DeLay, another leader secondarily associated with the failed revolt (VandeHei 1997; Seelye 1998c). Armey's doctrinaire belief in cutting government spending also won him some enemies. For example, rumors circulated that he was disliked by legislators with military facilities in their districts, including members of the House Depot Caucus, because Armey had spearheaded the creation of the base closure and realignment process which targeted many such facilities for closure, and he had recently allowed the House to consider legislative language that would prevent jobs at two closing depots from going to other military installations (Eilperin 1998a). Then there were complaints about Armey's garbled verbal style in media appearances and his unpolished public persona (Eilperin 1998a).

It was on this last count that Armey's primary rival, Steve Largent, stood out as a major threat. When Largent was first elected to Congress in 1994, he was perhaps the most famous Republican freshman elected that year, having been an NFL wide receiver for the Seattle Seahawks.[5] The Oklahoman was attractive, articulate, and comfortable in the media spotlight. Seen as a promising up-and-comer from his first days in Congress, other House members sought him out to make speeches and raise money, and they voted him "most likely to succeed" in his 1994 freshman class. Ideologically, Largent was slightly more to the right than Armey, and he had a solid reputation as a Christian social conservative, advocating for such causes as bans on abortion and gay marriage and support for legislation to "protect parents' right to use corporal punishment and make medical decisions for their children" (Jacoby 1998; Ota 1998).[6]

Largent had made his mark from the get-go as a backbencher willing to openly challenge GOP leaders. He was one of fifteen Republicans who voted to extend a government shutdown in 1996, a move opposed by Gingrich and other party chiefs who saw the shutdown as a public relations debacle (Jacoby 1998). Largent was also a member of the Gang of Eleven, a group of Republicans who openly objected to leaders' political tactics, and he held meetings in his office to plot the failed removal of Gingrich in 1997. There was an air of reform to his candidacy as well, insofar as he promised a change in GOP leadership after the disappointing midterm elections of 1998 (Barnett 1999; Carney 1998; Katz 1998; Koszczuk 1997). Besides ambition, Largent was likely driven by personal animosity toward Armey for his perceived betrayal of the coup plot. "Nobody trusts the leader," he publicly claimed (Merida 1998).

The third candidate, Jennifer Dunn, had been a member of the House since 1993 and was a fast-rising star in the GOP. Dunn was a former state party chair and, when she first arrived in Congress, some fellow Republicans thought she might eventually become the first woman Speaker of the House. Appointed to the Ways and Means Committee in 1995 and elected Conference secretary at the beginning of the 105th Congress, Dunn became the highest-ranking woman in the party when she was chosen to be Conference vice chair in July 1997. Despite her impressive rise in the ranks of leadership, however, she had some weaknesses as a candidate. The GOP was increasingly conservative, but she was more ideologically moderate than Largent or Armey and received mixed reviews from influential conservative groups, particularly on abortion-related proposals. Some even cynically wondered if, to the extent Dunn did vote conservatively, it was solely to aid her leadership aspirations.[7] In addition, she lacked a substantial base from which to launch a bid. The party had few moderates or women, and though GOP leaders had stood behind her in the past, she would be challenging one of them, was losing another to retirement (Gingrich) and, following disputes over who should be in charge of party messaging, had a frayed relationship with a third (Boehner) (Seelye 1998a; VandeHei 1998a; Vucanovich and Cafferata 2005; Walsh 1998).

The Campaign

Steve Largent heralded his candidacy on November 6, three days after the disappointing congressional elections, declaring that, just as it was for Democrats in 1994, the choice of majority leader "was a referendum on our Republican Leadership." The "*only* reason" to run for leadership, he opined, "is to *lead*, not to preserve a position of power." Largent proposed four strategic foci for the office of majority leader: "adopt a simple Republican agenda" that "we can clearly communicate and that unites Republicans, including our friends in the Senate"; "heal the alienation" in his party as well as among Democrats, "the Senate, and the Administration"; "merge a clear, consistent message with believable messengers"; and enhance the party's "coordination and organization."[8] He insisted that "communications is critical" (with his media skills no doubt in mind) and that the party needed "to avoid the train wrecks that we've had in the last two years with government shutdowns [and] with year-end budget-busting omnibus bills"(Eilperin 1998a).[9]

Perhaps anticipating a challenge, Armey had been quietly accumulating commitments from colleagues for months. When Largent threw his hat in the ring, Armey's office issued a statement acknowledging that the election was "a wake-up call" but noting that the incumbent leader had "spoken to over 130 members since election day, and heard broad support for rekindling the spirit of the Contract with America." He emphasized the advantages of continuity in leadership, while his communications director insisted that, "with Newt leaving, we need stability and experience" (Jacoby 1998).[10] In a letter to other House Republicans, Armey cited his "proven track record developing major projects that define our Party's vision" and promised to "craft a clear, powerful Agenda 2000," "go back to getting our [budget and appropriations] work done on time," and help the rank-and-file "be better communicators."[11]

Dunn, who at first reportedly planned to run for reelection as Conference vice chair, declared three days after Largent's announcement that she, too, would challenge Armey (Casteel 1998; Espo 1998; Katz 1998). In her statement of candidacy, she described herself as a "fresh face . . . delivering a clear message that will build broad support for our vision from all Americans." She obliquely referred to both her gender and the conservatism of the conference, asserting her capability to "broaden the base of the Party," and even mentioning that she was "a mother who named her son Reagan."[12]

Armey's campaign, which consisted of a seventeen-member whip team, canvassed for votes, sought influential endorsements, and tried to create an aura of inevitability. Whereas Armey's opponents appeared frequently on television, the Texan generally campaigned out of the spotlight. He and his backers acknowledged Largent's strong media presence but insisted it was no substitute for political skill, as when Armey supporter Joe Barton (R-TX) circulated a pro-Armey *Washington Times* editorial entitled "Pitting Image vs. Substance."[13]

Armey obtained public endorsements from top party leaders, committee chairs, and subcommittee chairs,[14] and obtained a commitment from Livingston, Gingrich's expected successor, to remain publicly neutral and not follow the lead of his ally DeLay by supporting Largent. Armey also scored endorsements from prominent individuals outside of Congress, including *Washington Times* correspondent Donald Lambro and Steve Moore of the libertarian Cato Institute (Casteel 1998; Clines 1998; National Center for Public Policy Research 1998; Stoddard 1998a; VandeHei 1998b).[15]

For a spur-of-the-moment bid, Largent's campaign was impressively elaborate, balancing insider and outsider strategies and employing rapid-response tactics to throw cold water on any news story claiming Armey was in the lead. Largent diligently worked the phones over the weekend before Dunn entered the race, and he assembled a whip team of twenty-four mostly junior members with broad regional representation who held nightly conference calls to strategize and tally vote commitments. He also benefited from testimonials by several representatives who, to a person, cited Largent's strength as a communicator.[16] For instance, Joe Scarborough (R-FL) observed that "Americans love what Republicans stand for—it's just their leaders they don't like. . . . Steve Largent can provide [a] new start while remaining faithful to the values of Ronald Reagan."[17] Largent's favored status among social conservatives also led to public backing from prominent conservative activist Paul Weyrich (Casteel 1998; Jacoby 1998; Merida 1998; National Center for Public Policy Research 1998).

Largent had a number of vulnerabilities that he tried to mitigate. His vocal social conservatism and his reputation as a rebellious backbencher was potentially off-putting to more mainstream Republicans. A further complication was that fellow Oklahoman J. C. Watts was simultaneously challenging Conference Chair John Boehner, a problem for those who sought more regional balance in a party already dominated by southerners. To try to broaden his support, Largent issued a press release touting endorsements from well-known moderates, including Ray LaHood (R-IL) and Jack Quinn (R-NY).[18] Promising to "put the conference's agenda ahead of [his] own,"[19] he

offered to "create an advisory board made up of members representing a cross-section of our conference."[20]

Dunn, meanwhile, had useful allies working on her behalf. Jim
Gibbons (R-NV) and Doc Hastings (R-WA) made phone calls and
counted votes for her, and they sent "Dear Colleague" letters extolling her ability to "convey a message," including one that reprinted
an editorial touting Dunn as a "suburban, female, family oriented"
representative of the GOP.[21] Other advocates included Rodney
Frelinghuysen (R-NJ), who pointed out Dunn's efforts "to reduce
the gender gap and expand our Republican base," and Mary Bono
(R-CA), who said that Dunn could "bring new and diverse leadership
to the House."[22] Dunn also touted her media appeal versus Armey's
and leadership experience as more extensive than Largent's. She
explicitly highlighted her gender, noting that as leader she would
"carry the banner for moms," and also offered to bring regional diversity lacking in leadership (Jacoby 1998; Preston 1998; Stoddard
1998a; VandeHei 1998b). Indeed, top House Republicans and consultants were keenly aware that having a woman as the GOP's public
face could yield important collective political advantages.[23]

The Washingtonian was not entirely successful in neutralizing her
liabilities, however. She reportedly received "a cool reception from
social conservatives" because of her voting record on abortion and
other social issues (Katz and Doherty 1998). Moderates did not see
her as a natural ally either, and just days after her entry, the Tuesday
Group, a group of moderate congressional Republicans, refused to
endorse her (Seelye 1998a; VandeHei 1998b). Moreover, her relatively late entry into the race cost her an opportunity to win support
from Republicans already committed to someone else. Her opponents even tried to counteract her advantage among women, with
Armey seeking public backing from female supporters while Tom
Coburn (R-OK) opined in a "Dear Colleague" letter that "women
voters respond to Steve [Largent]'s message because he is a likeable,
sincere, upbeat communicator."[24]

All three candidates sought to win the votes of newly elected Republicans. Armey visited the districts of sixteen of the seventeen

freshmen and invited them to visit him the weekend before the vote. Dunn, like Armey, had given campaign contributions to many of the freshmen and had actively campaigned for six of them. Largent, meanwhile, sent staffers to the airport to pick up new members upon their arrival in DC and lobbied them as they emerged from their first meetings on the Hill (Foerstel 1998; Fram 1998a; Javers 1998).

Dunn, Armey, and Largent also touted the number of vote commitments they had and low-balled their opponents' level of support. Eight days before the election, the Armey camp claimed over 100 votes in hand, only about 12 fewer than was needed to win. "I know a head fake when I see one," retorted Largent, and his campaign insisted the race would "go to at least a second ballot" and accused Armey of "bluffing and spinning, and . . . trying to create a sense of inevitability."[25] Though the Armey campaign frequently vowed their candidate had the most vote commitments, the fact that his count changed little as the election neared suggested that Armey's momentum had stalled (Casteel 1998; Gugliotta and Eilperin 1998b; Seelye 1998a, 1998d).

Neither Largent nor Dunn expected to win on the first ballot, so they—and, tellingly, Armey—were looking to secure commitments in a second round of voting. The key question was how many Largent or Dunn supporters would refuse to vote for Armey if their preferred candidate were eliminated. Some, like Dunn ally Greg Ganske (R-IA), argued that he saw "a very large anti-Armey vote." But much depended on who dropped out first: pro-Largent Republicans might vote for Dunn if Largent lost in the first round, as Ganske claimed, but it was unclear whether Dunn voters would readily lend their ballots to a conservative back-bencher like Largent (Merida 1998; VandeHei 1998c).

As the campaign continued, Largent's tactics became increasingly bold. From the beginning, he tried to persuade Dunn to abandon the race, even promising to create a new leadership position, assistant majority leader, just for her.[26] Dunn refused, but Largent continued to hold out that possibility until the day of the election, seemingly worried that she was robbing him of anti-Armey voters. Largent also complained that Armey's poor scheduling of House business had contributed to "at least twelve divorces" in four years, leading one Armey supporter to warn that Largent was "engaged in a kind of public campaign that hurts you in a member-to-member race" (Hallow 1998; Merida 1998; Seelye 1998b; Welch 1998).

Rumors flew that other candidates might run. Armey scored endorsements from Bill Thomas (R-CA) and Buck McKeon (R-CA), two lawmakers rumored to be eyeing a challenge. Republicans who remained dissatisfied with their choices then tried to draft Chief Deputy Whip Hastert, seeing him "as a possible bridge for moderates and conservatives," as one reporter put it. Armey feared that Hastert would draw disproportionately from his own reservoir of support, and when Hastert approached Armey to seek release from his prior commitment to vote for him, Armey refused. Although he apparently kept his word to vote for Armey and never formally declared his candidacy, Hastert supporters Mike Castle (R-DE), Tom Ewing (R-IL), and Marge Roukema (R-NJ) asked their colleagues to "reconsider commitments made prior to his being in the race" (Eilperin 1998a, 1998b; Fram 1998b; Hastert 2004).[27]

The Election

House Republicans met on November 18 to select their party's leaders. While Tom DeLay ran for whip unopposed, and Robert Livingston was nominated for Speaker without opposition, the GOP ousted two incumbents from their leadership posts: Conference Chair Boehner, who was defeated by Watts, 121–93, and NRCC chair Linder, who lost to Tom Davis, 130–77. A third election, for Dunn's newly vacated post of Conference vice chair, was won by Tillie Fowler (R-FL) after two rounds of balloting. The most anticipated fight of the day, however, was for majority leader. Largent was nominated by LaHood, while the widely respected, socially conservative lawmaker Henry Hyde nominated Armey (Stoddard 1998b). Despite never formally declaring his candidacy, Hastert's name was put forward too.

On the first ballot, Armey received 100 votes; Largent, 58; Dunn, 45; and Hastert, 18. As expected, Armey had come in first place. However, neither he nor any of his rivals had received an absolute majority, and each had fallen short of the votes they claimed they would get. Hastert was eliminated as the lowest vote getter, and a second round of balloting began. On that ballot, Armey won 99 votes, while Largent garnered 73 and Dunn 49. The result disappointed Dunn and belied the claim by some that Hastert's followers would naturally migrate to her (VandeHei 1998d). But Armey and his supporters also had reason to be alarmed: as had happened to Phil Burton in his race for leader in 1976 (see chapter 5), the leading candidate had shown no real gain in votes—and, in Armey's case, had actually *lost* a vote—suggesting a large faction, if not the majority, of the party would vote for anyone but him.

Armey and his aides breathed a sigh of relief, however, when the third ballot was tallied. Armey garnered 127 votes, enough to overcome Largent's 95. The majority leader had done well in securing second (technically, third) ballot commitments, and some speculated that ideological preferences had trumped anti-incumbency attitudes. As one moderate put it, "There clearly was an anti-Armey sentiment in the Conference, and people felt it was time to get rid of him. . . . But in the end the moderates just couldn't go with Largent. It was more like going with the old devil we know" (Peters 2001, 129; Seelye 1998e).

Though Armey would be one of the only GOP leaders from the previous Congress to continue in leadership, he would gradually lose influence to others. Majority Whip DeLay continued to demonstrate consummate skill in marshaling votes for key bills, and he held considerable sway within the conference (e.g., Dubose and Reid 2004). Ironically, the man who came in fourth place in the revolt—Dennis Hastert—would also exceed Armey in influence. When news of Bob Livingston's sexual improprieties came to light, leading him to withdraw abruptly from consideration as Speaker, DeLay and his allies quickly recruited Hastert to be Gingrich's successor (P. Baker 2000). Armey would continue to serve as majority leader under Hastert for four more years before retiring from Congress in 2002, at which point DeLay succeeded to the post without opposition.

Explaining Vote Choice

To estimate vote choice, we draw upon an Armey whip tally, taken not long before the election, which records whether lawmakers were committed to Armey, Largent, or Dunn.[28] (Votes for Hastert were not identified, so the first round of voting cannot be analyzed.) It also notes if a lawmaker was expected to vote for Armey on the last ballot (noted in the tally as "2nd ballot" or "ballot 2"), allowing us to estimate vote choice in the final round of voting. Armey's estimates of his own vote totals were more accurate than those he made of his opponents (103 for himself, versus 41 for Largent and 35 for Dunn, on the second ballot, and 118 for himself on the final ballot). We use multinomial logit regression to test the impact of various factors on vote choice on the second ballot, though the results should be interpreted cautiously because a test of the Independence of Irrelevant Alternatives (IIA) assumption suggests that non-Armey voters were less than ambivalent about their choices on the second ballot.[29] For the final ballot, we employ probit regression.

Recall that, according to the mixed-motive model, professional connections and salient goals will both help explain vote choice in leadership elections. To test the professional connection hypothesis, we include variables measuring if a lawmaker was from a candidate's state delegation and if a legislator served on Dunn's Ways and Means Committee or Largent's Commerce Committee. (Armey did not serve on any committee.) Electoral goals were salient largely due to campaign contributions by Armey and Dunn (but not Largent, who made none). In terms of policy goals, although the candidates rarely delivered explicit ideological appeals, ideology was an important undercurrent of the campaign, since Largent was widely seen as the most conservative candidate and Dunn the most moderate, so we expect DW-NOMINATE scores to help explain vote choice. Of particular salience was the issue of abortion, so we include prolife

rating scores for all three candidates. Because another potentially salient policy concern was Armey's position on base closings, we add a
variable measuring whether a lawmaker was a prominent and active
member of the Depot Caucus.[30] We also include a variable measuring whether a lawmaker was a member of the ideologically committed class of 1994, and therefore more likely to support fellow member Steve Largent and oppose Armey for his perceived betrayal of the
attempt to remove Gingrich, which was led primarily by members of
that class.

Finally, in terms of influence goals, we would expect Armey to
garner disproportionate backing from committee chairs and fellow
party leaders, whose votes he had overtly sought out. We also expect
that Largent's fellow members of the Gang of Eleven supported Largent and opposed Armey,[31] and that female Republicans were more
likely to support Dunn as a means of increasing the profile and influence of GOP women. We also include controls for age and tenure,
but we do not expect either to have had an effect, since none of the
candidates made direct campaign pledges to expand opportunities
for younger, less senior Republicans.[32] Also included is a measure of
electoral security (logged two-party vote received in the last election), though we do not predict that will matter either, because the
party's seat loss in 1998 was relatively small and Gingrich had taken
the brunt of the blame for it.

The results of our analysis of the second round of balloting appear
in table 6.1. The first two columns provide coefficients for each variable, which should be interpreted as relative to the base condition of
voting for Armey, and the last two columns show the relative change
in probability of supporting Largent or Dunn compared to Armey
following a one standard deviation increase in each predictive variable (or, for dichotomous variables, a change from 0 to 1). Committee
membership is not statistically significant, contrary to expectations,
but state delegation is separated completely by vote choice, so it is
omitted from the analysis to avoid inflated coefficients and unreliable standard errors. Campaign contributions do not appear to have
influenced vote choice, but policy goals are statistically significant.

Table 6.1. Analysis of Estimated Vote for Majority Leader, 2nd Ballot (1998)

Hypothesis	Independent Variable	Coefficients		Change in Probability	
		Largent	Dunn	Largent	Dunn
Professional Connection	On Largent committee	-1.01 (1.32)	-0.96 (0.85)	.24,.16 [-.07]	.20,.13 [-.06]
	On Dunn committee	-1.46 (1.95)	0.36 (1.10)	.24,.12 [-.11]	.19,.25 [+.06]
Goal Salience	Donation from Armey (logged)	-0.04 (0.04)	-0.06 (0.04)	.23,.21 [-.02]	.19,.15 [-.04]
	Donation from Dunn (logged)	-0.08 (0.06)	0.05 (0.05)	.23,.18 [-.04]	.19,.22 [+.04]
	DW-NOMINATE (1st dimension)	-1.28 (1.86)	-2.61 (2.28)	.23,.22 [-.01]	.19,.16 [-.03]
	Prolife rating	12.32* (5.65)	-2.93** (1.02)	.23,.59 [+.36]	.19,.09 [-.10]
	Active in Depot Caucus	4.00** (1.47)	3.27* (1.27)	.21,.51 [+.30]	.18,.34 [+.16]
	Class of 1994	1.53* (0.60)	1.80** (0.69)	.20,.31 [+.12]	.16,.32 [+.15]
	In leadership	-1.13 (0.82)	-2.23* (1.06)	.24,.17 [-.07]	.20,.07 [-.13]

		Other		
Committee chair	-16.20***	-2.57^	.24, .00	.21, .07
	(1.43)	(1.34)	[-.24]	[-.13]
Gang of 11	3.88**	-17.78***	.19, .64	.21, .00
	(1.14)	(1.04)	[+.46]	[-.21]
Female	-2.40*	2.22*	.24, .07	.17, .51
	(0.91)	(0.96)	[-.17]	[+.34]
% 2-party vote (logged)	-1.85	-0.32	.23, .20	.19, .19
	(1.54)	(1.43)	[-.03]	[+.00]
Age	-0.02	0.05	.23, .21	.19, .24
	(0.03)	(0.04)	[-.02]	[+.05]
Terms	-0.25	-0.12	.23, .17	.19, .16
	(0.15)	(0.10)	[-.06]	[-.02]
Constant	-12.56*	0.05		
	(6.11)	(2.13)		
N	178			
Log L	-99.30			
McFadden's R²	.43			
PRE	24.0%			

Note: Table entries are multinomial logit coefficients (compared to the base outcome, a vote for Armey) with robust standard errors in parentheses. The last two columns show the average predictive probabilities of supporting each candidate compared to support for Armey when each variable is changed from 0 to 1 (for dichotomous variables) or increased by one standard deviation (for continuous variables) with the difference in brackets.

^ p < .1; * p < .05; ** p < .01; *** p < .001 (2-tailed test).

In particular, prolife lawmakers are positively associated with a vote for Largent over Armey (with a substantial 36 percent increase in the relative probability of supporting Largent) and negatively associated with a vote for Dunn over Armey. DW-NOMINATE scores are unexpectedly insignificant, though this may be due to their correlation with prolife ratings.[33] As predicted, active Depot Caucus members were positively associated with a vote for Largent or Dunn relative to Armey—increasing the relative probability of voting for Armey's two opponents by a sizeable 30 percent and 16 percent, respectively —as were members of the class of 1994. In terms of influence-related variables, Armey appears to have drawn support from committee chairs and party leaders, as expected; chairs were drawn away from Largent in particular, with their relative probability of voting for Largent over Armey being near-zero. Members of the Gang of Eleven preferred Largent over Armey by a substantial margin (increasing the relative probability of voting for the Oklahoman by a whopping 46 percent) and steered away from Dunn (reducing the relative probability of voting for her over Armey to virtually nil).[34] Women were positively associated with a vote for Dunn over Armey (and 34 percent more likely to vote for her over the incumbent) and negatively associated with support for Largent compared to Armey. Control variables, including two-party vote, age, and seniority, are not statistically significant.

Though campaign contributions are statistically insignificant in explaining vote choice, they appear to have had at least some effect among freshmen Republicans, lawmakers who were otherwise unfamiliar with the candidates. Nine Republicans received money only from Armey; four of them committed to Armey, two to Largent, and none to Dunn (with the rest undecided). Eight received money from both Armey and Dunn; five of them committed to Armey and three to Dunn. In other words, a necessary precondition for Dunn to win the vote of a freshman was to give the freshman a donation, so her reluctance to contribute to many newcomers' campaigns may have cost her some of their votes.[35]

Table 6.2 displays the results of a probit analysis of the final round of balloting. Model 1 tests just the professional connections hypothesis, while Model 2 includes salient goals. This analysis provides less support for the mixed-motive model. On the one hand, the Texas delegation variable is statistically significant in both models and has a substantively significant effect (increasing the average likelihood of voting for Armey by 32 percent). Armey's campaign contributions are also statistically significant, and a one standard deviation increase in average donation (about $8,300) increased the likelihood of supporting Armey by a modest 8 percent. Also statistically significant is ideology, though the sign of the coefficient on the ideology variable indicates that Armey did better among conservatives, contrary to expectation. Committee chairs were 33 percent more likely to support Armey over Largent, and membership in the class of 1994 is just shy of statistical significance in explaining the likelihood of voting against Armey (p = 0.10). On the other hand, a number of variables used to test the model are statistically insignificant, including committee assignment, membership in the Oklahoma delegation, and some additional policy- and influence-related measures.[36]

In sum, we find that Republican legislators were swayed by a mix of professional connections and salient goals in making their vote choice for majority leader in early 1998, though that mix was more potent on the second ballot than the third. Armey was unable initially to win the votes of the class of 1994, socially liberal members, Gingrich coup plotters, key Depot Caucus members, or legislators from his opponents' state delegations. However, those groups were not large enough to nullify his support among Texans or his ability to make salient certain influence goals (by appealing to party leaders and committee chairs), electoral goals (via campaign contributions), and, on the final ballot, policy goals (of conservatives generally). Coupled with success in securing early vote commitments, an opponent in the final round who had less cross-party appeal, and running as the candidate who offered continuity in a time of instability, Armey was able to secure victory.

Table 6.2. Analysis of Estimated Vote for Armey as Majority Leader, 3rd Ballot (1998)

Hypothesis	Independent Variable	Model 1	Model 2	Change in Probability (Model 2)
Professional Connection	From Texas	1.34*	1.09^	.52, .84
		(0.53)	(0.56)	[+.32]
	From Oklahoma	-0.95	-0.64	.54, .33
		(0.61)	(0.75)	[-.21]
	On Largent committee	0.26	0.33	.53, .64
		(0.29)	(0.31)	[+.11]
Goal Salience	Donation from Armey (logged)	—	0.03*	.54, .62
			(0.01)	[+.08]
	DW-NOMINATE (1st dimension)	—	1.19^	.54, .60
			(0.67)	[+.07]
	Pro-Life Rating	—	0.40	.54, .57
			(0.40)	[+.04]
	Active in Depot Caucus	—	-0.53	.55, .37
			(0.45)	[-.18]
	Class of 1994	—	-0.41	.57, .43
			(0.25)	[-.14]
	In leadership	—	0.21	.53, .60
			(0.33)	[+.07]

Committee chair	—	1.09* (0.45)	.52, .84 [+.33]
Gang of 11	—	-0.28 (0.45)	.54, .45 [-.09]
Female	—	-0.34 (0.36)	.55, .43 [-.12]
Other			
% 2-party vote (logged)	—	0.60 (0.47)	.54, .58 [+.04]
Age	—	-0.00 (0.04)	.54, .52 [-.02]
Terms	—	0.04 (0.04)	.54, .59 [+.05]
Constant	0.03 (0.09)	-0.45 (0.78)	
N	220	219	
Log L	-146.04	-129.49	
McFadden's R^2	.04	.14	
PRE	2.9%	30.7%	

Note: Table entries for each model are probit coefficients with robust standard errors in parentheses. The final column shows the average predicted probabilities of supporting Armey when each variable in Model 2 is changed from 0 to 1 (for dichotomous variables) or increased by one standard deviation (for continuous variables) with the difference in brackets.

^ $p < .1$; * $p < .05$; ** $p < .01$; *** $p < .001$ (2-tailed test).

Revolt against the "Gut-Fighter":
The 1964–65 Race for Minority Leader

The revolt election against House Republican Leader Charles Halleck (R-IN), led by Conference Chairman Gerald Ford (R-MI) in January 1965, was one of the most consequential in American history. It not only garnered considerable attention in the public sphere (Mayhew 2000) but also ultimately led to Ford's selection as the thirty-eighth president of the United States.[37]

Halleck was a self-proclaimed "gut-fighter" from Indiana who had defeated the previous minority leader, Joe Martin (R-MA), in an intraparty revolt in six years earlier. Martin later remarked that Halleck "was hardly the man to pass [an opportunity] by. . . . When he felt absolutely sure of a majority, he moved in for the kill" (Martin 1960, 5). As GOP leader, Halleck had worked diligently and often successfully to increase Republican voting unity, forcing Democrats to look for votes for major bills from within their own divided party. He also sought to join forces whenever possible with southern Democrats in a conservative coalition that could deny Democrats a working majority.[38] And he had increased his party's public profile as one-half of the Ev and Charlie Show, a series of televised press conferences held jointly with Senate Republican Leader Everett Dirksen of Illinois (Scheele 1966).

Not every House Republican was satisfied with Halleck, however. His efforts at maximizing voting unity compelled GOP moderates to cast ballots that were politically or personally uncomfortable, while his willingness to let civil rights legislation reach the House floor in late 1963 infuriated southerners. Some Republicans argued that Halleck's legislative strategy and public persona made it appear that their party "opposes only for the sake of opposition" or was driven less by ideological principles than by what would attract conservative Democratic votes. Halleck could also come across as conceited and unwilling to consult with anyone outside his tight circle of allies, and he gave a cold shoulder to the "Young Turks," a group of Republican reformers who felt largely excluded from party decision making. His excessive drinking, which exacerbated his bad temper, was also a serious problem (Averill 1964c, 1964d; R. Donovan 1964; Kumpa 1964; Lyons 1963; Peabody 1976; Purdum 2014; Van Atta 2008).[39]

"General agitation for change in the leadership" came as early as mid-1964, when Republicans suffered through "a long, hot legislative session" which produced major liberal laws on civil rights, taxes, and poverty reduction. Arizona Senator Barry Goldwater's crushing loss to Lyndon Johnson in the 1964 presidential election dragged down congressional GOP candidates, and the party was left with just 140 seats in the House, its fewest since 1938. For some, the election merely "provided an excuse for promoting a revolt," but it also created new problems for Halleck. The conservative, older, and more senior Republicans who constituted his base were defeated in disproportionate numbers, and the election loss implied that Halleck's image and oppositional approach to governance was toxic to the GOP's reputation. Also, a smaller conference meant Halleck could no longer build majorities with southern Democrats—"the only kind of leadership Halleck is capable of," in the words of Halleck critic Robert Griffin (R-MI) (Peabody 1976; Scheele 1966; Wicker 1965).[40]

Unhappy Republicans called for a party-wide meeting to discuss possible internal reforms, but that did not assuage their doubts about Halleck. Griffin, Charles Goodell (R-NY), and a dozen or so others met and, after considering various possible challengers, decided to ask Ford to run against the incumbent leader.[41] Ford was young, attractive, and a former All-American football player with few enemies.[42] He was allied with party reformers yet solidly conservative, and he had already demonstrated he could successfully challenge a sitting party leader by defeating incumbent Conference Chair Charles Hoeven (R-IA) in 1963.[43] The Michigander was not a perfect candidate, however. He seemed to be ambivalent, if not reluctant, to run, just as he had not challenged Hoeven until pressed to do so. He had also done relatively little as Conference chair, and some saw him as insufficiently dynamic and a "persistent plodder" (Averill 1964b; Edwards 1964b; Kumpa 1964; Peabody 1976).[44]

When Ford agreed to take the plunge, he issued a statement that deemphasized ideological differences with Halleck and played up the importance of "leading rather than simply reacting," to rehabilitate the GOP's collective reputation. He also offered to make every Republican "a first team player" and implied that more influence would be granted to less senior members. Once he learned of Ford's intentions, Halleck immediately returned to the capital from a vacation in Florida and announced he would run to keep his post. The incumbent insisted he could not be faulted for the election outcome, and he called attention to his prior success at keeping the party unified, helping Eisenhower get his bills passed, and defeating or watering down Kennedy's and Johnson's legislative initiatives (Freeburg 1964c; Scheele 1966; Sterne 1964a).

Ford got his campaign off to a quick start, making phone calls to likely supporters before officially declaring his candidacy in order to nail down votes and because, according to one House Republican, "if they [other Republicans] felt that they were in on the decision [to run], they might . . . work for Ford."[45] Led by Griffin, Ford's campaign operation included about thirty members of Congress who provided information, lobbied lawmakers, and double-checked prior vote commitments. The primary targets were large state delegations like California, New York, Ohio, and Pennsylvania, though the campaign also reached out to smaller states, such as Kansas, and skeptical southern conservatives as well. Freshmen were also approached, but they proved "the hardest ones to read," perhaps because they feared retaliation by Halleck (Ford 1979; Peabody 1976; Rumsfeld 2011).[46]

In contrast to the Ford campaign, Halleck's was relatively unorganized, got off to a slow start, depended heavily on a small number of allies—mostly fellow Indianans and some party leaders—and lacked a systematic means of confirming lawmakers' commitments. "You aren't doing enough," warned Minority Whip Les Arends (R-IL), but Halleck replied that "he didn't think anybody could beat him because of all the favors he'd done for the members" (Peabody 1976).[47] Like Ford, Halleck focused on winning state delegations, zeroing in on their most senior members in the expectation that they would bring in-state colleagues with them. He tried to cash in on past favors, like distributing desired committee assignments and making campaign stops in fellow Republicans' districts. To counter Halleck's advantages, Ford and his team emphasized that, in Griffin's words, "the strength of the Republican Party was at stake."[48] Halleck had extensive personal connections with business lobbyists, but the Ford campaign took advantage of their own candidate's contacts, reputation, and seat on the Appropriations Committee to deter interest groups from taking sides, if not encourage them to openly support Ford. The Michigander also successfully convinced some major GOP figures, including Goldwater, to stay neutral (Peabody 1976; Scheele 1966).[49]

Both campaigns tried to garner positive media coverage. One Halleck ally distributed clippings by sympathetic reporters and columnists, while Robert Ellsworth (R-KS) sent out copies of a magazine interview in which Ford complained that Halleck had let conservative southern Democrats dictate the party's agenda and strategy. Campaign surrogates also appeared on an NBC news program to tout the advantages of their candidate and criticize the opposition (*Chicago Tribune* 1964; Peabody 1976; Sterne 1964b).

The Ford campaign faced two particular challenges. The first was how to win over the Wednesday Group, a collection of twenty moderate-to-liberal Republicans. Though many of its members believed Halleck saw them "as a band of liberal crackpots," according to columnists Rowland Evans and Robert Novak, not all were automatically inclined to vote for Ford, and some toyed with fielding a more ideologically moderate candidate from their ranks, like John Lindsay (R-NY) or Robert Stafford (R-VT).[50] Ford needed their votes but had to court them carefully because, as one of his allies explained, a Wednesday Club endorsement meant "we'll lose conservatives all over the place," including southerners who were already suspicious of Ford's open criticism of Halleck's "southern strategy."[51] The second challenge was to avoid getting entangled in other leadership contests occurring or threatening to occur simultaneously. Mel Laird (R-WI), a close friend of Ford's who was unpopular with moderates for strongly supporting Goldwater, proclaimed that he would run for Conference chair, and a number of more liberal-leaning Republicans became suspicious that Ford and Laird had made a secret deal to help each other. Meanwhile, conservatives worried that the Goldwater-appointed head of the Republican National Committee, Dean Burch, might be forced from office, making them uneasy about the prospect of siding with moderates to also oust Halleck (Evans and Novak 1964b, 1964c; *Herald Tribune* 1964; Kabaservice 2012; Peabody 1976; Rodgers 1964).[52]

By late December, the Ford team was "convinced that they had the votes to win," and Ford departed for a previously scheduled family skiing trip in Michigan. But Halleck suddenly began ratcheting up his campaign, sending out a "Dear Colleague" letter, hosting a cocktail party for incoming freshmen, and somehow securing a copy of the Ford campaign's whip list. Rushing back to Washington, Ford fought to stop an apparent swing in support toward Halleck. The incumbent leader managed to strike a deal with John Lindsay to get a few votes from the Wednesday Group in exchange for supporting the Group's candidate for chairman of the conference, Peter Frelinghuysen (R-NJ). Nonetheless, the Ford team reversed Halleck's momentum and, on the eve of the election, felt confident it was within striking distance of victory (Ford 1979; Peabody 1976; Scheele 1966).[53]

On Monday, January 4, House Republicans gathered to vote by secret ballot (then a relatively new practice, having been adopted by the party in 1959). They first cast their ballots in the election for Conference chair, which Laird won, 77–62, despite Halleck delivering some promised votes to Frelinghuysen.[54] Then came the long-awaited contest for minority leader. After vacating the first round of voting because an extra ballot was cast, Ford was narrowly elected, defeating Halleck 73–67 (Peabody 1976; Scheele 1966). Ford had managed to overthrow the "Gut Fighter," his second successful challenge to an incumbent in two years.

Jubilant over the result, younger reform-minded Republicans soon saw the party adopt reforms to expand their opportunities for influence. But in the longer run, Ford's victory would prove to have far greater political ramifications. In 1973, Ford—by then a prominent and popular minority leader—was the choice of President Richard Nixon to be his vice president, after the incumbent vice president, Spiro Agnew, resigned. Less than a year later, Nixon himself quit the White House, leaving Ford to become the next president of the United States. Had Ford never successfully challenged Charlie Halleck in 1965, presidential history might have gone in a very different direction.

If the mixed-motive model explains vote choice in this election, we should expect to find a statistically significant effect of both professional connections and salient goals. We test this with probit regression, estimating vote choice with a preelection "master" tally kept by Ford ally Donald Rumsfeld (R-IL) and augmented by information about vote choice gathered from newspaper accounts and interviews with lawmakers after the election.[55] In terms of professional connections, we examine whether lawmakers from Michigan and Indiana, plus members of Ford's Appropriations Committee, lent their support to their committee colleague running for office. Reelection goals were salient in the race, given the electoral disaster of 1964 and the Ford campaign's emphasis on improving the GOP's reputation with voters, so electorally vulnerable lawmakers—i.e., those narrowly elected in 1964—should be more likely to support Ford. In terms of policy, we would not expect left-right ideological preferences to be significant because both candidates were ideologically similar and neither raised many policy matters in his campaign, but we nonetheless control for them with legislator DW-NOMINATE scores.[56] Influence goals were salient, however. Age, tenure, or both should be significant, since Ford was younger and less senior than Halleck, was allied with Republicans frustrated about Halleck's "doctrinaire and rigid adherence to the old seniority rules," as John Anderson (R-IL) put it, and expressed an openness to distributing influence in the party more widely.[57] Chairs and party leaders are not expected to lean toward either candidate, because both candidates were in leadership roles and committee influence was not an explicit issue in their campaigns.[58] Finally, because southern Republicans were subject to cross-pressures—they were supportive of Halleck's southern strategy but disappointed by his lack of opposition to civil rights legislation—we control for southern representation but do not expect it to be statistically significant.

The results of the analysis are shown in table 6.3. Models 1 and 2

Table 6.3. Analysis of Estimated Vote for Ford as Minority Leader (1965)

Hypothesis	Independent Variable	Stringent Vote Estimate		Relaxed Vote Estimate		Change in Probability (Model 4)
		Model 1	Model 2	Model 3	Model 4	
Professional Connection	On Ford committee	0.78^ (0.41)	0.99* (0.46)	1.29* (0.53)	1.55* (0.63)	.53, .93 [+.40]
Goal Salience	2–party vote (logged)	—	−2.74* (1.26)	—	−2.69* (1.26)	.57, .48 [−.09]
	Age	—	−0.03^ (0.02)	—	−0.02 (0.02)	.57, .49 [−.08]
	Term	—	0.01 (0.05)	—	−0.04 (0.06)	.57, .52 [−.05]

Other

DW-NOMINATE (1st dimension)	—	−1.70* (0.81)	—	−1.40^ (0.77)	−.57, .49 [−.08]
In leadership	—	0.68 (0.62)	—	0.57 (0.64)	.56, .74 [+.18]
Committee ranking member	—	−0.19 (0.53)	—	0.22 (0.54)	.56, .63 [+.07]
South	—	−0.34 (0.41)	—	−0.46 (0.42)	.58, .42 [−.16]
Constant	−0.11 (0.11)	0.14 (0.92)	0.09 (0.11)	0.27 (0.89)	
N	139	139	139	139	
Log L	−94.30	−86.69	−91.15	−83.33	
McFadden's R^2	.02	.10	.04	.12	
PRE	9.0%	31.3%	0.0%	21.7%	

Note: Table entries for each model are probit coefficients with robust standard errors in parentheses. The final column shows the average predicted probabilities of supporting Ford when each variable in Model 2 is changed from 0 to 1 (for dichotomous variables) or increased by one standard deviation (for continuous variables) with the difference in brackets.

^ p < .1; * p < .05; ** p < .01; *** p < .001 (2-tailed significance test).

estimate a lawmaker as voting for Ford only if noted as such in the Rumsfeld tally or outside sources; Models 3 and 4 use a more relaxed vote estimate, counting as Ford votes also those marked as "leaning Ford" in the Rumsfeld count. In all four models, legislators not estimated as voting for Ford are assumed to have voted for Halleck. The results are consistent with both the professional connection and salient goal hypotheses. The Michigan and Indiana delegation variables must be dropped because all members of those delegations voted for their respective candidate—a strong indication that state delegation mattered—and membership on Ford's Appropriations Committee is both statistically significant and, as shown in the last column of table 6.3, has a substantial effect in Model 4 (increasing the average probability of voting for Ford from 53 percent to 93 percent). In terms of salient goals, Republicans who won by a wider margin in 1964 were more likely to vote against Ford, as expected, with a one standard deviation increase in two-party vote share (from a mean of 57 percent to 63 percent of the vote) increasing the average probability of voting against Ford by nearly 10 percentage points. Age is weakly significant in Model 2, and its correlation with term in office likely explains why the latter is not statistically significant.[59] Unexpectedly, first-dimension DW-NOMINATE scores are statistically significant in both models, suggesting conservatives preferred Halleck over Ford, but the finding is not robust, as the variable loses its significance when omitting Republicans with outlier DW-NOMINATE values.[60] As expected, party leaders, committee ranking members, and southerners were no more or less likely to support Ford when controlling for other factors.

In short, the Ford-Halleck race was one in which both professional connections and salient goals help explain why individual Republicans cast the ballots they did. As in any leadership race, we cannot rule out the influence of additional, unmeasurable factors identified as causally important by observers of the election, such as personal friendships, dislike of Halleck's temperament, and favors Halleck had done for other House Republicans in years past (Peabody 1976; Scheele 1966). Nonetheless, the mixed-motive model gives us considerable insight into the multiple factors that helped shape votes for party leadership candidates. Our analysis also shows why the 1964 election put Halleck at a significant disadvantage within his party: not only were collective electoral concerns salient, but two Republicans from his home state and several older, more conservative members of the party (all of whom were predicted to prefer Halleck over Ford based on the regression model) were among those who lost their seats that year.[61] This underscores how successful revolts may depend on how an election defeat reconstitutes a party's membership as well as its depressive effect on the survivors' morale.

The Underdog Loses: The 1968–69 Race for Speaker

The 1969 challenge against Speaker John McCormack (D-MA) was notable for being the first intraparty contest for the speakership in over forty years. Though McCormack easily won the challenge, mounted by the outspoken liberal reformer Morris Udall (D-AZ), it may have hastened McCormack's departure from Congress and, in the longer term, was an early harbinger of a liberal shift within the Democratic Party that would eventually supplant its older, more conservative congressional cadre (see chapter 3).[62]

During the 90th Congress (1967–68), a growing number of Democrats, especially junior liberal lawmakers, expressed concerns about McCormack, who had become Speaker following the death of Sam Rayburn in 1961. These included his unstinting support of the Vietnam War, his tepid, laid-back leadership style, and the fact that he was increasingly out of step with the concerns of newer House members. Following the 1968 elections, Udall declared his candidacy in a December 26 letter to colleagues.[63] He framed his campaign in general terms, calling for "change" and "fresh leadership," expressing alarm at the future electoral viability of the Democratic Party, and lamenting the declining power of the House versus the Senate and the White House.[64] Udall, who was considerably younger and less senior than McCormack, described his challenge as an effort to find "opportunities for younger and more marginal Members" competing with older party oligarchs for influence (Bolling 1965a; Carson and Johnson 2001; Evans and Novak 1967).[65]

It is difficult to gauge the degree to which Udall's ambition explains his decision to challenge McCormack. Despite the fact that Udall had eyed House leadership since coming to the House and had been an advocate for reform throughout the 1960s, he saw his race against McCormack as symbolic. He ran only after having failed to recruit someone else to do so, and he claimed that if he did manage to win in the caucus, he would allow another candidate to be the party's nominee on the House floor. Despite this ambivalence, Udall campaigned extensively for the position. Unsurprisingly, he found it hard to convince many Democrats to take the bold step of voting to remove their own party's incumbent Speaker. The Arizonan received no endorsements from major advocacy groups and little, if any, organized support from the liberal Democratic Study Group (DSG). Meanwhile, Udall's declaration prompted a flood of telegrams and letters to McCormack from fellow lawmakers pledging their support for him. Also problematic for Udall was that he was relatively liberal and his candidacy was often characterized as a "left-wing" challenge, but progressives and change-oriented Democrats constituted a minority in the party.[66] By the eve of the nominating election in caucus, Udall counted no more than 85 votes, not enough to win (Carson and Johnson 2001; Champagne et al. 2009; McGrory 1969; Nelson 2017; *Newsweek* 1969; Peabody 1976).[67]

As would be the case in his race for majority leader two years later, discussed in chapter 3, Udall's private count was significantly inflated, in part because he underestimated the durability of written commitments to McCormack. When the caucus met to nominate a Speaker in January 1969, Udall lost by a wide margin, 178–58, with four ballots cast for Ways and Means Committee chair Wilbur Mills (D-AR), one of those who had been discussed as a possible challenger to McCormack. Nonetheless, the results were the largest number of recorded votes ever cast against an incumbent Speaker in the caucus in the twentieth century. More importantly, the outcome signaled the growing influence of younger liberals; in fact, to shore up their support in the election, McCormack had agreed to their demand that the caucus meet monthly. Udall's challenge became one of a series of difficulties that would beset the aging Speaker, including the criminal indictment of a staffer, the prolonged illness of his wife, and a "no confidence" resolution introduced against him in the caucus by Jerome Waldie (D-CA). McCormack retired from the House in 1970, remaining long enough to get his revenge against Udall by lobbying against his candidacy for majority leader (Carson and Johnson 2001; J. Farrell 2001; Hunter 1970a; Nelson 2017; Peabody 1976; *U.S. News and World Report* 1970).

We test the explanatory power of the mixed-motive model in this race using probit regression. To estimate the vote choice of lawmakers, we draw upon press reports, letters, and telegrams kept by McCormack and postmortem vote estimations made by Udall. Data from both candidates allow us to crosscheck members' pledges and determine that only six lawmakers pledged to both candidates.[68] To capture the effect of professional connections, we include variables measuring whether a lawmaker was from the same state as McCormack (though not Udall, the lone Democrat from Arizona) or sat on either of Udall's committees (Interior and Insular Affairs, and Post Office and Civil Service). (McCormack, being Speaker of the House, served on no committees.) In terms of goals, we expect ideology to matter because Udall was widely recognized as the more liberal candidate, so we include DW-NOMINATE scores to estimate ideological preferences. Influence-related goals were salient as well. Since Udall was a junior member and his campaign was framed in part as giving more opportunities to younger legislators, we include measures of age and length of service of lawmakers and whether a Democrat was in leadership or chaired a committee.[69] We do not expect electoral goals to be significant because the size of the party's seat loss in 1968 was relatively small and there is no evidence that the congressional elections were of major concern among Democrats.

The results appear in table 6.4. Models 1 and 2 show the estimated effects of the independent variables using a more stringent measure of voting for Udall: those counted by Udall as a supporter and either

Table 6.4. Analysis of Estimated Caucus Vote for Udall as Speaker (1969)

Hypothesis	Independent Variable	Stringent Vote Estimate		Relaxed Vote Estimate		Change in Probability (Model 4)
		Model 1	Model 2	Model 3	Model 4	
Professional Connection	From Massachusetts	0.08 (0.62)	0.44 (0.64)	-0.08 (.62)	0.32 (0.60)	.21, .28 [+.08]
	On Udall committee	0.46^ (0.26)	0.07 (0.27)	0.48^ (0.25)	0.12 (0.27)	.20, .23 [+.03]
Goal Salience	DW-NOMINATE (1st dimension)	—	-2.49*** (0.66)	—	-2.23*** (0.59)	.21, .12 [-.09]
	Age	—	-0.06*** (0.02)	—	-0.06*** (0.01)	.21, .10 [-.11]
	Term	—	0.01 (0.04)	—	0.00 (0.04)	.21, .21 [+.00]

Other	—	0.14	—	-0.43	.21, .19
		(0.61)		(0.59)	[-.02]
2-party vote (logged)					
Constant	-1.04***	1.31	-0.88***	1.25^	
	(0.11)	(0.68)	(0.10)	(0.64)	
N	240	239	240	239	
Log L	-106.58	-84.54	-120.96	-96.54	
McFadden's R²	.01	.22	.02	.21	
PRE	0.0%	2.5%	0.0%	6.0%	

Note: Table entries for each model are probit coefficients with robust standard errors in parentheses. Models 1 and 2 use the most stringent estimate of vote choice; Models 3 and 4 use a less stringent estimate. The final column shows the average predicted probabilities of supporting Udall when each variable in Model 4 is changed from 0 to 1 (for dichotomous variables) or increased by one standard deviation (for continuous variables) with the difference in brackets.

^ p < .1; * p < .05; ** p < .01; *** p < .001 (2-tailed significance test).

confirmed as a Udall voter by, or missing from, the McCormack data (N = 40). Models 3 and 4 are a more relaxed measure, coding a Democrat as voting for Udall if identified as such in either the Udall or McCormack data (N = 50).[70] The results provide strong evidence for the mixed-motive model. The Udall committee variable is modestly statistically significant in Models 1 and 3, though its substantive effect is small (raising the average probability of voting for Udall by just 3 percent). The Massachusetts delegation variable is not statistically significant, but this may be an artifact of the delegation's relatively small size, because at least six of the eight Massachusetts members supported the Speaker. Conservatism is negatively associated with a vote for Udall, as predicted, and younger lawmakers were more likely to vote for the challenger, with a one standard deviation increase in age (about ten years) reducing the average probability of voting for Udall by 11 percent. The seniority variable is not statistically significant, a consequence of its high correlation with age.[71] The leadership and committee chair variables must be excluded because not a single party leader or committee chair voted for Udall, strongly suggesting both variables help explain vote choice. Finally, electoral vulnerability proves statistically insignificant, as expected.[72]

The findings confirm that goals made salient in the campaign, coupled with the professional connections derived from state delegations, contributed to the voting calculations of lawmakers in the election.[73] This spelled doom for Udall, a candidate from a tiny state delegation in a party where senior conservatives outnumbered younger liberals.

Floor Challenges against Speakers

The Speaker of the House is the only leader subject to both a nomination vote within his party and a vote of the entire chamber, usually at the start of a given Congress. He or she is also the only House officer who can be removed by the chamber at any time via a privileged floor motion, known as a motion to vacate the chair. As a result, Speakers and Speaker candidates are potentially susceptible to a very particular type of leadership revolt: removal or nonselection when a subset of their party joins with the bulk of the minority party to vote against them on the floor.

In the nineteenth and early twentieth centuries, defections against one's party nominee for Speaker were not uncommon, due to the presence of sizeable intraparty factions and more lax party discipline. Floor revolts against Speakers vanished after the 1920s, but starting in the mid-1990s, the number of lawmakers willing to vote against their party's nominee on the floor began to grow again, and there were several serious floor revolts and attempted revolts against incumbent Speakers and party nominees for Speaker. As mentioned above, in 1997 a group of disgruntled House Republicans met in secret to devise a method to oust incumbent Speaker Newt Gingrich, a plot that unraveled when Majority Leader Dick Armey leaked word of it to Gingrich. In 2013, John Boehner lost the votes of twelve Republicans in the chamber's vote for Speaker, just seven shy of the nineteen needed to deny him a majority of ballots. Two years later, twenty-five Republicans did the same—the largest defection by a Speaker's party since the nineteenth century—and while Boehner survived, it may have helped convince him to resign from Congress less than a year later (Blake 2015; Green and Bee 2016; Jenkins and Stewart 2013).[74]

The procedure employed to select a Speaker on the chamber floor is unique among leadership elections. The vote is public and ballots are cast in alphabetical order, which means lawmakers whose last names come earlier in the alphabet may influence the votes of legislators whose names come later—and, more importantly, it allows party leaders, advocacy groups, and constituents to identify rebels and thereby reward or punish them. It is also possible to deny a nominee the speakership even if she lacks a challenger, because ballots cast as "present" or for any hypothetical candidate count against the party nominee. As a result, not voting for the nominee of one's party could result in the opposing party's nominee being selected Speaker, putting greater pressure on potential rebels to fall in line. This suggests that floor votes for Speaker are entwined more closely with norms of party loyalty than are other leadership elections (Green 2016; Green and Bee 2016).

Though these features of the Speaker selection process make it unlikely that the mixed-motive model applies to it, we nonetheless test the model on a recent case of floor rebellion: the January 2013 election for Speaker, which nearly defeated Republican nominee John Boehner. As with other leadership races, we employ probit to test various explanatory variables. Those variables include measures of shared state delegation (Ohio), electoral safety (the logged percent of two-party vote), ideology (first dimension DW-NOMINATE scores), term in office, age, and whether a lawmaker served in leadership or as a committee chair.[75] (As Speaker, Boehner served on no committees, so that type of professional connection cannot be tested.) Opposition to Boehner was reportedly strongest among especially conservative Republicans, so we expect DW-NOMINATE scores to be statistically significant. Leaders, by contrast, should be less likely to defy party norms and vote against Boehner on the floor. There were also two goal-related concerns salient to a handful of Republicans: if the party supported one's primary opponent, or if a lawmaker lost his choice committee assignment as punishment for rebellious behavior in the previous Congress (Blake 2015).[76] We thus include dichotomous variables capturing these two concerns.

The results, shown in table 6.5, could be interpreted as providing some support for the mixed-motive model. Several key factors are perfectly separated by the vote for Boehner—serving in the Ohio delegation, as a party leader, or as a committee chair—and must therefore be dropped from the analysis. Age is not statistically significant, but seniority is just shy of statistical significance ($p = 0.11$), and conservative Republicans were more likely to vote against Boehner, as predicted.[77] Most strikingly, goal-related variables associated with particularized benefits are not only statistically significant but have massive substantive effects: Republicans who beat a party-endorsed primary opponent were 40 percent less likely to vote for Boehner, and those punished by GOP leaders were 74 percent less likely to

Table 6.5. Analysis of Estimated Floor Vote for Boehner as Speaker (2013)

Hypothesis	Independent Variable	Model	Change in Probability
Goal	DW-NOMINATE	−3.04*	.95, .90
Salience	(1st dimension)	(1.33)	[−.05]
	Age	−0.02	.95, .94
		(0.02)	[−.01]
	Term	0.07	.95, .97
		(0.04)	[+.01]
	Punished in 2012	−3.12*	.96, .22
		(1.35)	[−.74]
	Beat party-endorsed	−2.00**	.96, .56
	primary opponent	(0.72)	[−.40]
Other	2-party vote (logged)	−1.12	.95, .94
		(0.97)	[−.01]
	Constant	4.55**	
		(1.52)	
	N	231	
	Log L	−28.41	
	McFadden's R²	.40	
	PRE	16.7%	

Note: Table entries for the model are probit coefficients with robust standard errors in parentheses. The final column shows the average predicted probabilities of voting for Boehner when each variable is changed from 0 to 1 (for dichotomous variables) or increased by one standard deviation (for continuous variables) with the difference in brackets.
^ $p < .1$; * $p < .05$; ** $p < .01$; *** $p < .001$ (2-tailed significance test).

cast a ballot for the Ohioan. This suggests that those who had specific grievances with the incumbent leader—versus more general concerns about salient goals—were most willing to take the bold step of rejecting their party's nominee for Speaker on the House floor.

These results could also be taken as evidence that the floor vote for Speaker is a function of how committed lawmakers are to party loyalty as a norm. For instance, Republicans who had been robbed of a committee assignment had already shown a propensity to eschew intraparty cooperation, while a prior analysis of the election found a relationship between voting against Boehner and an inherent tendency toward rebellion (Green 2016; Thorp 2012). To do something as daring as oppose one's party nominee for Speaker may require not just salient goals and a lack of personal connections but an aversion to cooperating with fellow partisans altogether.

Conclusion

Leadership revolts, while less common than races for open leadership positions, have potentially dramatic impacts, whether they succeed in ousting the incumbent or not. Since 1960, revolts against incumbent leaders have contributed to the retirement or resignation of two Speakers, ended the careers of several other incumbent leaders, and led one lawmaker on a path to the presidency. Although every race has its unique features, our analyses of multiple revolt elections are consistent with the mixed-motive model of vote choice in leadership elections. In many cases, ideology is statistically significant, but other factors are also, including age, leadership status, serving as a committee chair, electoral class, and, in one case, lawmakers' relative electoral security.

Our findings, and the rarity of revolt elections, also suggest a possible qualification to the principal-agent theory of congressional leadership, which holds that elected congressional leaders selected by their party caucus act on behalf of majority party interests to ensure reselection as leader (Rohde and Shepsle 1987; Sinclair 1995). Incumbent leaders are more difficult to remove than one would think, even if a sizeable number of same-party lawmakers support their ouster. The risks and uncertainties associated with a revolt likely deter many would-be challengers from making a play for an occupied leadership post, and leaders themselves will aggressively fight emerging challenges as well as actual ones, using resources like campaign donations to shore up support (see chapter 2). As a result, while the paucity of revolts could be a sign that congressional leaders generally serve as effective and loyal agents, it is also possible that leaders have more flexibility to depart from the wishes of their party than principal-agent theory posits without suffering from a successful revolt (Peabody 1967).

In the next and final chapter, we review our findings and discuss their implications for leadership elections in other legislatures. We also explore other possible explanations of vote choice in congressional leadership elections, review the ways that leadership election politics have changed over the past six decades, and speculate how they may change in the future.

seven

CONCLUSION

Party leadership posts are coveted by many members of Congress. Every so often, two or more of those lawmakers decide that the benefits of running for an elected leadership position outweigh the costs. When that happens, their colleagues face an important and potentially difficult decision: who should lead them? Most do not make that decision lightly, for they know that party leaders can have a profound influence, both individually—on their ability to achieve their goals—and collectively, on the future of their party, the legislature, and the country.

We have argued that legislators' vote choice cannot be explained by a single factor, such as ideological preference or personal friendship. Rather, a mix of relational and instrumental variables contributes to the selection of a party leader. Specifically, lawmakers' vote for leader is influenced by professional connections they may share with one or more candidates for office, as well as personal goals made salient by the candidates, their campaigns, and the political context. Some mix of these motives, depending on the candidates who run, the campaigns they wage, and the broader context of the leadership race comes into play when members of the House of Representatives have the opportunity to choose one candidate or another for a leadership position in their party.

In this chapter, we review our examination of the factors behind candidate emergence and our analyses of vote choice in fourteen contested leadership elections in the U.S. House of Representatives since 1965. We then discuss additional possible explanations of vote choice, how applicable our findings may be to other legislative settings, and how the politics of leadership races has changed in the past and may change in the years ahead.

Ambition and the Emergence of Leadership Candidates

Though the primary focus of this study has been on how members choose among leaders, in chapter 2 we reviewed some of the reasons lawmakers might consider running for an elected leadership office and why they ultimately choose to do so. Our case studies of leadership elections subsequently revealed some discernible commonalities in why some legislators seek to be a party leader.[1] One is the possession of intangible character traits that make some members more ambitious than others. At least fifteen of the thirty-six candidates in races examined in the previous chapters were reputed to be innately ambitious, often harboring ambitions for leadership from their earliest days in Congress. A number saw themselves, or were seen by colleagues, as rising stars in their party. At the other end of the spectrum, six candidates (Wayne Hays, Ed Jenkins, John Lewis, John McFall, James O'Hara, and B. F. Sisk) were sufficiently ambivalent as to enter their race late or to engage in lackluster campaigning. Interestingly, all six lost their bids, whereas eight of the fifteen highly ambitious candidates were successful.[2]

Another commonality among leadership candidates is being the beneficiary of mentor-protégé relationships, peer recruitment, or both. Fourteen candidates we discussed fit this description. Some were recruited by top leaders, like Tip O'Neill, who encouraged Jim Wright's candidacy, and Bob Michel, who supported Ed Madigan and Bob Walker, while others were recruited by rank-and-file members to run. A large percentage appear to have followed an iterative process of sounding out close allies, receiving encouragement from them, and then citing that encouragement when surveying others.

Our cases suggested two other common patterns. A handful of candidates emerged with the explicit goal of blocking the ambitions of others. Ed Madigan, John Murtha, Steve Largent, and Richard Bolling all ran at least in part to hinder the candidacies of rivals or unwanted opponents (albeit unsuccessfully). Finally, some lawmakers appear to have been motivated to run for leadership out of concerns about their party and Congress as a whole. In many cases that we examined, at least one candidate sought to frame the race as "change versus the status quo" in some respect. Though that framing may have been more strategic than genuine at times, there is evidence to suggest that at least some of these candidates, such as Morris Udall in 1968, were genuinely unhappy about the state of affairs and believed a change in leadership was essential to improve matters.

The Mixed-Motive Model and Leadership Vote Choice

In previous chapters we tested our mixed-motive model of vote choice for fourteen leadership elections. As shown in table 7.1, in all cases we found evidence to support the predictions of that model. First, at least some professional connections with individual candidates, forged by a shared state, shared committee, or both were statistically significant in every race. Shared states were an especially frequent explanation of vote choice: in all but two of the races, either every lawmaker from a candidate's state delegation voted for that candidate, or all state delegation variables were statistically significant in explaining vote choice. The substantive effect of shared states and committees was also noteworthy, with an average effect (when estimable) on the probability of voting for a candidate on the first ballot (or, in the 1998 majority leader election, the second ballot) of 27 percent for a same-state candidate and 13 percent for a same-committee candidate.[3] Second, we found that the preponderance of salient goals in each race helped explain vote choice. In every election but two, more than half of the variables used to measure salient goals were not only in the expected causal direction but also statistically significant (or had to be omitted because they explained vote choice perfectly or nearly perfectly). To be sure, in seven of the fourteen elections, other variables assumed not to matter proved statistically significant—ideology in two cases and, in three others, the age of lawmakers, the latter suggesting that there may be important generational considerations that lawmakers take into account (such as in heir apparent races). The mixed-motive model also did less well in explaining certain races, such as the 1989 election for Democratic leader and the second round of balloting for majority leader in 1971. Nonetheless, the results were generally consistent with our claim that in party leadership elections, a combination of professional connections and salient goals matter in shaping vote choice.

One explanatory variable that was often statistically significant was ideology. While this may suggest that the ideology hypothesis of vote choice has merit, in most cases (eight of ten) ideology was made salient by the nature of the election, and in only three races was it statistically significant (or not) contrary to what the mixed-motive model would predict. Also, ideology was significant in every Democratic Party race (six of six), but in only half of Republican Party races (four of eight), underscoring differences in how the parties valued ideological variations.

Besides ideology, perhaps the most noteworthy factor driving vote choice is campaign contributions. After Henry Waxman (D-CA) formed an LPAC as part of his successful campaign to win a subcommittee chairmanship in 1979, ambitious rank-and-file lawmakers began forming LPACs of their own (Currinder 2009, 24–31). Past studies have shown that this made strategic sense insofar as donating money to partisan colleagues correlates with advancement in Congress (Cann 2008; Currinder 2009; Heberlig and Larson 2012; Powell 2009). But we have shown here for the first time that it also correlates at the level of individual vote choice, even after controlling for other possible explanations of voting behavior. In six of the nine non-Speaker races between 1980 and 2006 that we analyzed, campaign donations from candidates were statistically significant and positively associated with support for that candidate. In one of the two open-seat races in which the vacancy materialized unexpectedly, the candidates had given little or no campaign funds to their peers, strongly suggesting that monies are distributed by potential candidates when there is an expectation that a leadership race is in the works. In several instances, contributions also correlated positively with the votes of freshmen lawmakers, with whom candidates are unlikely to have professional or personal connections.

Table 7.1. Summary of Findings

Race	Type	Statistically Significant or Predicts Success/Failure Perfectly?				
		Shared State	Shared Committee	Salient Goal Variables	Ideology	Unanticipated Variables
GOP Leader (1965)	Revolt	all	all	2 of 3	yes	ideology
Dem Speaker (1969)	Revolt	some (50%)	all	4 of 5	yes	none
Dem Leader (1971), 1st ballot	Open	all	all[a]	4 of 6	yes	2-party vote, committee
Dem Leader (1976), 1st ballot	Challenge to heir	all	some (75%)	9 of 10[a]	yes	2-party vote
GOP Leader (1980)	Open	all	some (50%)	5 of 7	no	none
GOP Whip (1980)	Open	all	some (50%)	3 of 5	yes	ideology
Dem Leader (1989)	Open	all	none	2 of 4[a]	yes	age, terms
GOP Whip (1989)	Open	some (50%)	some (50%)	4 of 7	no	none

GOP Whip (1994)	Open	all	some (33%)	4 of 6[a]	no	none
GOP Leader (1998), 2nd ballot	Revolt	all	none	7 of 10	no	none
Dem Whip (2001)	Open	all	none	3 of 4	yes	none
GOP Leader (2006), 1st ballot	Challenge to heir	all	all	8 of 10[a]	yes	age, terms
Dem Leader (2006)	Challenge to heir	all	all	3 of 3	yes	age, leader, ranking on committee
Speaker (2013)	Revolt	all	n/a	5 of 7	yes	none

Note: "Some," "all," or "yes" indicates that at least 1 variable in that category (a) was significant at p < .10 or greater in at least 1 model specification, or (b) had to be omitted because it predicted success or failure perfectly. Shared state and committee include only those states and committees hypothesized to be statistically significant in explaining vote choice. Shaded cell = ideology was one of the hypothesized salient goals.

[a] The sign of one variable is in the opposite direction of that hypothesized (Sisk committee in the 1971 race, age in the 1976 race, ideology in the 1989 election for Democratic leader, McCollum contributions in 1994, and Shadegg donations in the 2006 election for GOP leader).

At first glance, it may seem hard to believe that a $500 or even a $5,000 contribution would influence one's vote in a leadership race, given that the average lawmaker raises many times that amount to run for election. But it makes more sense when one considers how campaign donations create a sense of obligation by their recipients and serve as a powerful signal that the donor cares about the recipient and, by extension, the party. Those involved with past leadership races have acknowledged that money matters, often for these reasons. A former Democratic leader called campaign fundraising "a big deal" in leadership selection, while one Hill aide told us that money was "without question" important because "it shows you are a team player."[4] "That's part of what gets you into leadership—the money you can raise," as one Republican staffer who was involved in several leadership races put it.[5] "Money, whether we like it or not, is a pretty powerful tool," explained W. G. "Bill" Hefner (D-NC), who lost a 1986 race for whip to Tony Coelho, chair of the party's campaign arm, the Democratic Congressional Campaign Committee (DCCC) (Calmes 1986). Coelho agreed that "when somebody gives you a helping hand, no matter how big it is, you are appreciative" (J. Farrell 2001, 398).

Donating money is also an indication that a candidate can perform an increasingly important duty of House leaders: party-wide fundraising. "Money plays a big role," a Republican staffer told us. "Rank and file members want someone who can raise money. . . . If you are putting together a profile of what people want in a leader . . . being able to raise money is a key factor."[6] Noted a Democratic leadership aide, "It's convincing the members that you are there for them and you are going to help them. While $1000 isn't going to sway the vote, it's part of the aggregate. . . . It's more an indirect indicator of the ability and willingness to help."[7] In addition, archival evidence from some of the races we examined, such as internal memos by candidates indicating to whom they have given donations, supports the claim that leadership candidates provide contributions with the expectation that they drive lawmakers' voting decisions.

Other Explanations of Vote Choice

Our statistical analyses hardly explain all of the variation in vote choice in party leadership elections. The average (median) percent of voting variation explained by "full" regression models (the R^2 statistic) is 23 percent, and while some of the models yield a proportional reduction in error (PRE) as high as 72 percent, the average (median) PRE is only 27 percent.[8] Although this represents a decided improvement in our understanding of leadership vote choice, it begs the question of what other possible factors might account for this unexplained variation. Based on our research and the observations of others who have studied party leadership races in the House, we identify two basic types of causal factors: individual-level, including personal relationships and goals unique to specific members of Congress, and macrolevel, like candidate reputation, position and style, and campaign tactics. We briefly review the explanatory plausibility of each.

Individual-Level Factors

Perhaps the most commonly cited individual-level reason a legislator votes one way or another for a leadership candidate is the personal relationship she has with one of the candidates (i.e., the personal-relationship hypothesis discussed in chapter 1). As in any collective institution, friendships exist within Congress (e.g., Champagne et al. 2009; Green 2016), and it seems reasonable to assume that leadership candidates would look for any way to get votes, including tapping into personal relationships they may have with others. Those relationships, which also affect a candidate's decision to run in the first place (see chapter 2), could be based on friendships or social familiarity; common identities, like a shared hometown, religion, ethnicity, or occupation; or spousal, family, or even romantic relationships.[9]

Current and former lawmakers and staff have noted the value of personal relationships in leadership races. Some examples:

- "I think relationships are probably the biggest thing. . . . The Boehners of the world are the masters of personal relationships in the House."[10]
- In his 2006 race for majority leader, John Boehner sought support from "a lot of individuals that he was close to," including "Devin Nunes, from California, whose office was next to Boehner."[11]
- By participating in sports activities and prayer breakfasts "you develop a rapport with Members" and "you go about trying to build on [personal relationships] to build a campaign for office."[12]
- "Ideas and principles matter, but . . . it's friendships . . . [Kevin] McCarthy is the friendliest guy around . . . [for example,] he remembers everybody's birthday."[13]
- Regarding Tom Price (R-GA), who considered running for majority leader in 2015: "Tom's been here for a long time, and I've probably said two words to the guy. . . . I've got to know that I can come up to you when the [crap]'s hitting the fan [on the House floor] and be, like, 'Tom, listen: This is my problem with this bill' or 'I need you to be with me on this,' and it not be awkward or distant, because I don't really know you" (Gehrke 2015).
- According to an aide to congressman Tom DeLay, leadership races are "totally like a popularity contest. It's more like a high school election" (Goldstein 1994).

Accounts of some individual races point to bridges built or burned with colleagues due to personal interactions that affected their voting behavior. For instance, in his challenge against Charlie Halleck in 1965, Gerald Ford received the votes of Joe Martin (R-MA), who had been ousted as leader by Halleck in 1959, and Howard Callaway (R-GA), who was a good friend of Ford ally Robert Griffin.[14] Hale Boggs's "personal friendship" with southerners reportedly helped him win the votes of enough of them in his 1971 race for majority leader to overcome the erratic behavior that had made many Democrats lose faith in him (Shannon 1971). Morris Udall speculated that he lost of the vote of Kenneth Gray (D-IL) in that same election because Udall's subcommittee had taken charge of a bill Gray believed rightly fell under his own committee's jurisdiction (see chapter 3). The race for majority leader in 1976 is probably the most famous example of personal relationships influencing vote choice: Richard Bolling's pomposity did not endear him to many Democrats, and Phil Burton's abrasive personality may have cost him the single precious vote he needed to beat Jim Wright.[15]

Given the difficulty in observing and systematically measuring such relationships, we cannot disprove the personal-relationship hypothesis. For some individual lawmakers in particular races, personal relationships may contribute to their voting calculation. Nevertheless, as we have shown in previous chapters, one cannot distill vote choice in leadership elections into a simple matter of personal relationships between candidates and the rank-and-file. It may also be the case that some friendships or other personal connections are an outgrowth of preexisting professional connections, like shared state delegation or committee assignment, and not the underlying causal factor behind the decision to back a particular candidate.[16] Moreover, the personal-relationship hypothesis cannot readily explain the vote choice of new members of Congress, who are almost certain to lack close ties to any of the candidates and must therefore calculate their voting preference based on other factors.

Another individualistic factor that could account for unexplained variation in vote choice is a unique benefit or advantage that accrues to a lawmaker if one particular candidate wins. For instance, a legislator might be able to join a desirable committee if a candidate from that committee is elected to leadership, relinquishing his committee seat (e.g. Peabody 1976, 179). Maybe a certain favor has been promised to a member of Congress—an overseas trip, help with a specific bill, a visit to one's congressional district, assistance with fundraising—in exchange for support. Or, conversely, a member of Congress opposes a candidate because her election will impose some personal cost. For instance, Morris Udall speculated that he lost the vote of Wayne Aspinall (D-CO), the "crusty and autocratic" conservative chairman of the Interior and Insular Affairs Committee, in 1971 because Aspinall feared Udall's departure from his committee to become majority leader would allow Phil Burton, an outspokenly liberal committee member, to have greater influence (Jacobs 1995, 218–21).[17] We cannot possibly control for all such individualistic reasons for selecting a particular candidate, but it seems reasonable to assume that they play a role in the voting behavior of at least some lawmakers some of the time.

Macrolevel Factors

One macrofactor that could influence the voting preferences of lawmakers is a candidate's reputation among the rank-and-file. There are two dimensions to candidate reputation. The first is reputation internal to the party. As a former leadership candidate explained to us, "personal character and attributes sometimes trump ideology" in shaping vote choice.[18] "A lot of it . . . is like running for student body president," said one erstwhile GOP aide; "It's a popularity contest."[19] Another echoed this sentiment, remarking that "it's a popularity contest to some extent . . . you have to be well-liked in the conference."[20] Especially important may be a reputation among one's colleagues for competence, service, and loyalty to the party (e.g., Wicks 2001).[21] Candidates who have been in a position to help others—serving on Appropriations, say, or heading the party's campaign committee— may become known as service-oriented even by those to whom they have not provided explicit assistance. Internal reputation is likely linked to what lawmakers think is the right array of skills for a specific leadership post, which not only differ between posts but change over time as well.

The other dimension of reputation is how a candidate is perceived externally, by the public, by influential individuals and groups outside Congress, or by the opposite party. Some candidates are better at the internal aspects of legislative leadership, whereas others might be superior media spokespersons, campaigners, or fundraisers. In a number of races, such as the 1976 campaign for majority leader, at least one candidate made a point of highlighting their public persona, presumably because they believed it would help them win votes. Public reputation has probably become more important as party leaders have been increasingly expected to serve as media-oriented figures (Harris 1998; Sinclair 1995). It may be even more valuable when combined with a positive evaluation within the party. As one former Democratic leader told us, members want "someone they can trust, someone who has good political intelligence, *someone who is presentable* . . . and, you know, someone they like."[22]

It is difficult to say how much a candidate's reputation, public or private, influences votes in a leadership election. A positive reputation cannot hurt, and good public image in particular could sway those of the rank-and-file who are especially concerned with their party's collective goals or protecting and enhancing its brand (Cox and McCubbins 1993; Grynaviski 2010; Kiewiet and McCubbins 1991; Lee 2016; Z. Smith 2007). Yet there are races in which the more charismatic and well-spoken candidate lost, such as Morris Udall (in both his 1969 and 1971 leadership races) and Guy Vander Jagt (in his 1980 race for majority leader). A candidate's positive internal image may be less an independent influence on vote choice than an offshoot of his or her efforts to satisfy colleagues' goals. For instance, Tony Coelho raised a great deal of campaign funds for candidates, which improved his reputation within the Democratic Party but, perhaps more importantly, yielded support among fund recipients. In his race for Democratic Caucus vice chair in 2005, Joe Crowley (D-NY) noted that fundraising was "one way to quantify what you are doing for the team" (Billings 2005).

Another macrolevel factor that may matter is the position and leadership style of candidates. A number of lawmakers who run, for instance, are insurgent candidates—not a part of the established leadership structure and regime—and they can attract the votes of junior lawmakers who lack influence (e.g., the 1965 and 2006 races for Republican leader and the 1969 race for Speaker). But whether insurgents do better or worse than establishment candidates is likely tied to the overall perception of the party's leadership by the rank-and-file, which is inherently variable and perhaps linked to time-bound considerations of the party's current problems or opportunities. What we can say, however, is that insurgents are no more or less likely to win than establishment candidates. Table 7.2, which lists the fourteen races we examine and notes those with a clear contrast in candidates between these two types, shows success by nearly an equal number of each.

Candidates might be able to garner more votes if they have leadership styles perceived as more appropriate or desirable to the position being contested. For instance, in the 1980 race for Republican minority leader, Bob Michel may have had an advantage insofar as some lawmakers saw the position's primary responsibility as coalition building—Michel's strength—rather than public communication, which his opponent, Guy Vander Jagt, insisted it could be (see chapter 4). As Barber Conable (R-NY) wrote to Vander Jagt in 1980, though he thought that he and Michel were both talented, he could not support Vander Jagt for minority leader because "my concept of the minority leader's function is primarily legislative," and while Vander Jagt was "more the political leader," Michel was "more the legislative floor leader."[23] And in 1994, Bob Walker's candidacy, built around his past success as a thorn to Democrats, may have suffered when Republicans took majority control of the chamber, changing the whip's job into one where policy development and bill passage, not position-taking and bipartisan coalition-building, were central. Some have argued that candidates with a more confrontational, "bomb-thrower" style became increasingly popular in the Republican Conference in the 1980s, improving their chances in leadership elections until they eventually triumphed over their more conciliatory opponents, starting with Newt Gingrich in 1989 (Connelly and Pitney 1994, 54–58; Harris 2006; Lee 2016, 100–105).

There is something to be said for the argument that style matters, and it may well be that a candidate's leadership style or perceived skill set (such as legislative effectiveness) is an important part of some lawmakers' calculation of their vote preference. Who those

Table 7.2. Characteristics of Leadership Races

Race	Type	Establishment vs. Insurgent?	Winner: Establishment or Insurgent?	Was Winner 1st to Declare Candidacy?
GOP Leader (1965)	Revolt	yes	insurgent	no
Dem Speaker (1969)	Revolt	yes	establishment	yes
Dem Leader (1971)	Open	yes	establishment	no
Dem Leader (1976)	Challenge to heir	no	n/a	no
GOP Leader (1980)	Open	yes	establishment	yes
GOP Whip (1980)	Open	yes	establishment	no
Dem Leader (1989)	Open	no	n/a	no
GOP Whip (1989)	Open	yes	insurgent	yes
GOP Whip (1994)	Open	yes	insurgent	yes
GOP Leader (1998)	Revolt	yes	establishment	no
Dem Whip (2001)	Open	no	n/a	yes
GOP Leader (2006)	Challenge to heir	yes	insurgent	no
Dem Leader (2006)	Challenge to heir	no	n/a	yes
Speaker (2013)	Revolt	no	n/a	yes

lawmakers might be is difficult to estimate with much precision. Furthermore, as we have seen, the vote choice of lawmakers in races featuring stylistically different candidates is also swayed by factors that may have little to do with leadership style. Michel, for instance, won many votes because of his strategic distribution of campaign contributions, and Gingrich appealed to fellow southerners seeking greater regional influence in leadership. Candidates may also win in spite of their leadership style, not because of it. Gingrich's bomb-throwing style was troubling to some legislators, and a switch of just two votes—which, as we have noted, could have happened for any number of reasons unrelated to Gingrich's style—would have made Ed Madigan the party's whip (Connelly and Pitney 1994, 56).

Another macrofactor that could play a role is the identity and background of other incumbent leaders or candidates in other leadership races. For instance, efforts to achieve ideological or regional balance might make particular candidates more or less attractive, depending on who else is already in leadership. The appeal of Jim Wright as a relatively conservative southern candidate for leadership in 1976, for example, may have been based in part on the fact that the Speaker-elect, Tip O'Neill, was from the more liberal northeast. Such efforts to balance or to "round out" a leadership team might also result from generational or stylistic differences. Dick Cheney, for instance, was recruited to run for RPC chair in 1980 by Bob Michel, hoping in part it would "attract support and energy among my fellow freshmen and thereby lessen their fervor for Vander Jagt" (Cheney 2011, 135). And in more recent years, efforts to achieve broader racial or gender representation within the leadership have been more prominent in leadership campaigns. Still, the success of candidates' claims to offer such "balance" is conditioned by the range of other factors, and some of our cases illustrate its limitations. For instance, Bob Walker and Ed Jenkins each argued for his candidacy based on the need for a better regional balance in their respective parties, but neither won.

Finally, broad campaign tactics might influence votes. A common claim is that candidates are less likely to win when they pursue outsider strategies—garnering positive editorials in newspapers, appearing in the media, and having lobbyists and former lawmakers advocate for them—than if they use insider strategies, focusing on member-to-member appeals and relationships (Polsby 1962 [1992]; Peabody 1976, 494–97). As David Bonior put it, "running for a leadership position is an inside game—lobbyists and others on the outside have almost no influence on how members cast their votes" (Bonior 2018, 319). One congressman told a reporter that "if you're talking to the media, you're really not talking to the people you need to be talking to" (M. Fuller 2014). "I don't think interest groups play a big role," one GOP aide told us. "I don't know of any members who vote for a leader because of lobbying."[24] The races we have examined would seem to support that assertion, but only to a degree. Lawmakers who refrain from doing the necessary grunt work of building coalitions—lobbying, developing campaign themes, addressing lawmaker goals—are less likely to win, and outsider strategies are no substitute. Yet in many races, multiple candidates used outside strategies, including the eventual winner. Some candidates, like Gerald Ford (R-MI), made efforts to neutralize their opponent's outside strategy, asking lobbyists or high-profile actors not in Congress to refrain from making endorsements. Others may have relied on outside lobbying more covertly, as happened in the 2006 race for Democratic leader when a mysterious group issued a last-minute public attack against Jack Murtha for prior alleged ethical lapses. As Peabody wrote, "a negative column can start a rumor; a favorable column can help soften up a possible convert" (Peabody 1976, 193). The safest conclusion to reach is that outsider strategies are not sufficient to win, but they can signal the possession of outsider-oriented skills which are increasingly important to leadership (Brown and Peabody 1992), and they may still be necessary to compete, especially if one's opponents are using them too.[25]

On multiple-round ballots, another campaign tactic may be influential: second-tier candidates making deals to give their votes to each other upon elimination. Allegations of these sorts of arrangements were made in the 1971 and 1976 elections for Democratic leader and the 2006 race for Republican leader, with mixed success. Deals of this kind may indeed shape the outcome of multiround elections and could explain why our regression models explain a smaller proportion of variation in vote choice in second- and third-round ballots.[26] This does not preclude the applicability of our mixed-motive model, however, because those deals are often made between candidates whose supporters share common goals or professional connections with both candidates, so at least some of them might have "naturally" voted for their rivals anyway.

Timing is another campaign-related factor that could matter. The scheduling of the election, for instance, affects the time available to candidates to secure votes: holding an election early can benefit those who are ahead in vote commitments, while a later election date gives those who are behind an opportunity to catch up. Last-minute scheduling changes can even play a role in determining attendance. Louise Slaughter (D-NY) claimed she lost her race for vice chair of the Democratic Caucus in 1994 because "they moved the vote up by a day, and all my supporters had already gone home for the night" (Shaffrey 2000b).

The most important element of timing is when a candidate chooses to declare his candidacy and start asking for vote commitments. Because lawmakers are loath to break the commitments they make to candidates, those who secure a vote first may keep that vote regardless of who their rivals may be, leading to a "race for the commitments" (Kantin 2002). Said one Democratic congressman, "I find that in politics the first person who asks you [for your vote] is usually the one you support."[27] Interviews and accounts of some races suggest that starting a campaign earlier than your opponents is important for this reason. After his failed 1969 race for Speaker, Morris Udall noted that he lost the vote of Robert Tiernan (D-RI) because "Boland & others got there first."[28] In a private letter written to Newt Gingrich, Mickey Edwards (R-OK), who was running for Research Committee chair, lamented that Republicans were not only committing to candidates from the same committee or state, but also to those "who asked them first."[29] David Bonior attributed his loss to Bill Gray in a race for Democratic whip because Gray had gotten advance notice that the incumbent whip, Tony Coelho, was about to quit, allowing Gray to secure votes ahead of him. Two years later, Bonior got the jump on *his* opponents when the House Doorkeeper told him that Gray was going to resign. "As is often the case in leadership races," noted Bonior, "an early start was crucial" (Bonior 2018, 315).

The previous examples suggest that some legislators do vote for whomever asks for their support first, and only the most foolhardy candidate would deliberately delay entering a race and seeking votes. However, we lack sufficient data to answer the question of how many lawmakers' votes are won this way, and we are skeptical that, in terms of the ultimate outcome, it makes a difference in any but the closest elections. For some races that we examined in this study, early entry was attributed to helping a candidate win, or was at least correlated with victory. Still, as the last column of table 7.2 notes, in only half of the cases in this study did the eventual winner jump into the race before any challengers. Moreover, they may have won for other reasons, and it is reasonable to suppose that their early entry signaled that they were also savvier candidates who might also run better-prepared campaigns that would help them win. Lawmakers unlikely to support a candidate are more likely to remain uncommitted or even try to recruit others to run—as happened in the 1976 race for majority leader—than vote for that candidate.

One other campaign tactic that might affect lawmaker vote choice is that of a candidate who proclaims he already has a majority of votes, implying that those who oppose him will be on the losing side. The hope is to create a so-called bandwagon effect, a tipping point at which other caucus members believe that the candidate will win and vote accordingly (Laitin 1994; Schelling 1978). As Jim O'Hara, failed candidate for majority leader in 1971, put it, "the typical Congressman doesn't really care *who* is Majority Leader as much as he wants to be with the winner" (King 1971; see also Hunter 1971a). Some candidates, as we have seen in previous chapters, will try to plant positive news stories that indicate they are in the lead. This may be especially important in elections decided by multiple rounds of voting, in which a candidate needs to win sufficient commitments early on to suggest he is strong enough to be victorious on subsequent ballots, so that supporters of the lowest vote-getter in the first round will lean toward backing the likely winner later (Peabody 1976, 213). Jim Wright, for instance, wrote in a private memo that he hoped to do well enough on the first ballot "to establish a Victory psychology and attract more 'band wagon' switches on the second ballot."[30]

Is there a bandwagon effect? Though it is impossible to say for sure, we expect the tactic turns no more than a handful of undecided votes,[31] and we have found no evidence that it affects the actual outcome of races. Lawmakers are likely to be familiar with, and thus skeptical of, such claims, and they have stronger reasons to support candidates than simply because someone is expected to be the winner. In many campaigns (the 1971, 1976, and 1998 races for majority leader, for instance) at least one candidate declared that he had a majority of votes, yet did not or, at a minimum, had failed to win a majority on the first ballot. Furthermore, if the bandwagon tactic were effective, we would expect to see few leadership elections decided by a narrow margin. Yet of the eighty-eight House party leadership elections held between 1965 and 2016 that led to publicly reported caucus or conference votes, nearly one third (twenty-nine) were decided with a vote margin between the winner and the loser(s) of less than 10 percent. Bandwagon effects, if any, are most likely to emerge—and less likely to matter—when one candidate is so much stronger than her opponents that the outcome is already all but certain (Peabody 1976, 177, 198).

Leadership Races in Other Legislatures

One question that emerges from our analysis is how applicable our findings are to leadership races in other legislative chambers. To the extent that our theoretical approach depends on features of the U.S. House that can be found elsewhere—a relatively small membership, lawmakers who desire to achieve individual goals, party leaders who are expected to help with those goals—we would expect the mixed-motive model to help explain vote choice in other legislatures too. Yet subtle differences across chambers may alter the calculations of the rank-and-file in leadership elections. We assume, for example, that lawmakers have at least three primary goals: reelection, policy, and influence (Fenno 1973). But legislatures with term limits may have many more representatives who are unable to run for reelection and thus are less concerned with that particular objective. Other legislatures may have parties with more participatory decision-making processes, limiting the ability of their occupants to shape policy or gain much internal influence. And party leaders in some legislatures may be too weak to help bring lawmakers' goals to fruition; this might make leadership elections in such contexts more personal than political.

Variations in the size of a legislature could also have a significant effect. Leadership candidates in chambers larger than the U.S. House may depend even more heavily on professional connections and broad appeals to lawmaker goals, since it is less likely they have personal connections with many lawmakers to rely upon, and it is less efficient to conduct vote buying on an individual basis. By contrast, elections in smaller chambers may be influenced to a greater extent by personal relationships between candidates and the rank-and-file. Size also has a practical effect on the ability to test the mixed-motive model with statistical analysis. In the U.S. Senate, for instance, political parties are usually between one-third and one-fourth the size of their counterparts in the House, which reduces the odds of finding statistically significant effects in a regression test.

Leadership Races, Past and Future

The House of Representatives is not a static institution; it has changed considerably over the past several decades. These changes, some of which were referred to obliquely in previous chapters, have affected the politics of party leadership elections in the chamber in important ways. Those changes also suggest how those politics could alter in the years ahead.

One important shift in prior decades has been a modest growth in the number of elected leadership positions in the House. Since 1960, both parties have created new positions or made existing positions electable by the full party, rather than appointed or chosen by committee.[32] The reasons for this expansion are many, including increased responsibilities of the party leadership, a greater demand for building and maintaining party unity, legislators' desire to be included in decision making, and the need to distribute leadership posts as consolation prizes to those defeated in leadership races (J. Fuller 2014; Loomis 1984; Meinke 2016; Sinclair 1995). On the one hand, this has expanded the number of opportunities for ambitious lawmakers, potentially reducing competition for any given leadership post. On the other hand, the number of lawmakers desiring leadership offices seems to have grown too, at least initially. The average number of candidates running for a contested position (excluding floor votes for Speaker) rose from 2.25 between 1961 and 1970 to 2.47 between 1981 and 1990, but then shrank slightly since (to 2.35 between 1991 and 2016). Should either party in the House choose to create more elected leadership positions in the future, it may—depending on the desirability of those positions—increase the number of candidates running for leadership.

A second change has been in the relative competitiveness of leadership positions across parties. Generally speaking, in the 1960s and 1970s Republicans were more prone to contested elections for leadership positions, while Democrats followed a leadership ladder in which lower-positioned leaders became the heir apparent for vacant positions above them (Nelson 1977; Peabody 1976). There remain discernible and persistent differences between Democrats and Republicans, albeit not in the ways identified in the past. With the Democrats turning their whip position from appointive to elective in 1986, top party leaders' ability to control conflicts for leadership posts waned. The relative stability of the Democrats' selection patterns, especially compared to Republicans, gave way, and House Democrats became more prone to open competition, particularly after the 1980s. Republicans' leadership selection process became somewhat less conflictual, though the party still has more open competition elections for leadership vacancies than Democrats and continues to face more revolt-type races. The key takeaways are that neither party is immune to intraparty conflict in leadership selection and that such conflict seems likely to continue.

A third and even greater change since the 1960s has been the monetization of leadership races. In the past, candidates might informally and indirectly steer campaign money to lawmakers in the hopes of securing their vote. That changed with the exploding cost of congressional campaigns and new campaign finance rules in the 1970s which mandated the disclosure of campaign fundraising and expenditures. As previously noted, Henry Waxman inaugurated the now-common practice of using LPACs to raise and distribute funds to their partisan colleagues (Brown and Peabody 1992; Cann 2008; Currinder 2003; Heberlig and Larson 2012). The size and publicity of financial contributions as a campaign tool has expanded considerably since then. When asked how leadership races had changed over time, a former Republican leader, who had been in the House from the 1970s through the 1990s, simply answered: "Money . . . the amounts of money . . . the leadership PACs, which I think are a perversion."[33] "It shouldn't be called a 'Leadership PAC," Barney Frank (D-MA) acerbically remarked. "It should be called 'I wanna buy my way into the Leadership PAC'" (Dorment 2014). Recent developments in campaign finance law may further expand the role of money and give critics like Frank even more reason to complain. The rise of "dark money," "super PACs," and other instruments of campaign finance since the early-2010s may potentially overshadow the role of LPACs, both because they provide a new pipeline of cash and because their untraceability makes them attractive to lawmakers wary of the appearance of being bought. This, in turn, may give increased leverage to wealthy outsiders seeking to shape the outcome of leadership races.

A fourth major change over time has been in the kinds of services party leaders are expected to provide. Through the mid-twentieth century, congressional leaders had limited public visibility and were valued less for their public persona than for their political and procedural skills. But that quickly changed. As early as 1965, Gerald Ford

(R-MI) was prized by many colleagues as a telegenic candidate for minority leader. In the 1980s and early 1990s, more lawmakers insisted their leaders and leadership organizations needed to be better oriented toward communication. Today it is a given that a congressional leader must have an attractive public persona, be competent in the art of public relations, and pursue a legislative and political agenda with an eye toward press and media strategy (Sinclair 1995, 2006; Meinke 2016; Harris 1998, 2010, 2013; Malecha and Reagan 2011). Such candidates do not always win, but it is now virtually unquestioned that a candidate for nearly any party leadership post be able to perform well on Sunday news shows, conduct interviews and press conferences, and deliver speeches that extol the virtues of their party (Brown and Peabody 1992, 360).

A fifth difference between the 1960s and the 2010s is the level of participation by the public and outside groups in leadership elections. Races for leadership posts were once almost entirely a matter of inside baseball, receiving little media attention and of importance to only a handful of lobbying groups. Today, with ubiquitous media coverage of Congress, the expanded use of social media, and a plethora of national interest groups (particularly ideological ones), leadership races can attract considerable attention from outsiders and, in the view of one former congressman, "more effort by outside groups to have an impact" on the outcome.[34] "It's easier to communicate with people now," said one GOP aide in an interview. "Maybe outside groups can say or do things in media and other outside platforms than can impact a race."[35] Leadership campaigns in the past two decades have increasingly been characterized by running tallies of commitments to each candidate by reporters, hourly updates of how individual lawmakers stand, and pressure from constituents and organized interests to vote one way or another. The struggles of John Boehner and Nancy Pelosi to keep party members from defecting against them in floor votes for Speaker highlight the electoral incentives lawmakers face to vote in one direction or another. Even if a ballot remains secret, the clear trend is toward greater engagement by the wider public in leadership races. Greater public attention to congressional parties and leadership elections likely means that changing expectations of voters may help some candidates over others. We have already seen how women and ethnic minorities, once sidelined in the House, can be an asset to a party seeking to present an image of diversity and inclusiveness. In the future, candidates from other ethnic, racial, or identity groups, like Muslims or the LGBTQ community, may become more desirable. More generally, the rising clout of particular cliques within parties may help elevate certain candidates seen as representing those factions.

Despite these diachronic changes, leadership elections have kept constant in many key ways. Candidates still lobby colleagues one-on-one; they form campaign teams to support their bids for office; they offer benefits and favors in exchange for votes; they frame their candidacies in ways to benefit themselves and tarnish their opponents; and they harvest professional connections for votes. As one Republican staffer told us, "I don't know if [leadership races] have changed that much. I think there is a lot of continuity—things have changed in terms of the mechanics and the technology, but the underlying factors of why members support one candidate over another have not changed that much."[36]

In short, we may see more ethnically diverse leadership candidates, drawing more heavily on outside financial support, than we have in the past, with voters, interest groups, and new media playing more significant roles in shaping lawmakers' vote choice. But so long as the central elements shaping the House's leadership elections—the size of the chamber, the service orientation of party leaders, committees and states as the bases for professional connections—do not change, professional connections and salient goals will remain fundamental to how the rank-and-file decide who will lead them.

Leadership elections usually occur in the interval between the November congressional elections and the start of the new Congress. An anticipated vacancy generally prompts multiple lawmakers to contemplate running for the soon-to-be open post, and one or more legislators may begin campaigning, at least informally, many months in advance. When unexpected vacancies happen, such as when an incumbent leader dies or suddenly resigns, would-be candidates often scramble to build a campaign and gauge support for their candidacies. A contested leadership election may also take place if an incumbent leader is challenged; these also customarily occur after the November elections.

Candidates typically begin by informing their closest congressional colleagues of their interest and gauging if they concur that a bid for office is wise. If enough of them do, those colleagues are subsequently enlisted as campaign managers or surrogates, serving as part of a campaign team of typically one to two dozen others. They and the candidate will approach fellow members of Congress, ask for their votes, and make a reasonable determination of how they will actually cast their ballots. As one staff veteran of multiple GOP leadership races described it, "You start with a small cadre of people who are your good friends [and who] encouraged you to run. . . . Then these people help you decide how to reach out to other members."[1]

A time-tested strategy in any campaign for elected office is to divide the electorate into groups, or "pockets of potential strength or weakness," and target each group accordingly (Bradshaw 1995; Cicero 2012; Herrnson 2012; Oliver 2012). Strategic coalition-building of this sort is pursued by congressional leadership candidates, too. Those with whom a candidate shares a personal connection, particularly legislators from the same state or committees, are an important set of potential voters. Other key factions may include colleagues with shared ethnic or racial backgrounds, gender, home region, positions of influence (i.e., fellow committee chairs or party leaders), electoral class, or membership in a legislative caucus. As the same congressional aide noted, "Your state delegation—you go there first, my [election year] class, same committee . . . these are the normal building blocks of a campaign."[2]

Additional sets of party members get particular attention as well. Some campaigns target opinion leaders, lawmakers with well-regarded reputations, or colleagues with their own networks of influence in the hopes they can bring additional votes their way. These include the deans of state delegations, committee chairs, or other prominent figures. One Republican leadership aide went so far as to declare that chairs of committees can "serve almost as [campaign] whips in their own right," so "if you can get committee chairs, that's the first place to go."[3] Freshmen members, or individuals running for Congress for the first time, are another important group, particularly if sizeable in number. They are often treated differently, however, since they are less familiar with the candidates and may have a unique set of concerns, such as building their legislative reputations, securing plum committee assignments, or establishing a modicum of electoral security.

Much like the process used to evaluate legislator preferences on upcoming bills or amendments (Evans and Gandy 2009), leadership candidates commonly grade the level of support they have from their colleagues, ranging from a definite favorable vote to strong opposition. A staff veteran of multiple Democratic leadership races put it this way: "It's usually like, are they definitely with you? That would be a 1, voting for you on the first ballot. 2 [is] leaning toward you; 3, undecided; 4, leaning away from you; 5, would never ever vote for you."[4] Candidates and their proxies will often approach lawmakers several times to confirm their preferences and persuade those who are undecided or leaning toward a favorable vote. If the race involves three or more candidates, a lawmaker may be asked to commit on second or subsequent ballots. To minimize the probability of error, wise candidates will personally confirm the estimates given them by others and ask the same legislators multiple times in order to check for any potential slippage in support.

Persuasion is probably the most common tactic used to sway lawmakers to vote for a candidate. But side-payments—past favors, or promises of future ones, in exchange for votes—are also employed. The most frequent sort of side-payment in today's Congress is money donated to colleagues' reelection campaigns, and most ambitious lawmakers create leadership political action committees (LPACs), the instruments by which they can legally raise and distribute funds to other lawmakers and congressional candidates (Currinder 2003; Heberlig and Larson 2012). There are countless other, less easily quantifiable benefits available as well, such as helping a lawmaker get her bill enacted, holding a committee hearing on a colleague's topic of interest, or supporting someone's bid for a desired committee assignment or another position in leadership.

This personal, member-to-member campaigning is usually supplemented by wider-scale tactics. Supportive "Dear Colleague" letters from allies are a common tool used to advertise one's breadth of support within the party and ensure those allies are truly in your camp. Just as in any race for an elected post, party leadership candidates will often develop a small set of campaign themes—redistributing influence within the party, improving the party's electoral performance, managing the chamber better—and advertise them in letters, press releases, and public appearances (Bradshaw 1995, 40, 42; Sides et al. 2012, 133–37; Sweeney 1995, 28). "Bandwagon" strategies are also frequent, with candidates exaggerating the number of vote commitments they have in the hopes of winning over undecided legislators, scaring away late challengers, and encouraging weaker rivals to drop out. Some candidates use "outsider" strategies as well, enlisting opinion writers and sympathetic reporters to extol their virtues or asking lobbying groups to approach individual members of Congress on their behalf.

The actual election of a party leader follows a common sequence of events. After the full party gathers, each candidate is formally nominated by one or more colleagues. The nominators, who usually deliver speeches on behalf of their candidate, are generally selected based on their prominence, reputation, and ability to demonstrate a breadth of appeal (e.g., Peabody 1976, 209). Voting then follows by secret ballot. Both the Democratic and Republican parties use a majoritarian, Multiple Round Single Elimination (MRSE) process.[5] If two candidates are vying for the post, whichever one receives a majority is declared the victor, but if there are more than two candidates, and none achieves a majority on the first ballot, the candidate receiving the fewest votes is eliminated and the party proceeds to the next round of balloting, and voting rounds continue until one candidate receives a majority. Occasionally, a candidate who comes close to last will nonetheless withdraw, and sometimes a legislator who is about to be declared the loser will ask that his or her rival be selected by acclimation before the final vote count, acknowledging the likely outcome and avoiding intraparty disunity.

Selection of the Speaker of the House is conducted somewhat differently. When a party votes internally for Speaker, it is technically only nominating a candidate. The final vote is conducted on the floor of the House during the first day of a new Congress. All members cast their vote orally, in alphabetical order. Technically, this means the majority party's candidate for Speaker could be defeated, but there is a strong norm against voting for anyone other than your party's nominee, and in practice, the House elects the candidate nominated by the majority party.

NOTES

Abbreviations of Archival Collections

DDP — Deborah Pryce Papers, Ohio Congressional Archives, Ohio State University, Columbus.

DDR — Dan Rostenkowski Papers, Loyola University Chicago Archives and Special Collections, Loyola University of Chicago.

DSG — Democratic Study Group Records, Manuscript Division, Library of Congress, Washington, DC.

EGS — E. G. "Bud" Shuster Papers, Pasquerilla Library, St. Francis University, Loretto, PA.

ELJ — Ed L. Jenkins Papers, Richard B. Russell Library for Political Research and Studies, University of Georgia Libraries, Athens.

EPB — Edward P. Boland Papers, Special Collections, John J. Burns Library, Boston College, Chestnut Hill, MA.

GRF — Gerald R. Ford Congressional Papers, 1949–73, Gerald R. Ford Presidential Library and Museum, Ann Arbor, MI.

GVJ — Guy A. Vander Jagt Papers, 1957–92 [H92–1165], Hope College, Holland, MI.

HDC — Records of the House Democratic Caucus, Manuscript Division, Library of Congress, Washington, DC.

JCW — Jim Wright Collection, Mary Couts Burnett Library, Texas Christian University, Fort Worth.

JPM — John P. Murtha Congressional Papers, Archives and Manuscript Collections, University of Pittsburgh, Pittsburgh.

JWM — John W. McCormack Papers, Howard Gotlieb Archival Research Center, Boston University, Boston.

ME — Mickey Edwards Collection, Carl Albert Research Center Archives, University of Oklahoma, Norman.

MKU — Morris K. Udall Papers, Special Collections, University of Arizona Library, Tucson.

NLG — Papers of Representative Newt Gingrich, Special Collections, University of West Georgia, Carrollton.

PB — Philip Burton Papers, Bancroft Library, University of California, Berkeley.

RAG Richard A. Gephardt Collection, Missouri History Museum, St. Louis.

RB Richard Bolling Papers, Miller Nichols Library, University of Missouri-Kansas City, Kansas City.

RHM Robert H. Michel Collection, Dirksen Congressional Research Center, Pekin, IL.

RKA Richard K. Armey Collection, Carl Albert Research Center Archives, University of Oklahoma, Norman.

RLP Robert L. Peabody Research Interview Notes, 1964–67, Gerald R. Ford Presidential Library and Museum, Ann Arbor, MI.

USC U.S. Capitol Historical Society Oral History Interviews, Library of Congress, Washington, DC.

Chapter 1. Choosing the Leader

1. Other possible changes in congressional party leadership include an elected leader replacing an appointed one and the elimination or creation of a leadership position in the party (Nelson 1977, 928). Although we do not examine races for elected committee chairs, we expect the dynamics of those races to be similar to party leadership races, particularly when they are determined by the full party. See, e.g., Bolling 1965b and Obey 2007, 215–17.

2. The vote for Speaker of the House does not use a secret ballot; see chapter 6.

3. The chair of the Democrats' version of the NRCC, the Democratic Congressional Campaign Committee (DCCC), is currently appointed by the party's top leader. There are also numerous appointed deputy and assistant whip positions. For descriptions of the roles and functions of some of these other leaders, see Kolodny 1998 and Meinke 2016.

4. See for example Grofman, Koetzle, and McCann 2002; Harris and Nelson 2008; Jessee and Malhotra 2010; Patterson 1963; and Posler and Rhodes 1997.

5. Interviews with former Democratic leader, May 18, 2016; former Democratic leader, March 10, 2016; and former Republican member of Congress, March 22, 2016. Some whip counts we uncovered indicate that certain lawmakers do think in terms of candidate ideology. In the 2006 Democratic leader race, for instance, the Murtha whip count noted that Dan Lipinski (D-IL) "wants [a] conservative." Whip count, Box 145, Folder: JPM Majority Leadership Race, JPM.

6. Interview with former Republican member of Congress, March 22, 2016.

7. Barber Conable Jr. to Guy Vander Jagt, November 12, 1980, Box 149, Folder: Leadership Races (97th Congress), 1981, GVJ.

8. Interview with former Republican member of Congress, March 22, 2016.

9. See also Bradshaw 1995, 40; Faucheaux 2003, 73.

10. In previous studies we have used committee and region as proxies for policy goals (Green 2006; Green and Harris 2007). Harris (2006) combines shared committee, state, and entering class into a single measure of personal connections, but here we define "personal" as friendships and close alliances that may exist separately from connections forged through common professional duties or identities, and we assert that members of shared electoral classes will not develop strong ties except in certain contexts.

11. Interview with former Democratic leader, March 10, 2016.

12. Interview with Democratic member of Congress, July 8, 2016.

13. Interview with former Republican member of Congress, March 22, 2016. Candidates sometimes lobby other state delegations to vote for them as a unit, or states themselves offer their votes as a bloc in exchange for benefits (e.g. Newhauser 2014).

14. Interview with Republican aide, June 3, 2016.

15. Interview with Democratic member of Congress, July 8, 2016.

16. Robert Peabody interview with Don Rumsfeld, December 30, 1964, Robert L. Peabody Research Interview Notes, Box 1, RLP; and authors' interview with former Republican member of Congress, March 22, 2016.

17. Letter to Newt Gingrich from Mickey Edwards, April 2, 1987, Box 1077, Folder: Correspondence—Mickey Edwards, NLG.

18. In terms of principal-agent theory, the idea is that lawmakers choose an agent (the party leader) who is most likely to carry out their goals as principal (Sinclair 1995).

19. We have discovered individual examples of this in some leadership races. In the 2006 race for Democratic leader, for instance, the Murtha whip count noted that Stephanie Herseth (D-SD) was a Hoyer supporter but included the parenthetical query, "should we talk to Max Sandlin??" Sandlin, a former congressman, was Herseth's soon-to-be husband. Murtha Whip count, Box 145, Folder: JPM Majority Leadership Race, JPM.

20. For more on the influence of age and seniority in leadership races, see Bibby and Davidson 1967, 143; Kelly n.d.; and Peabody 1976.

21. Interview with House Republican aide, June 3, 2016; interview with House Republican aide, June 9, 2016.

22. Whether lawmakers are persuaded by broad-based or targeted appeals, or even need to be persuaded at all, depends in part on the lawmakers themselves. According to one Republican aide, "Some will say, 'Yes, I'm with you no matter what.' Others will try to leverage the situation" and "ask for . . . priorities on the floor." Interview with House Republican aide, May 2, 2016.

23. For instance, Phil Burton's (D-CA) failure to ask Thomas "Lud" Ashley (D-OH) for his vote may have cost him his bid to become majority leader in 1976 (Jacobs 1995, 321; see chapter 5). In a more recent example, Renee Ellmers (R-NC) explained that she supported underdog Jason Chaffetz (R-UT) over Kevin McCarthy (R-CA) for Speaker in 2015 because McCarthy "has not spoken to me personally for my vote, and Jason Chaffetz has . . . I can't vote for someone who doesn't ask for my vote" (Wong and Marcos 2015).

24. Interview with House Republican aide, May 2, 2016.

25. Interview with former Democratic leader, March 31, 2016.

26. Interview with Democratic member of Congress, July 8, 2016.

27. The composition of the party's leadership in the other chamber could also matter. For example, some believed that because Texan Jim Wright was Speaker, it hurt fellow "oil patch" Democrat Senator Bennett Johnston of Louisiana when he ran for Senate majority leader in 1989 (Harris and Green 2017).

28. Since aggregate election results can influence the goal of internal influence (e.g., one cannot be a committee chair if one's party is in the minority), concerns with election results might be captured indirectly by measures of this latter goal. Peabody argued that, besides personality, congressional election results were the most important factor that consistently influences leadership elections (Peabody 1976, 303–6). However, we find that this is true in only some races. See also chapter 6.

29. Another important contextual variable is the rules of balloting, since the method used to record voter preferences can affect the results and candidates may alter their campaign strategies accordingly. The basic procedure (voting in rounds, with the lowest-recorded candidate eliminated after each round until one candidate receives a majority of the ballots cast), which has been unchanged over the period we examine, does

create opportunities for strategic voting, as is seen in other countries that use such a process (D. Farrell 2001). We discuss the voting process further in the appendix.

30. We use the natural log of vote percentages and campaign contributions by leadership candidates to minimize the rightward skew of the data. DW-NOMINATE scores are used to estimate ideology (Poole and Rosenthal 1997), but since they may in fact measure degree of party voting loyalty (Lee 2009), we rerun our models with membership in ideological caucuses (e.g. the Progressive Caucus, the Republican Study Committee) when such membership data is available. Leadership includes serving as Speaker (if in majority), majority leader, minority leader, majority whip, and minority whip. For Republicans, it also includes Conference chair, vice chair, and secretary; GOP policy committee chair; chair of the NRCC; chief deputy whip (or whips, if multiple); and, between 1965 and 1994, GOP research committee chair. For Democrats, it also includes Caucus chair and vice chair (or secretary); chair of the DCCC; chief deputy whip (or whips, if multiple); and, starting in 1999, assistant to the leader.

31. In those cases where such internal data is unavailable, we use the commitments that legislators publicly make in support of candidates (e.g., the Pelosi-Hoyer case in chapter 3 and the Boehner, Blunt, and Shadegg race in chapter 5). We exclude the candidates' own votes from the analyses.

32. Multinomial logit has advantages over multinomial probit (Dow and Endersby 2004), but the former depends on the so-called Independence of Irrelevant Alternatives (IIA) assumption, which holds that an individual's choice would not be affected by the other possible choices (or, in this case, that legislators who chose one candidate would be equally likely to support any of the other candidates) (Cheng and Long 2007). This is a questionable assumption in many multicandidate races, but unfortunately, multinomial probit was unable to estimate coefficients in most instances.

33. This is a particular problem if the omitted variable is correlated with one or more variables that are in the regression model. For instance, if a candidate finds a way to covertly send interest group campaign contributions to freshmen, but those contributions are not included in the regression, a variable measuring freshman status may prove statistically significant, erroneously suggesting that being a freshman—rather than the recipient of campaign contributions—explains vote choice.

34. An alternative to running regression analyses for each individual race would be to analyze the pooled vote data for all of the leadership

elections we examine. Although the larger number of observations would give us greater analytical leverage, that approach would preclude controlling for factors unique to each race.

35. An alternative solution would be to use a penalized log-likelihood model (Firth 1993; Zorn 2005), but that model does not permit the estimation of the marginal effects of individual variables on the dependent variable, is unable to calculate goodness-of-fit measures, and cannot be used with multinomial dependent variables (i.e., races with three or more candidates). Nonetheless, we reran all probit analyses with penalized log-likelihood (specifically, the *firthlogit* command in Stata) and footnoted any resulting differences in statistical significance. Overall, the results closely matched those in the probit models.

36. Minutes of the House Democratic Caucus, December 6, 1976, p. 63, Carton 13, Folder 9, PB.

37. As will be seen in subsequent chapters, candidates routinely exaggerate the number of votes they have in order to create a bandwagon effect, give their supporters confidence, encourage candidates to drop out, and deter others from entering the race (Peabody 1976, 198). Occasionally a candidate has predicted the exact number of votes he ultimately received, as happened in the Democratic whip races of 1986 (by Tony Coelho, D-CA) and 1991 (by David Bonior, D-MI).

38. Candidates tend to do worse when counting the votes of their competitors, possibly because legislators are loath to admit supporting a rival to a candidate directly (e.g., Peabody 1976, 187).

39. Leaders' whip counts and postvote analyses occasionally identify legislators considered untrustworthy. For example, Morris Udall noted after his failed 1971 majority leader race that Shirley Chisholm (D-NY) "told different stories to different people." Office Memo, "Leadership Wrap-Up," January 21, 1971, Box 78, Folder: House Leadership Campaign Files, 1968–71, MKU.

40. Interview with House Republican aide, June 3, 2016.

41. There are also ways for leadership campaigns to check the votes of legislators who have made shaky commitments, such as shadowing lawmakers or even peeking at their ballots to ensure they have voted as promised (e.g., Jacobs 1995, 318). Legislators whose commitment is not considered trustworthy, and who fail to show their ballots to a candidate's "lieutenant," may also raise red flags with candidates. Interview with House Democratic aide, November 30, 2006.

42. Oppenheimer and Peabody 1977, 43; interview with former Republican member of Congress, March 22, 2016; Jackson 1986; Peabody 1976, 197.
43. Interview with former Democratic leader, March 10, 2016.
44. Ibid.
45. Interview with William Pitts, April 6, 1965, RLP.
46. Interview with former Democratic leader, May 18, 2016.
47. It may be harder for candidates to determine vote commitments on multiple ballots, since some lawmakers may commit to supporting a candidate after the first ballot while others may commit to a vote once their preferred candidate is eliminated (Peabody 1976, 197).
48. This includes five floor votes for Speaker in which a sizeable proportion of a party voted against their own party's nominee (either in the majority or the minority). See chapter 6.
49. Some would categorize this race as a challenge to the heir apparent, but it does not meet our definition of that category; see chapter 5.

Chapter 2. Why Run?

1. Interview with Republican leadership aide, May 2, 2016.
2. Political scientists have studied the ambitions of would-be officeholders in the congressional electoral context for decades. Notable examples include Fowler and McClure 1989; Gaddie 2004; Gaddie and Bullock 2000; Jacobson and Kernell 1983; Kazee 1994; Lawless 2012; Maestas et al. 2006; Maisel and Stone 1997; and Schlesinger 1966.
3. Peabody (1976) claimed that "perhaps as many as three-fourths of a given House or Senate do not really see themselves as potential congressional leaders" (473).
4. Interview with Republican leadership aide, June 3, 2016.
5. Interview with Democratic leadership aide, May 4, 2016.
6. Interview with former Republican leadership aide, June 9, 2016.
7. Interview with former Republican leadership aide, May 4, 2016.
8. Interview with former Republican member of Congress, March 22, 2016.
9. Ibid.
10. Interview with Republican leadership aide, June 3, 2016.
11. Interview with former Democratic leader, May 18, 2016.
12. Interview with former Democratic leader, March 10, 2016.

13. Champagne et al. (2009) also contend that "mentor-protégé relationships dominated House politics and significantly affected U.S. history in the second half of the twentieth century" (14).

14. A similar dynamic may exist in the Senate as well (Lee and Oppenheimer 1999). Interestingly, some House districts seem to correlate with leadership aspirations even as their occupants change. Pelosi came from the same district as Caucus Chair Phil Burton (D-CA); Richard Gephardt represented Caucus Secretary Leonor Sullivan's (D-MO) district; and David Bonior (D-MI) represented the same House district as leadership candidate James O'Hara. This may be more than coincidental. One former leader told us that it was a "natural inclination for people from" his state "to at least consider running for leadership" because it had a tradition of electing party leaders. Interview with former House Democratic leader, March 31, 2016.

15. Interview with former Democratic leader, March 10, 2016.

16. Interview with former Democratic leadership aide, May 4, 2016.

17. Interview with former Republican leader, March 22, 2016.

18. Interview with Republican leadership aide, May 2, 2016.

19. Ibid.

20. Interview with former Democratic leader, March 31, 2016.

21. Sometimes serving as a committee chair can put a member in good stead for a leadership bid, as was the case for Sam Rayburn, Tom Foley, and John Boehner.

22. Interview with Republican leadership aide, June 3, 2016.

23. Lawless (2012) found that recruitment by individuals with political influence can spur men and women alike "to think seriously about a candidacy" for public office (22).

24. Interview with former Democratic leader, March 10, 2016.

25. Interview with former Democratic leader, March 31, 2016.

26. Interview with former Republican leadership aide, June 3, 2016.

27. Oral history interview with Sue Myrick, Office of the Historian, U.S. House of Representatives, March 14, 2016, p. 27, History, Art, and Archives, U.S. House of Representatives, history.house.gov/Oral-History/Women/Representative-Myrick (accessed March 20, 2018).

28. This is consistent with Lawless's analogous finding that women who seek public office are more likely to seek lower-level local offices than men (Lawless 2012, 75).

29. "Detailed Agenda for 10/23 Meeting," Box 29, Folder 31: Chairmanship Races, 2002, 2004, 2006, RG: 57/d, DDP.

30. The health of existing leaders can also lead to surprise vacancies and spur of the moment campaigns (Irish 2001, 189). There is perhaps no more dramatic example than the sudden disappearance (and presumed death) of Hale Boggs in October 1972, which prompted the election for House majority leader between Tip O'Neill and Sam Gibbons (Champagne et al. 2009, 204–17; Peabody 1976).

31. Interview with former Democratic leader, March 10, 2016.

32. "Some Thoughts on How to Win While Losing," Box 78, Folder 78/1: Aftermath—Thoughts on Losing Speaker's Race, 1969, MKU.

33. Interview with former Democratic leader, May 18, 2016.

34. Interview with former Republican leadership aide, June 9, 2016.

35. Generally speaking, House Democrats have made leadership selection in the party more consensus-based, orderly, and stable than Republicans, though that stability has waned in recent years (Harris 2006; Nelson 1977; Peabody 1967, 1976).

36. Still, Newt Gingrich seemed to "nudge" Bob Michel out of the position during the 103rd Congress, talking to colleagues and "leaving the clear impression that he would run in the next Congress whether or not Michel retired" ("Michel Announces Retirement" 1994, p. 19; Hook 1993).

37. Kerry to Dick, November 7, 1994, "Re: Tomorrow Night and Beyond," Box 40, Folder 32, RKA.

38. Interview with former House Republican member, March 22, 2016.

39. Peabody has called races such as these "routine advancement" because the other candidate or candidates had little chance of winning (Peabody 1976, 267).

40. Similarly, Martin Frost ended his challenge to Nancy Pelosi for minority leader only two days after announcing, based on a calculation that "he could not win" (Ferrechio 2002).

Chapter 3. Open Competition Races I

1. For more on the race, see Peters and Rosenthal 2010.

2. Hoyer's 1st dimension DW-NOMINATE score in the 107th Congress was slightly more conservative (−0.335) than Pelosi's (−0.461).

3. Interview with former Democratic leadership aide, May 4, 2016.

4. Interview with former Democratic member, March 10, 2016.

5. We used LexisNexis and other internet searches to identify 85 Pelosi supporters (72 percent of her total vote) and 49 Hoyer supporters (52 percent of his total vote).

6. The variable was weakly statistically significant ($p < .10$) when using penalized log-likelihood (*firthlogit*, see chapter 1, note 35) to estimate Model 2 with omitted variables. The statistical significance (or lack thereof) of other variables remained unchanged.

7. Excluding outlier values of age, DW-NOMINATE, and seniority variables; excluding lawmakers unopposed for reelection; and excluding freshmen does not alter the statistical significance of the coefficients (though removing outliers or lawmakers unopposed for reelection does make the Intelligence Committee variable statistically significant [$p < .10$]). Adding a squared term variable does not noticeably alter the results. Term in office is moderately correlated with ranking status and age, but eliminating that variable does not alter the significance of the remaining variables. DW-NOMINATE is correlated with two-party vote, but dropping the former variable has no effect on the statistical significance of the latter.

8. The remaining four freshmen who expressed support for one of the candidates received equal amounts (or nothing) from both; they split their votes evenly between them. Replacing the contribution variables in Model 2 with variables equal to one if a lawmaker received any money from either candidate does not alter the results.

9. A more detailed discussion of this race can be found in Champagne et al. 2009 and Peabody 1976.

10. Others who reportedly considered running or were seen as likely candidates included Dan Rostenkowski (D-IL), Tip O'Neill (D-MA), and Hugh Carey (D-NY) (Hunter 1970b; King 1971; O'Neill 1987, 258–59). Richard Bolling (D-MO) originally entered the race but then dropped out (Weaver 1970). John Moss (D-CA) was a candidate briefly but withdrew after the California delegation voted to back Sisk, and Eddie Boland (D-MA) at one point called himself "an unannounced candidate" (King 1971; O'Neill 1987; Peabody 1976).

11. In his speech nominating Boggs to be majority leader, Edward Hébert (D-LA) noted Boggs's "thirty years of burning ambition that enabled him to climb to leadership." Democratic Caucus Minutes, January 19, 1971, Box 3, Folder 7: 92nd 19–20–21 January 1971, HDC.

12. Interestingly, Boggs's DW-NOMINATE score, -0.415, placed him furthest to the left of all five candidates.

13. His DW-NOMINATE score (-0.322) was the furthest to the right of the five candidates.

14. Udall had been downplaying his DSG membership in recent years. O'Hara was a former chairman of the DSG as well (Hunter 1970b;

Peabody 1976, 170; "Summary, DSG Chairmen/Executive Committee Members," Box II:6, Folder 4, DSG).

15. Udall's DW-NOMINATE score was −0.371, versus O'Hara's −0.413.

16. Former president Lyndon Johnson reportedly lobbied the Texas delegation against Udall for that reason (J. Farrell 2001, 284–85).

17. According to Tip O'Neill, Udall was also popular for establishing automatic pay raises for members of Congress (O'Neill 1987, 257).

18. We do not define this race as a challenge to the heir apparent. Albert had been whip before becoming leader in 1962, but there was "no tradition which dictate[d]" this at the time (Polsby 1962 [1992], 247). McCormack, who was leader under Sam Rayburn, had only been whip when the Democrats lost their majority status in 1952 and Rayburn took his place as party leader. Peabody characterized it as an "open competition" race and went no further than to suggest that a "ladder of succession" from whip to leader "seemed to be developing" at the time (Peabody 1976, 215–16, 282–83).

19. The reason for this change in personality is unclear. Peabody speculates it was a combination of work pressures, a close reelection campaign, and alcohol abuse (Peabody 1976, 159).

20. For more on the recruitment of Sisk, see Anderson 1970 and Evans and Novak 1970b.

21. Sisk's DW-NOMINATE score, −0.325, was second most rightward of the five running for majority leader.

22. See also the memo (presumably by Udall) outlining "why Bolling's Outside Strategy Failed," Box II:122, Folder 6, DSG.

23. Memo, Box II:122, Folder 6, DSG. Udall hoped that he could make Boland whip in exchange for his support (King 1971, 55).

24. "Final Push—Soft or Undecided," Memo, Box 78, Folder 28: Head Count, MKU. Udall tried to win the vote of the chair of his own committee, Wayne Aspinall (Interior), but Aspinall feared a victory by Udall would pave the way for his nemesis, Phil Burton (D-CA), to win a subcommittee chairmanship (Udall "Leadership Wrap-Up" Memo, January 21, 1971, Box 78, Folder 17: Working Papers (1), MKU). See also chapter 6.

25. McCormack told at least one fellow Massachusetts Democrat, Louise Day Hicks, to not vote for Udall. "Leadership" Memo, January 14, 1971, Box 78, Folder 28: Head Count, MKU.

26. Udall believed Rostenkowski and his patron, Chicago Mayor Richard J. Daley, were sufficiently unpopular among southerners, and with Carl

Albert (see note 38), that this alliance could hurt Boggs (Udall "Leadership" Memo, January 14, 1971, Box 78, Folder 28: Head Count, MKU). Rostenkowski and Daley may have also lobbied against Udall in his 1969 race for Speaker.

27. See also "Leadership" Memo, January 14, 1971, Box 78, Folder 28: Head Count, MKU.

28. The DSG optimistically believed at least a "handful" of Hays or Sisk supporters would vote for either Udall or O'Hara in later ballots, allowing one of them to win. "A Liberal Majority If . . . ," Box II:122, Folder 6, DSG.

29. Udall, however, believed Hays truly did want the post. "House Head Count," House Leadership Campaign Files, 1968–71, Box 78, Folder 3: Head Count, MKU.

30. The DSG also kept close tabs on the race, including head counts. See Box II:122, Folder 6, DSG.

31. Intriguingly, the DSG Papers contain two typewritten drafts of essays critical of Hays, Boggs, and Sisk with language that subsequently appeared in *New Republic* editorial columns. *New Republic* 1970, 1971; "A Liberal Majority Leader, If . . ." and untitled essay, Box II:122, Folder 6, DSG.

32. The bandwagon tactic could also include publicly undercounting opponents' totals. See "Leadership" memo from Udall, January 14, 1971, Box 78, Folder 28: Head Count, MKU.

33. Office Memo, "Leadership," January 14, 1971, Box 78, Folder 28: Head Count, MKU.

34. "ADA Opposes Sisk in Majority Leader Race," ADA Press Release, 1971, Box II:122, Folder 6, DSG.

35. Udall still counted Brasco as a favorable vote. Office Memo, "Leadership Wrap-Up," January 21, 1971, Box 78, Folder 17: Working Papers (1), MKU.

36. They also agreed to eliminate the lowest vote getter after the second round of balloting, to prevent low vote-getters from winning by pulling more support in subsequent ballots (Peabody 1976, 204 n. 9).

37. It is unclear whether Hays had received something from Boggs in exchange for leaving the race. Hays had proposed a hundred-dollar bet with his fellow candidates that he would not come in last place, but no one took him up on it (Evans and Novak 1970c).

38. Rostenkowski, who had just unexpectedly lost his reelection bid to be Caucus chair, had humiliated Albert by forcing him off the podium

during the 1968 Democratic Convention and, thinking of running for Speaker himself, had ordered the Illinois delegation to withhold its support for Albert as Speaker (J. Farrell 2001).

39. Counting all certain and likely vote estimates by Udall, with two revisions based on outside sources (King 1971; Peabody 1976), the totals on the first ballot are 87 Boggs, 69 Udall, 21 Sisk, 25 Hays, and 26 O'Hara, and on the second ballot 122 Boggs, 81 Udall, and 6 Sisk, with the rest undetermined and excluded from the analysis. Udall count dated January 21 [1971], Box 78, Folder 17: Working Papers (1), MKU.

40. Though some issues presumably crossed party lines in the race, we were unable to identify a cross-cutting issue that was not highly correlated with DW-NOMINATE. For instance, O'Hara's supporters had higher average AFL-CIO vote rating scores for the 91st Congress than any other candidate's (an average COPE score of 87.6, versus 79.9 for Udall). But COPE scores correlate highly with 1st dimension DW-NOMINATE scores (r = −0.85), and unsurprisingly, adding them to the model eliminates the statistical significance of the latter.

41. O'Hara was also an assistant whip (Peabody 1976), but given the relatively small prominence of assistant whips in the leadership structure at the time, we do not expect party leaders to have been more likely to support O'Hara over the higher-ranked Boggs.

42. However, when excluding outliers for term and DW-NOMINATE, the Sisk Committee becomes weakly significant (p < .10) for Udall and Hays. In addition, the Boggs committee variable becomes significant in explaining Sisk, DW-NOMINATE is no longer statistically significant for Sisk, Interior committee membership becomes weakly significant (p < .10) for Hays, and the term variable loses its significance for Hays.

43. If DW-NOMINATE is replaced with a variable measuring membership in the liberal-leaning DSG, it is statistically significant in explaining support for Udall or O'Hara over Boggs—possible further evidence for the role of ideology, if not a consequence of both candidates' association with the group.

44. This variable could be a proxy for region, since the only opponents of the Voting Rights Act serving in the 92nd Congress were from the South.

45. When omitting the term variable, age is statistically significant and positive in explaining a vote for Sisk over Boggs, and two-party vote is weakly significant (p < .10) for Udall and O'Hara. The term variable drops out when adding a squared term variable. Excluding freshmen results in Hays's state becoming statistically significant for Udall,

two-party voting losing significance for Udall, and northern state becoming weakly significant (p < .10) for Hays.

46. The term variable becomes statistically insignificant when adding a squared term variable in the final round of voting. Dropping that variable makes both the age and election margin coefficients positive and at least weakly significant (p < .10). Excluding outliers, freshmen, or Democrats unopposed for reelection has no effect on the statistical significance of the remaining variables. The results in Model 2 are unchanged when adding omitted variables with a penalized log-likelihood model.

47. Udall speculated that more individualistic factors may have played a role. For instance, he thought that Kenneth Gray (D-IL) had voted against him out of professional jealousy, because a bill had been referred to Udall's subcommittee rather than his own (King 1971, 63).

48. For a more detailed discussion of the race, see Harris and Green 2015.

49. Gephardt had a −0.382 1st dimension DW-NOMINATE score in the 101st Congress; Jenkins had a score of −0.141.

50. Michael Wessel to Tom O'Donnell, Deborah Johns, and Andie King "Re: Leadership Race," May 26, 1989, Box 684, Folder 3, RAG.

51. Ibid.

52. Jenkins letter to "Southern Members Only," Box 4, Folder 13: Majority Leadership Race 1989, Series 3B, ELJ.

53. Rostenkowski may have also opposed Gephardt because Bolling was a rival of his and because Gephardt was possibly associated with a previous attempted coup against Speaker Tip O'Neill, an ally of Rostenkowski (J. Farrell 2001, 650).

54. Jenkins campaign notes, undated, Box 4, Folder 13: Majority Leadership Race 1989, Series 3B, ELJ.

55. "General Mailings," Box 4, Folder 13: Majority Leadership Race 1989, Series 3B, ELJ.

56. Ed Jenkins to Don Edwards, June 6, 1989, Box 4, Folder 13: Majority Leadership Race 1989, Series 3B, ELJ.

57. "[Democrats] Who Have Received Contributions from the Ed Jenkins for Congress Committee," Box 4, Folder 13: Majority Leadership Race 1989, Series 3B, ELJ.

58. Jenkins campaign notes, Box 4, Folder 13: Majority Leadership Race 1989, Series 3B, ELJ.

59. Jenkins campaign notes, undated, and Sammy Smith to Earl Leonard, June 7, 1989, Box 4, Folder 13: Majority Leadership Race 1989, Series 3B, ELJ.

60. "General Mailings" and text of Lewis's nominating speech, Box 4, Folder 13: Majority Leadership Race 1989, Series 3B, ELJ.

61. We were able to estimate 156 votes for Gephardt, 25 short of the total he received. Because Gephardt's most comprehensive tally had relatively few Democrats marked as solid supporters, we estimated Gephardt votes by combining all Democrats marked on the whip sheet as "yes" or "leaning yes" with Democrats marked as a "1" on the same tally, Democrats marked "for me" on a Gephardt call list, and Democrats noted as "firm Gephardt" on a Jenkins whip sheet. Neither Gephardt nor Jenkins had many firm estimates of commitments to vote for Jenkins, so we assume all other lawmakers voted for Jenkins. See Gephardt's handwritten and typewritten member lists, n.d., May 27, 1989, and May 29, 1989, Box 684 Folders 3 and 4, RAG; and, Jenkins's undated member list, Box 4, Folder 13: Majority Leadership Race 1989, Series 3B, ELJ.

62. Despite Jenkins's outreach to those who supported aid for the Nicaraguan Contras, there is no evidence that Contra funding was an issue in the selection of party leader. Including a proxy for that support (derived from a vote for Reagan's Contra aid package in February 1988) does not markedly change the regression results.

63. Jenkins claimed to have given funds to more Democrats than could be confirmed in FEC data. A dummy variable equal to 1 if Jenkins gave (or claimed to give) money to a colleague proved statistically insignificant when included in the statistical models.

64. Southern state representation becomes significant when using penalized log-likelihood, which allows for the state delegation variables to be included; it also results in the term in office variable losing its statistical significance.

65. The seniority variable loses its statistical significance when running Model 2 without outlier values of age and term, without lawmakers who were unopposed for reelection, or without freshmen. Age and term in office are moderately correlated with other explanatory variables, and when excluding one, the other loses its statistical significance.

Chapter 4. Open Competition Races II

1. Thirty open competition races in the House GOP were for positions that had no equivalent in the House Democratic Caucus, or that Democrats did not choose by election.

2. It followed the failed confirmation of Sen. John Tower (R-TX) as defense secretary.

3. On March 21, Gingrich wrote to Robert Walker (R-PA), in an apparent reference to his candidacy for whip, "You called and said I should do it so I am." Letter to Robert Walker, March 21, 1989, Box 176A, Folder: Speaker Newt Gingrich, RSW.

4. Transcript of taped interview with Robert Michel, p. 30, Box "Personal 2," Folder: Personal: Member Notes, RHM.

5. Perhaps Hyde's most dogged advocate was Gerald Solomon (R-NY), who told the conference he would nominate Hyde for whip and who tried to build momentum for his write-in candidacy with a press release headlined "Support of Hyde for GOP Whip Grows." Dear Republican Colleague Letter, March 16, 1989, Box 81, Folder 19, ME; Gerald Solomon Press Release, March 20, 1989, Box 2353, Folder: Whip Race Info, NLG. At least two lawmakers later opined that Gingrich saw Hyde as his strongest challenger and might have withdrawn had Hyde run (Z. Smith 2012, 221 n. 116; interview with Robert K. Dornan by Frank van der Linden, March 23, 1989, Box 1, Folder: Dornan, Robert K., USC). Gingrich supporters Robert Dornan (R-CA) and Duncan Hunter (R-CA) may have tried to assuage doubts about Gingrich's viability as Michel's successor when they wrote to colleagues that Hyde could take Michel's post next, "NO MUSICAL CHAIRS REQUIRED." Dear Colleague letter, March 16, 1989, Box 81, Folder 14, ME.

6. Lewis's mid-March news conference in which he announced his withdrawal ended on an odd note when Gerald Solomon suddenly revealed his plans to draft Hyde for the race. Hyde called it a kind but "Quixotic gesture" (Kenworthy and Phillips 1989, Phillips 1989b).

7. Transcript of taped interview with Robert Michel, p. 31, Box "Personal 2," Folder: Personal: Member Notes, RHM.

8. The candidates' 1st dimension DW-NOMINATE scores in the 101st Congress were 0.362 for Gingrich and 0.302 for Madigan; their second dimension scores were -0.09 for Gingrich and -0.349 for Madigan.

9. Reporters repeated this theme throughout coverage of the race (e.g., Kenworthy and Phillips 1989; Toner 1989a).

10. Transcript of taped interview with Robert Michel, p. 34, Box "Personal 2," Folder: Personal: Member Notes, RHM.

11. Clift and Brazaitis 1996, 240; interview with Robert K. Dornan by Frank van der Linden, March 23, 1989, Box 1, Folder: Dornan, Robert K.,

USC; transcript of taped interview with Robert Michel, pp. 34–35, Box "Personal 2," Folder: Personal: Member Notes, RHM.

12. A March 14 memo from Gingrich lists 50 Republicans considered "priorities" to persuade, of whom 22 would later be counted as Gingrich supporters. Since he eventually received 87 votes, it means 65 were in favor of Gingrich at that point. However, Bob Dornan (R-CA) later recounted that the number of commitments that day was only in the fifties. See Box 2353, Folder: Whip Race Information, NLG; and interview with Robert K. Dornan, March 23, 1989, USC.

13. This may have been a genuine overcount on Madigan's part. Tom DeLay, who was helping Madigan, later swore that multiple Republicans had falsely committed to Madigan. Interview with Robert K. Dornan by Frank van der Linden, March 23, 1989, Box 1, Folder: Dornan, Robert K., USC.

14. Bob Walker later claimed that because Madigan surrogate Tom DeLay "played hardball" to get their votes, he may have inadvertently steered a couple of lawmakers away from Madigan (Z. Smith 2012).

15. Transcript of taped interview with Robert Michel, p. 38, Box "Personal 2," Folder: Personal: Member Notes, RHM.

16. Ibid.

17. That sheet noted 87 votes for Gingrich and 88 for Madigan, but we dropped one Madigan supporter who was absent and recoded another (Robert Coughlin [R-PA]) who had switched to Gingrich at the last minute (Hastert 2004, 94); undated list of all House Republicans, Box 2353, Folder: Whip Race Info, NLG. If the unreadable ballot was cast for Madigan, our estimated count matches the final vote tally.

18. Sixty-three House Republicans in the 101st Congress had signed the letter. See "List of Co-Signers of the Gingrich Letter," Box 673, Folder: Ethics Handout, NLG. The letter was not signed by Michel, and the committee's investigation ultimately led to Wright's resignation (Barry 1989).

19. When omitting outlier values of DW-NOMINATE, terms in office, and percent of the two-party vote, the leadership variable becomes statistically significant and negative (B = -5.17, se = 0.58), while the Wright letter variable loses its statistical significance. Adding a squared term variable results in both the term and squared term variables becoming at least weakly significant ($p < .10$). Dropping freshmen from the analysis results in statistically insignificant coefficients for South

and age, but omitting lawmakers who were unopposed for reelection in 1988 does not alter the statistical significance of any of the explanatory variables.

20. Harris (2006) combines COS membership with membership in the 92 Group into a new variable. This variable is statistically significant and positive (B = 0.66, se = 0.28) when used instead of COS membership, and the Wright letter variable becomes statistically insignificant as well, suggesting that both variables are capturing the influence of a more aggressive tactical mindset.

21. Southern representation may also overlap ideological preferences; omitting the South variable results in a weakly significant coefficient for the DW-NOMINATE variable (B = 1.24, se = 0.68).

22. Koopman (1996) offers a different explanation of the results, focusing more on the role of factions within the GOP.

23. Rhodes would later blame Newt Gingrich for instigating that near insurrection (Rhodes 1995).

24. Memo to Congressman Gingrich from Roger France, August 16, 1979, Box 294, Folder: Opposition to Democrats, NLG. For more on the race, see Harris and Green 2015.

25. Fred W. Beuttler oral history with Robert H. Michel, September 5, 2007, part 1, pp. 16-17, Collection 153, Folder: Oral History Transcripts 2007, RHM.

26. Guy Vander Jagt to Gene Snyder, December 21, 1979, Folder: GVJ Correspondence—Political Minority Leadership, 1980-81 (1), GVJ.

27. Guy Vander Jagt to Newt Gingrich, undated, Folder: GVJ Correspondence—Political Minority Leadership, 1980-81 (1), GVJ.

28. In fact, Michel was somewhat to the right of Vander Jagt, based on DW-NOMINATE scores (0.322 in the 97th Congress, versus Vander Jagt's 0.210), and only in the late 1970s had Vander Jagt begun voting more conservatively (L. Cannon 1980).

29. See Everett McKinley Dirksen Congressional Research Center, "Anatomy of a Congressional Leadership Race," http://dirksencenter.org/leadershiprace/index.htm (accessed September 9, 2017).

30. Interview with former Republican aide, August 15, 2016.

31. See Rousselot's "Western and Plains Tally Sheet," in Leadership Series Box 2, Folder: 96th Leadership Contests, 1980 (2), RHM.

32. Jim Sparling letter, "Subject: Minority Leadership Election," October 29, 1980, Box 151, Folder: Political Minority Leadership, 1979-80, GVJ.

33. "Talking Points for Electing Guy Vander Jagt Minority Leader," Box 151, Folder: Correspondence—Political-Minority Leadership, 1980–81 (2), GVJ.

34. "Remarks Prepared to Introduce Michel," Press Series, Box 28, Folder: Michel, Robert (1), RHM.

35. For instance, in the 1979 race to succeed John Anderson (R-IL) as Conference chairman, Republican freshmen were said to have "drafted" Henry Hyde (R-IL) to run in part because they were looking "for someone who will look good on 'Meet the Press,' effectively articulate Republican issues and be a floor leader" (Russell 1979a).

36. Jim Sparling letter, "Subject: Minority Leadership Election," October 29, 1980, Box 151, Folder: Political Minority Leadership, 1979–80, GVJ.

37. Newt Gingrich to Republican Freshmen, November 14, 1980, Box 151, Folder: Correspondence—Political—Minority Leadership, 1980–81 (2), GVJ. Gingrich's endorsement of Vander Jagt, and its implied criticisms of Michel, set the stage for years of tension between Gingrich and Michel.

38. Michel letter to incoming freshmen, November 7, 1980, Leadership Series, Box 2, Folder: Leadership Contests, 1980 (1), RHM.

39. Colleague letter to David Dreier (sent to all freshmen), November 21, 1980, Leadership Series, Box 2, Folder: Leadership Contests, 1980 (1), RHM.

40. Steve Stockmeyer to Guy Vander Jagt, "Re: Committee Appointments," Box 151, Folder: Political Minority Leadership, 1979–80, GVJ.

41. Ibid.

42. See, e.g., "Talking Points for Electing Guy Vander Jagt Minority Leader," Box 151, Folder: Correspondence—Political-Minority Leadership, 1980–81 (2), GVJ.

43. Bob Whittaker to Guy Vander Jagt, December 3, 1980, Box 151, Folder: Correspondence—Political-Minority Leadership, 1980–81 (2), GVJ.

44. Vander Jagt Campaign Document, November 17, 1980, Box 151, Folder: Political Minority Leadership, 1979–80, GVJ.

45. All nine Republicans who were uncommitted on Vander Jagt's count, and recorded as either blank or no votes on Michel's tally, were freshmen. Michel later recalled that only two lawmakers had falsely pledged to vote for him. Transcript of taped interview with Robert Michel, p. 35, Box "Personal 2," Folder: Personal: Member Notes, RHM.

46. The Vander Jagt tally is dated November 26, 1980, twelve days before the election; Box 151, Folder: Political Minority Leadership, 1979–80,

GVJ. The Michel tally is undated but appears to have been taken sometime between mid-November and December 6, 1980; House Republican Members list, undated, Leadership Series, Box 2, Folder: 96th. Leadership Contests, 1980 (3), RHM.

47. We exclude the estimated votes of lawmakers who committed to both candidates on both tallies, who are marked as uncommitted or undetermined on both tallies, or who are marked as opponents on one candidate's tally but as uncommitted on the other candidate's tally.

48. Both Michel's committee and Vander Jagt's state have statistically significant effects in the full model if DW-NOMINATE, term, and two-party vote are excluded.

49. The statistical significance of two-party vote does not change in Models 2 or 4 when lawmakers who were unopposed for reelection in 1980 are excluded.

50. Amounts were noted in a tally of member support dated November 13, 1980, Leadership Series Box 2, Folder: 96th, Leadership Contests, 1980 (1), RHM.

51. Adding a variable equal to 1 if a lawmaker served on the NRCC does not dramatically alter the results in Models 2 or 4, but the variable itself is negative and weakly significant (B = −0.92, se = 0.34 in Model 2, B = −0.57, se = 0.31 in Model 4). Terms are moderately correlated with age and committee status, but omitting the variable measuring seniority does not alter the statistical significance of either variable in Model 2 or 4. The term variable loses its statistical significance in Model 2 (but not Model 4) when adding a squared term variable. Eliminating outlier values for DW-NOMINATE scores and term in office does not appreciably affect the results in Models 2 or 4. When using a penalized log-likelihood model (see chapter 1, note 35) to include omitted variables in Models 2 and 4 (see above), the only variable that changes in statistical significance is terms in office, which is no longer significant in Model 2.

52. Excluding freshmen from Model 2 has no effect on the statistical significance of the variables in the model, but when doing so in Model 4, the Michel donation variable must be omitted because it perfectly predicts a vote for Michel, and the Vander Jagt contribution variable becomes weakly significant (B = −0.06, se = 0.03).

53. Two freshmen received a contribution from both; they split their votes.

54. We also ran the same model with the dependent variable equal to one if the lawmaker was counted for both candidates (N = 27; see table 4.2). Illinois Republicans are less likely to do so (B = −0.85, se = 0.45), while age and DW-NOMINATE prove at least weakly statistically significant (p < .10) in explaining the likelihood of being double-counted, suggesting that older and more ideologically moderate Republicans were more likely to commit to both candidates.

55. Skip Bafalis, Clair Burgener, John Paul Hammerschmidt, Tom Corcoran, Joe McDade, and Bill Harsha Dear Colleague letter, November 8, 1978, and Bud Shuster, News Release, December 13, 1979, Series I: Congressional Papers, Sub-Series A: United States, Box 36A, Folder 32, EGS.

56. Fred W. Beuttler oral history with Robert H. Michel, October 15, 2007, p. 9, Collection 153, Folder: Oral History Transcripts 2007, RHM.

57. Lott, however, was also known as one of the party's "Blow-Dry Guys," a group of relatively partisan lawmakers seeking ways to challenge Democrats; the group also included Newt Gingrich, Bob Walker, and Jack Kemp (Green 2015, 18–19).

58. Lott's 1st dimension DW-NOMINATE score was 0.33; Shuster's, 0.375.

59. Dear Republican Colleague letter, November 12, 1980, and Dear Colleague letter, October 1, 1980, Series I: Congressional Papers, Sub-Series A: United States, Box 36A, Folder 32, EGS.

60. Bud Shuster to Freshmen Republican Members, November 14, 1980, Series I: Congressional Papers, Sub-Series A: United States, Box 36A, Folder 32, EGS. Shuster also sent congratulatory telegrams to more senior Republicans who won reelection, with the (unsurprising) exception of Lott and seven of his top supporters and campaign organizers. Shuster "Telegram to Incumbents Who Won," 1980; Series I: Congressional Papers, Sub-Series A: United States, Box 36A, Folder 32, EGS.

61. Bud Shuster's "Republican Conference Roll" document; Series I: Congressional Papers, Sub-Series A: United States, Box 36A, Folder 32, EGS.

62. "Whip Race Post-Mortem—Mistakes," December 10, 1980, Series I: Congressional Papers, Sub-Series A: United States, Box 36A, Folder 32, EGS.

63. Undated document, "Lott Strategy?" Series I: Congressional Papers, Sub-Series A: United States, Box 36A, Folder 32, EGS. If Shuster was right, it is unclear how many southern votes Lott could actually

command. According to whip counts taken by Michel and Vander Jagt (see above), at least eleven southern Republicans who opposed Shuster (including Lott) voted for Michel. On the other hand, at least nine other southern Republicans who opposed Shuster voted for Vander Jagt.

64. Interview with former Republican member of Congress, March 22, 2016; Bud Shuster's "Republican Conference Roll" document; Series I: Congressional Papers, Sub-Series A: United States, Box 36A, Folder 32, EGS.

65. "Republican Conference Roll," Series I: Congressional Papers, Sub-Series A: United States, Box 36A, Folder 32, EGS.

66. No DW-NOMINATE scores are available for three lawmakers who left the 97th Congress prematurely—Tennyson Guyer (R-OH), Jon Hinson (R-MS), and David Stockman (R-MI)—so they are excluded from Model 2.

67. The statistical significance of the coefficients does not change when eliminating outliers, Republicans who ran unopposed, freshmen, or terms in office (which are moderately correlated with two-party vote, committee ranking, and age). Terms in office loses its statistical significance when a squared term variable is added. Controls for membership on Shuster's Policy Committee and Lott's Research Committee are statistically insignificant when added to the model. Estimating the effects of omitted variables via a penalized log-likelihood model does not alter the statistical significance of the remaining variables.

68. Gerald Solomon briefly considered, but ultimately abandoned, a challenge against Gingrich for party leader.

69. For more on this race, see Green and Harris 2016.

70. Interview with former Republican member of Congress, March 22, 2016.

71. However, DeLay's 1st dimension DW-NOMINATE score in the 104th Congress, 0.653, was not far from Walker's score of 0.686.

72. Bill McCollum Press Release, "McCollum Will Seek Reelection, Will Run for House Republican Whip," October 12, 1993, Box 153a, Folder: Whip Race 1993, RSW.

73. McCollum's DW-NOMINATE 1st dimension score in the 104th Congress was 0.410.

74. Interview with former Republican member of Congress, March 22, 2016; "The Whip Race," Box 153a, Folder: The Whip Race 1993, RSW. Others who were considered possible candidates were Nancy Johnson (R-CT), John Boehner (R-OH), and Armey. Walker produced a twenty-

one-page chronology of the whip race that provides key facts and dates related to his campaign. "The Whip Race," Box 153a, Folder: The Whip Race 1993, RSW. Key dates listed here and below are from this document, except where otherwise identified.

75. Robert S. Walker, Dear Colleague letter, October 8, 1993, Box 153a, Folder: Whip Race 1993, and "Who are some of the Members Voting for Bob Walker in the Whip Race," Box 170a, Folder: Whip Race 1993–94 (2), RSW.

76. See various letters, Box 170, Folder: Whip Race 1993–94 (2), RSW.

77. Tom DeLay, Dear Colleague letter, April 11, 1994, Box 153b, Folder: Whip Race 1994, RSW.

78. James V. Hansen, Dear Colleague letter, March 10, 1994, Box 171a, Folder: Whip Race 1994 (2), RSW.

79. "Regional Diversity—Hallmark of Majority Leadership," Box 170a, Folder: Whip Race 1993–94 (2), RSW.

80. Interview with former Republican member of Congress, March 22, 2016.

81. Mike Mihalke, "Challenger/Open Seat Strategy," Box 153a, Folder: Whip Race 1993 (2), RSW.

82. Memorandum to Walker Whip Team, Re: "Update 8/4/94," Box 153a, Folder: Whip Race 1993, RSW.

83. Agenda for October 10 Whip AAs Meeting, Box 153a, Folder: Whip Race 1993, RSW.

84. See, e.g., Dear Colleague letter by James Sensenbrenner (WI), May 18, 1994, Box 170, Folder: Whip Race 1993–94 (2), RSW. As one Republican congressman later put it, Walker's "message somewhat got trampled." Interview with former Republican member of Congress, March 22, 2016.

85. We combine two counts: one taken on November 15, about two weeks before the election, and one taken on December 3 of just freshmen, two days before the election; see the November 15, 1994, document (time-stamped 9:22 A.M.), Box 170a, Folder: Whip Race 1993–94 (2) and Box 170a, Folder: Whip 2 (1), RSW.

86. This means that the 10 "lean yes" and 18 "undecided" legislators are counted together with the 117 "no" and 3 "lean no" as having voted against Walker.

87. Walker also documented nonmonetary service he provided to lawmakers, such as campaign visits and personal phone calls. When rerunning the model with a dummy variable measuring whether a legislator

received such service, the variable proves nearly statistically significant (p = 0.104). "The Whip Race," RSW.

88. The Walker committee variable remains statistically significant in Model 2 if contributions from DeLay are omitted, as well as when the coefficients are estimated with a penalized log-likelihood model (which also results in the term variable losing its statistical significance).

89. Omitting outlier values of the explanatory variables, excluding freshmen, or excluding Republicans who ran unopposed in 1994 has no effect on the statistical significance of the variables in Model 2. Adding a squared term variable yields a statistically insignificant coefficient for the term variable. The Walker data also notes lawmakers who were undecided; when using the variables in Model 2 to predict the likelihood of being undecided, only one comes close to statistical significance: logged two-party vote (B = -2.24, p < .10), suggesting that those in more marginal districts were more likely to be undecided.

Chapter 5. Challenges to the Heir Apparent

1. In addition to the three we examine, the other two were the race for the Democratic nominee for Speaker in 1971 between Carl Albert (D-OK) and John Conyers (D-MI) and the 2014 race for Republican leader between Kevin McCarthy (R-CA) and Raúl Labrador (R-ID). We do not include the 2002 race for Democratic leader between Whip Nancy Pelosi and Harold Ford (D-TN) because the previous leader, Dick Gephardt, had been Caucus chair, and only one of the past three leaders had previously served as whip. We count the 1971 election for Democratic leader as an open race, though some claimed the whip position was the heir apparent at the time (see chapter 3).

2. Interview with Republican leadership aide, May 2, 2016.

3. See Nelson 1977, 923. One of the two Democratic leaders who had not previously been whip, Dick Gephardt (D-MO), was arguably not violating this norm of succession. When Gephardt was elected leader in June 1989, filling a vacancy caused by the election of Tom Foley to the speakership, there was no heir apparent: the whip position had been vacated when Tony Coelho (D-CA) resigned from Congress.

4. Wright's victory did maintain a different norm of succession, the "Austin Boston" connection, in which northern (usually Bostonian) and southern (usually Oklahoman or north Texan) Democrats alternated as occupants of succeeding rungs of the leadership ladder. For more on

this race and this broader pattern of succession, see Champagne et al. 2009 and Green and Harris 2015a.

5. Though Robert Peabody (1976) did not believe that the Democratic whip's succession to majority leader was sufficiently institutionalized at the time for McFall to be considered an heir apparent, we consider it as such based on our definition of heir apparent. See e.g. Jacobs 1995, 304–5; King 1980, 231; and Oppenheimer and Peabody 1977, 34.

6. McFall's DW-NOMINATE score in the 95th Congress (1977–78) was −0.465.

7. He had also pressed for a rules change that granted delegates a vote in their committee and in the Democratic Caucus (Jacobs 1995, 220). While Wright would largely neutralize Burton's support among (southern) lawmakers with cotton industries, Burton's help for pro-coal Democrats may help explain some of the support he eventually received.

8. Burton had the most liberal DW-NOMINATE score (−0.629) of all the candidates.

9. He had in particular earned the loyalty of Interior Committee Democrats by expanding their power at the expense of its autocratic chair, Wayne Aspinall (D-CO) (Jacobs 1995).

10. Tip O'Neill was reportedly so alarmed by Burton's ambitiousness that in 1974 he pressed Albert to announce his retirement early so he could get a head start over Burton in the race for Speaker ("Washington Wire" 1974).

11. They include Glenn Anderson (CA), Frank Annunzio (IL), Richard Bolling, John Brademas (IN), James Corman (CA), Robert Leggett (CA), Tip O'Neill, Leo Ryan (CA), Ed Roybal (CA), Ike Skelton (MO), Frank Thompson (NJ), Joe Waggonner (LA), and Charlie Wilson (CA) (Jacobs 1995).

12. His DW-NOMINATE score in the 95th Congress was −0.507, slightly to the left of McFall's.

13. Bolling's emphasis was more on reform than on legislation. He "wants to get the pipes in order," as one observer put it, while Burton "is more worried about the quality of the water coming through" (Baron 1976).

14. In a letter to Dan Rostenkowski, Wright thanked the Illinois Democrat for the "encouragement you have expressed verbally" that he said "contributed significantly to this decision." Wright to Rostenkowski, July 27, 1976, Folder: 22–21: Majority Leader Race, 1976, Series 1: General Files, 1952–94, DDR.

15. Wright's DW-NOMINATE score at the start of the 95th Congress (1977–78) was −0.383.
16. Philip Burton to Dan Rostenkowski, June 7, 1976, Folder: 22–21: Majority Leader Race 1976, Series 1: General Files, 1952–94, DDR; John Burton Dear Colleague letter, November 17, 1976, Carton 13, Folder 12, PB.
17. Richard Bolling to Dan Rostenkowski, undated, Folder: 22–21: Majority Leader Race, 1976, Series 1: General Files, 1952–94, DDR.
18. Wright also circulated a two-page memo outlining his vision for the job, which included being an "advocate, conciliator, and innovator." "The Responsibilities of the Majority Leader as I View Them," July 27, 1976, JCW.
19. Dear Colleague letter from Jim Wright, November 17, 1976, DDR.
20. Letter to Dan Rostenkowski from Jim Wright, November 15, 1976, DDR.
21. Minutes of the House Democratic Organizing Caucus, December 6, 1976, pp. 64, 67–69, Carton 13, Folder 9, PB.
22. Minutes of the House Democratic Organizing Caucus, December 6, 1976, p. 57, Carton 13, Folder 9, PB.
23. Letter to Dan Rostenkowski from Jim Wright, November 15, 1976, DDR.
24. Burton might have worked with *Roll Call* reporter (and later Burton aide) Myron Struck to publish a story reporting that Burton was likely to win and that Wright had more commitments than Bolling (Oppenheimer and Peabody 1977; Struck 1976).
25. See also undated "Dan Prescott" member list, Box 794, JCW.
26. Letter to Dan Rostenkowski from Jim Wright, November 15, 1976, DDR.
27. Minutes of the House Democratic Organizing Caucus, December 6, 1976, p. 72, Carton 13, Folder 9, PB. Under the rules, any candidates who tied in two consecutive rounds of voting would be eliminated. This would later mean another missed opportunity for Burton to win the race: had Bolling and Wright tied on the second and third ballots, Burton would have been the automatic victor (Oppenheimer and Peabody 1977, 84 n. 9).
28. Though Burton denied having told his supporters to throw their votes, biographer John Jacobs uncovered evidence that at least four Burton supporters had voted for Wright on their own initiative (Jacobs 1995, 319).

29. The Bolling campaign may have promised to help Wright if he were the last candidate standing against Burton. Burton had insisted that all rounds of voting immediately follow each other, fearing a delay could give opponents time to mobilize against him, but ironically, this denied Burton precious time to lobby for votes on the final ballot (J. Farrell 2001). According to John Jacobs, on the last ballot Joe Waggonner (D-LA) lobbied southern Democrats against Burton, Frank Thompson (D-NJ) got three same-state colleagues to switch from Burton to Wright, and Dan Rostenkowski convinced Lud Ashley (D-OH) to flip from Burton to Wright (Jacobs 1995).

30. For instance, Wright's staff compiled the comparative voting records of Burton and Wright in 1979 and 1980 ("Comparative Voting Record" memo, Box 794, JCW).

31. When the choice of McFall was removed from either Model 1 or Model 2, a seemingly unrelated estimation test (*suest* in Stata) failed to reject the Independence of Irrelevant Alternatives assumption for Bolling, but did reject it for Burton in Model 1. This is what one would expect, given Burton received just one more vote in the second round of balloting, with the remaining 30 McFall votes split between Wright and Bolling.

32. See also Minutes of the House Democratic Organizing Caucus, December 6, 1976, p. 53 and 70, Carton 13, Folder 9, PB. Burton and Wright, allegedly distributed campaign funds to other party members and freshmen candidates, and Bolling encouraged outside groups to make such donations (R. Baker 1989; Jacobs 1995; Oppenheimer and Peabody 1977). Wright later made much of his election-year visits to congressional districts, and his papers include a list first-time congressional candidates whose districts Wright visited in 1976 (Wright 1996, JCW). A dummy variable equal to one if Wright visited the district proves negative and statistically significant when explaining support for Burton over Wright in Model 1 of the first round of balloting.

33. Amendment to H.R. 16029, roll call no. 543. We use votes against the resolution under the assumption that Democrats elected after that vote were more likely to oppose the war and are thus coded the same as those who voted for the amendment. Another possibly prominent issue, Wright's opposition to the 1964 Civil Rights Act, is more difficult to measure with a recorded vote because only eighty Democrats in the 95th Congress had participated in the final passage vote of the act, and their vote choice is almost perfectly correlated with region (South vs. non-South).

34. Minutes of the House Democratic Organizing Caucus, December 6, 1976, pp. 49–50, Carton 13, Folder 9, PB.

35. Lawmakers from the oil-rich states of Arkansas, Oklahoma, and Texas had reason to vote against Burton because he had used Caucus rules to pass a resolution eliminating the oil depletion allowance. Bolling was born and educated in the South, but we do not expect that would have drawn many southerners to his candidacy (Jacobs 1995; Naughton 1976; Oppenheimer and Peabody 1977).

36. See the Jim Wright member lists noted "JW," "Non-Committed," and "Committed," undated, Box 794, JCW.

37. These are the "Members Believed For" memos, undated, General Files, 1952–94 Box 38, Folder 4: Majority Leader Race, 1973–76, DDR; and the undated "Dan Prescott" member list, Box 794, JCW. Many of the lawmakers on the "Members Believed For" memos are denoted with question marks, and we do not count them as definitive votes in our first, more restrictive tally.

38. These include Jacobs 1995; Oppenheimer and Peabody 1977; and Frey and Jewett 2009; "Tally Sheet July 28," Box 375, Folder 12, RB; "159 Natural constituency," Box 13, Folder 12: Profile: House Majority, PB; tellers and nominators identified in the Democratic Caucus minutes; lawmakers who served on a candidate's whip team; and those signing a "Dear Colleague" letter on behalf of a particular candidate. If the vote is unclear in the restrictive estimate, we recode it for a certain candidate only if the propensity of additional sources indicates a vote for that candidate. As a result, we count Norm Mineta (D-CA) as voting for Burton, even though many Democrats (including Burton) believed he voted for Wright (Jacobs 1995, 325). We also recoded Frank Annunzio (D-IL) from Wright to Bolling, because he served as a vote teller for Bolling; Jim Lloyd (D-CA) from Burton to McFall, because he later claimed to have voted for McFall; Leo Ryan (D-CA) from Burton to unclear because he disliked Burton; Joe Waggonner (D-LA) from Wright to Bolling because he reportedly worked on Bolling's campaign; and Mendel Davis (D-SC) because he was reportedly a Burton supporter (Frey and Jewett 2009; Jacobs 1995; Oppenheimer and Peabody 1977). The July 28 Bolling memo estimates votes of three lawmakers that contradict those cited elsewhere, but we opted to leave the original estimate for those lawmakers unchanged.

39. On the first ballot, our narrow estimate gives Burton 23 votes, Wright 88, Bolling 33, and McFall 17, while our broad estimate gives Burton

51, Wright 86, Bolling 48, and McFall 28 (the rest unclear or unknown). On the third ballot, our narrow estimate gives Burton 128 and Wright 126, while the broader estimate counts 137 for Burton and 140 for Wright (the rest unclear or unknown). Paul Simon (D-IL) may have voted present on all three ballots, but since this is speculative, we count him as voting for one of the candidates. We do not assume that those voting for Burton or Wright did so on all three ballots, and several Democrats likely switched their votes at least once between them (Jacobs 1995; Oppenheimer and Peabody 1977).

40. To test the robustness of DW-NOMINATE as a measure of ideology, we reran the regression analyses with membership in the liberal Democratic Study Group as a substitute measure. In Models 1 and 2, the coefficient was positive and at least weakly significant (p < .10) in explaining a vote for Burton or Bolling over Wright, a further indication that ideology mattered, though that could also be because Bolling and Burton were DSG members, and Burton had served as a chairman of the group ("Summary, DSG Chairmen/Executive Committee Members," Box II:6, Folder 4, DSG).

41. The age variable loses its statistical significance when omitting terms in office from Model 2.

42. The results in both models are essentially unchanged when estimated without outliers (highly conservative or very senior Democrats), except that two-party vote loses its statistical significance for McFall in Model 1 and DW-NOMINATE loses its significance for Bolling in Model 2. Omitting freshmen results in the class of 1974 losing statistical significance for Bolling but gaining significance for Burton, and term in office loses significance for Bolling. Dropping the DW-NOMINATE variable does not alter the statistical significance of the other policy-oriented variables in Models 1 or 2.

43. One tally was made by Myron Struck, a Burton aide, and the other is a Burton count compiled by an unidentified individual (Carton 13, Folder 12, PB). "Lean" votes on the second tally were counted as votes cast for that candidate.

44. See note 38. We ignore any notes of uncertainty about lawmaker vote choice if the vote was already identified via the stringent estimate. For only three lawmakers do we alter their relaxed vote estimate for the third ballot: Douglas Applegate (D-OH) and Lawrence McDonald (D-GA), whom John Jacobs states definitively as voting for Wright and Burton, respectively, and Lloyd Meeds (D-WA), who was so "concerned

with the prospect" of a Burton victory that he helped recruit Bolling (Jacobs 1995; Oppenheimer and Peabody 1977).

45. When replacing DW-NOMINATE scores with DSG membership, the latter is not statistically significant in either regression model. Excluding outlier Democrats (more conservative and senior lawmakers) has no effect on the statistical significance of the remaining variables in Model 1, but in Model 2 the state delegations lose their statistical significance, while the chairman variable becomes weakly significant ($p < .10$). The term variable loses its significance when a squared term variable is added. The age variable loses its statistical significance when unopposed Democrats or freshmen Democrats are omitted from either model, and the Vietnam War variable becomes significant in Model 2 when DW-NOMINATE scores are excluded. When using a penalized log-likelihood model to estimate the effects of omitted variables (see chapter 1, note 35), the statistical significance (or insignificance) of coefficients is unchanged in Model 2, while in Model 4 the Texas delegation variable loses its significance and the chairman variable becomes significant at the $p < .10$ level.

46. Oppenheimer and Peabody argue that news coverage had little impact on the outcome, apart from the stories about scandals. McFall aide Irv Sprague later speculated that McFall could have come in third on the first ballot, but had lost at least a third of his votes because of the foreign lobbyist scandal (Oppenheimer and Peabody 1977).

47. There may have been other regional or state-related considerations that influenced vote choice. For instance, eighty percent of the Ohio delegation voted for Burton on the third ballot (relaxed estimate), perhaps because of the lingering influence of Wayne Hays or Burton's past support for black lung compensation (Jacobs 1995).

48. Boehner's 1st dimension DW-NOMINATE score for the 109th Congress was 0.682; Blunt's, 0.633. Both were fifty-six years old.

49. Interview with Republican leadership aide, June 9, 2016.

50. John Boehner, "For a Majority That Matters," pp. 3–4, Box 36, Folder 53: Republican Leadership Races, Majority Leader, 2006, DDP.

51. Shadegg's 1st dimension DW-NOMINATE score for the 109th Congress was 0.935.

52. Interview with Republican leadership aide, June 9, 2016.

53. Ibid.

54. Ibid.

55. The 2 write-in votes technically allowed Shadegg to stay in the race for the second ballot.

56. One staff member close to the Boehner campaign later estimated that "99 percent" of Shadegg's first ballot support went to Boehner. Interview with Republican leadership aide, February 24, 2006.

57. We count Bill Thomas as a vote for Boehner, and we exclude Wayne Gilchrest (R-MD), who originally endorsed Boehner but switched to Blunt and was listed as a supporter on both candidates' lists, and Gary Miller (R-CA), who publicly supported Boehner but was absent from the vote (Cillizza 2006; O'Connor 2006c). Del. Luis Fortuño (R-PR), who endorsed Blunt, was excluded from the analysis because he could not vote on the House floor and thus had no DW-NOMINATE score. To test for any systematic difference between publicly committed members and all others, we ran probit regression with a dependent variable measuring whether a Republican made a public commitment. Texans were more likely to announce their vote publicly, and more senior members and conservatives were less likely to do so (p < .10).

58. Boehner campaigned against excessive earmarks inserted into appropriations bills (Wehrman 2006). This might have worried members of the Appropriations Committee, but a variable measuring membership on that committee is not statistically significant when included.

59. Concerns about the party retaining its majority were raised by some members (Weisman 2006b). In addition, Boehner emphasized problems with the party's reputation under the current leadership, and one Boehner aide later recalled that "members thought the majority was hanging in the balance" and worried about which candidate would best improve "the overall brand of the House Republican Conference." Interview with Republican leadership aide, June 9, 2016.

60. The contribution variables retain their signs and statistical significance when replaced by dummy variables equal to 1 if a lawmaker received any contribution from each candidate.

61. When replacing DW-NOMINATE with membership in the Republican Study Committee as a proxy for ideological conservatism, the RSC variable is positive and weakly significant (p < .10) in explaining a vote for Shadegg over Blunt.

62. These contrary signs are probably due to the support of Shadegg by a few senior but relatively young Republicans, including Paul Ryan (R-WI), Dave Weldon (R-FL), and Charlie Bass (R-NH). If all lawmakers who were unopposed for reelection are excluded, the statistical significance of the remaining variables is unchanged.

63. When adding a squared term variable, both term and squared term are statistically significant when explaining a vote for Boehner, but the first is positive while the second is negative. Rerunning the analysis without outlier values results in the election variable becoming weakly significant (p < .10) in explaining a vote for Boehner, and terms in office loses its statistical significance in explaining a vote for Shadegg.

64. Interview with Republican leadership aide, February 24, 2006.

65. Murtha's 1st dimension DW-NOMINATE score in the 110th Congress was −0.222, versus −0.323 for Hoyer.

66. Interview with House Democratic aide, November 30, 2006.

67. Dear Democratic Colleague letter from Steny Hoyer, November 8, 2006.

68. Interview with House Democratic aide, November 29, 2006.

69. Dear Democratic Colleague letter, November 13, 2006.

70. Interview with Democratic aide, November 29, 2006; interview with Democratic aide, November 30, 2006.

71. Interview with Democratic aide, November 30, 2006.

72. Whip count, Box 145, Folder: JPM Majority Leadership Race, JPM. Our thanks to Sean Kelly for helping secure these data. We check Murtha's whip count against public commitments made in the race, which one of us used to test the goal salience hypothesis in an earlier work (Green 2008).

73. This confirms the claim of one legislative aide who noted Murtha suffered from "a lot" of defections and that Hoyer was a better vote-counter (interview with Democratic aide, November 29, 2006; see also Yachnin and Bresnahan 2006).

74. One of the six, Elijah Cummings (D-MD), is noted in Murtha's whip count as having switched from Hoyer.

75. None of the variables we use in our models are statistically significant in explaining the likelihood of being undecided or refusing to state a preference.

76. The four nonvoting Democratic delegates are excluded because no DW-NOMINATE data is available for them. Murtha's whip sheet marked all four as voting for or leaning toward Hoyer.

77. One California Democrat, Brad Sherman, was noted in the Murtha whip count as someone who "will look to Nancy."

78. The results differ somewhat from those in Green 2008. Most notably, Green did not find DW-NOMINATE scores to be statistically significant, likely a consequence of his partial estimate of a different measure

of ideology (W-NOMINATE) and use of public commitments to estimate vote choice.

79. DW-NOMINATE is strongly correlated with two possible proxy measures of issue-specific policy concerns, opposition to the Iraq War (estimated by Democrats' votes on a May 2005 amendment urging the president to develop a troop withdrawal plan) and abortion rights (measured by each Democrat's average rating from the prochoice group NARAL in the 109th Congress). When using those measures instead of DW-NOMINATE, the Iraq war variable proves negative and statistically significant in both probit models, suggesting Murtha's early opposition to the war brought him some votes.

80. To test the robustness of the finding for DW-NOMINATE, we reran Models 1 and 3 using as substitutes membership in the (conservative) Blue Dog, (conservative) New Democrat, and (liberal) Progressive Caucuses. The latter two were statistically significant in the stringent model, and the first was significant in the relaxed model. When running the relaxed vote model without outlier values for the term variable (i.e., more than fifteen terms in office), the party leader variable is no longer statistically significant. Term drops out when adding a variable measuring squared terms in office. A penalized log-likelihood model also results in some variables losing their statistical significance, including California delegation and ranking committee member (Model 2 only) and party leadership and age (Model 4 only).

Chapter 6. Revolts

1. Legislative party leaders are, in theory, subject to removal at any time with a motion in Caucus or Conference to vacate a position (or, in the case of a Speaker, a motion to vacate the Speaker's chair, discussed below). But the most common threat of a revolt against an incumbent occurs when leadership elections are scheduled, i.e., just prior to the beginning of a Congress.

2. The fifth occurred in January 2011, when nineteen Democrats voted against Nancy Pelosi on the House floor as the party's nominee for Speaker. We count elections within a party to nominate an individual to be Speaker as the first type of revolt.

3. These include the elections of 1964 for Republicans (which was followed by two revolts), 1974 for Republicans (followed by one revolt), 1994 for Democrats (two revolts), 1998 for Republicans (three revolts),

2006 for Republicans (two revolts), 2008 for Republicans (two revolts), and 2010 for Democrats (two revolts, both against Nancy Pelosi). Peabody argues that a seat loss of at least thirty increases the odds of leadership change (Peabody 1976, 490).

4. The Armey campaign would compile a list legislative accomplishments to draw a contrast with Largent's thinner legislative record. See Dean Clancy to Majority Leader Armey, November 6, 1998, Box 54, Folder 17, RKA. See also Becker 2005.

5. Largent technically began service in November 1994, when he was chosen in a special election to finish the term of Republican Jim Inhofe.

6. Largent's DW-NOMINATE score in the 106th Congress was 0.743, versus Armey's score of 0.669.

7. Dunn's 1st dimension DW-NOMINATE score in the 106th Congress was 0.504.

8. Steve Largent, Dear Colleague letter, November 6, 1998, RG 57/d Box 36, Folder 47: Republican Leadership Races, Majority Leader, 1998, DDP.

9. Largent Dear Colleague letter, November 6, 1998, and "Steve Largent's Vision for the GOP," undated document, RG 57/d Box 36, Folder 47: Republican Leadership Races, Majority Leader, 1998, DDP.

10. Armey Press Release, November 6, 1998, RG 57/d Box 36, Folder 47: Republican Leadership Races, Majority Leader, 1998, DDP.

11. Dick Armey letter to Republican Colleagues, November 6, 1998, RG 57/d Box 36, Folder 47: Republican Leadership Races, Majority Leader, 1998, DDP.

12. Jennifer Dunn, Republican Colleague letter, November 10, 1998, RG 57/d Box 36, Folder 47: Republican Leadership Races, Majority Leader, 1998, DDP.

13. Joe Barton, Dear Colleague letter, November 17, 1998, RG 57/d— Box 36, Folder 47: Republican Leadership Races, Majority Leader, 1998, DDP.

14. See Dear Colleague letters on Armey's behalf in RG 57/d Box 36, Folder 47: Republican Leadership Races, Majority Leader, 1998, DDP.

15. See Lambro's editorial "Pitting Image vs. Substance;" Joe Barton, Dear Colleague letter, November 17, 1998, RG 57/d—Box 36, Folder 47: Republican Leadership Races, Majority Leader, 1998, DDP.

16. "What Members are Saying About Steve Largent," undated document, RG 57/d Box 36, Folder 47: Republican Leadership Races, Majority Leader, 1998, DDP.

17. Joe Scarborough, Dear Colleague letter, November 12, 1998, RG 57/d Box 36, Folder 47: Republican Leadership Races, Majority Leader, 1998, DDP.

18. "Largent Enjoys Strong Support as Election Nears," Press Release, November 16, 1998; Jack Quinn Dear Colleague letter, November 12, 1998; Ray LaHood Dear Colleague letter, November 11, 1998, RG 57/d Box 36, Folder 47: Republican Leadership Races, Majority Leader, 1998, DDP.

19. "Steve Largent's Vision for the GOP," undated, RG 57/d Box 36, Folder 47: Republican Leadership Races, Majority Leader, 1998, DDP.

20. Steve Largent, Dear Republican Colleague letter, November 13, 1998, RG 57/d Box 36, Folder 47: Republican Leadership Races, Majority Leader, 1998, DDP.

21. Doc Hastings Dear Colleague letter, November 10, 1998, and Jim Gibbons and John Peterson Dear Colleague letter, November 13, 1998, RG 57/d Box 36, Folder 47: Republican Leadership Races, Majority Leader, 1998, DDP. The editorial referenced in Hastings's letter was "Jennifer Dunn Is Ready to Lead a Gentler GOP," *Seattle Times*, November 10, 1998. Other letter writers for Dunn included John Peterson (PA), Rodney Frelinghuysen (NJ), Bob Franks (NJ), Mary Bono (CA), Doc Hastings (WA), George Nethercutt (WA), Jack Metcalf (WA), Rick White (WA), James Walsh (NY), and Greg Ganske (IA).

22. Rodney Freylinghuysen Dear Republican Colleague letter, November 13, 1998, and Mary Bono Dear Republican Colleague letter, November 13, 1998, RG 57/d Box 36, Folder 47: Republican Leadership Races, Majority Leader, 1998, DDP.

23. Undated document, "Communications College," Box 2263, Folder: Communication Project, NLG; Cindi Williams to David Winston, "Subject: Media Training," November 18, 1997, Box 2420, Folder: Gender Gap, NLG; and memo from Goeas, Tringali, and Stephenson to Armey, April 8, 1997, Box 2228, Folder: Leadership Communications, NLG.

24. Member Assignment Document, Box 54, Folder 17, RKA; Tom A. Coburn Dear Colleague letter, "Largent Closes Gender Gap," undated, RG 57/d Box 36, Folder 47: Republican Leadership Races, Majority Leader, 1998, DDP.

25. "Largent Enjoys Strong Support as Election Nears" Press Release, November 16, 1998, RG 57/d Box 36, Folder 47: Republican Leadership Races, Majority Leader, 1998, DDP.

26. Ibid.

27. Tom Ewing, Mike Castle, and Marge Roukema, Dear Colleague letter, November 17, 1998, RG 57/d Box 36, Folder 47: Republican Leadership Races, Majority Leader, 1998, DDP.

28. Armey Vote Count, undated, Box 54, Folder 17, RKA.

29. We were able to estimate a multinomial probit model, which does not depend on the IIA assumption, by excluding certain variables (chair and Gang of Eleven Membership), and the results were largely similar, with the following exceptions: Dunn contributions and terms became statistically significant for explaining a vote for Dunn, but gender did not, and terms became statistically significant for explaining a vote for Largent.

30. This includes the Republican cochair of the caucus, James Hansen (R-UT), five Republicans who spoke against the 1997 amendment on the floor, and seven other Republicans identified in media reports as high-profile members of the Caucus.

31. Membership in the Gang of Eleven comes from Koszczuk 1997. According to Barnett (1999), Steve Chabot (R-OH) and Sue Myrick (R-NC) were rumored to be members as well (see also VandeHei 1997).

32. Largent was youngest, at forty-four; Armey and Dunn were both fifty-eight. Armey was most senior, in his eighth term, while Largent and Dunn were both starting their third term.

33. When abortion scores are excluded, the ideology coefficient becomes statistically significant and negative when explaining support for Dunn over Armey (B = -4.55, se = 2.03).

34. When omitting lawmakers who were unopposed for reelection in 1998, the leadership variable is no longer statistically significant when explaining a vote for Dunn. The statistical significance of campaign contributions does not change when replacing these variables with dummy variables equal to one if the candidate gave any money to a colleague. The statistical (in)significance of the coefficients are unchanged when omitting outlier values for DW-NOMINATE and terms in office.

35. Excluding freshmen from the model makes DW-NOMINATE and age variables weakly significant (p < .10) when explaining a vote for Dunn over Armey.

36. Dropping the terms variable or lawmakers unopposed for reelection from Model 2 has no effect on the statistical significance of the remaining variables. When running Model 2 without outliers, DW-NOMINATE loses its statistical significance; when excluding freshmen, the class of

1994 variable becomes statistically significant; and when excluding Republicans unopposed in the 1998 elections, the Texas variable loses its statistical significance.

37. For more on the race, see Green and Harris 2015b; and Peabody 1976.

38. For more on the conservative coalition in Congress, see Polsby 2004.

39. See also the following interviews in the Peabody Research Interview Notes, Box 1, RLP: William Cramer, April 12, 1965; Paul Findley, March 30, 1965; Charles Goodell, January 6, 1965; John Lindsay, January 14, 1965; Richard Poff, January 26, 1965; and John Saylor, March 1965. Some of the quotes appear, slightly modified, in Peabody 1976.

40. Robert Peabody interview with Robert Griffin, December 29, 1964, RLP; see also Peabody interview with Richard Poff, January 26, 1965, RLP.

41. For more on the recruitment of Ford, see Averill 1964d; J. Cannon 1998; Ford 1979; Peabody 1976; Rumsfeld 2011; Sterne 1964a; and Robert Peabody interviews with Robert Griffin, December 29, 1964; and Robert Griffin and Charles Goodell, January 15, 1965, RLP.

42. Ford was fifty-two and in his ninth term, and the sixty-five-year old Halleck was starting his sixteenth term.

43. For more on that race, see Peabody 1976; Rumsfeld 2011; and Scheele 1966.

44. See also Robert Peabody interview with Paul Findley, March 30, 1965, RLP.

45. Robert Peabody interview with Robert Ellsworth, January 18, 1965, RLP.

46. Transcript of Roger Mudd interview with Robert Griffin and Charles Goodell, January 6, 1965, and Robert Peabody interviews with Alphonzo Bell, January 11, 1965; Robert Ellsworth, January 18, 1965; Robert Griffin, December 29, 1964; Robert Griffin and Charles Goodell, January 15, 1965; and Richard Poff, January 26, 1965, RLP.

47. Robert Peabody interviews with Paul Findley, March 30, 1965; Robert Griffin and Charles Goodell, January 15, 1965; and William Pitts, April 6, 1965, RLP.

48. Robert Peabody interview with Robert Griffin and Charles Goodell, January 6, 1965 (but see Peabody 1976, 133).

49. Transcript of Roger Mudd interview with Robert Griffin and Charles Goodell, January 6, 1965; and Robert Peabody interviews with Robert Ellsworth, January 18, 1965, and Robert Griffin, December 29, 1964, RLP.

50. See also Evans and Novak 1964a; Kumpa 1964; Sterne 1964a; and Robert Peabody interviews with John Lindsay, January 14, 1965; Silvio Conte, January 19, 1965; and Thomas Curtis, February 3, 1965, RLP.
51. For instance, Richard Poff (R-VA) later recalled that freshmen from Alabama, Georgia, and Mississippi were skeptical of Ford because they "smelled a deal between the Ford forces and the Wednesday Club." Robert Peabody interview with Richard Poff, January 26, 1965, RLP. See also Peabody interview with Catherine May, February 1, 1965, RLP.
52. Robert Peabody interviews with Frank Morse, January 26, 1965, and Gerald Lipscomb, January 19, 1964, RLP.
53. Transcript of Roger Mudd interview with Robert Griffin and Charles Goodell, January 6, 1965, and Robert Peabody interviews with Robert Griffin, January 6, 1965; Robert Lindsay, January 14, 1965; and William Pitts, April 6, 1965, RLP.
54. For more on Laird's race for Conference chair, see Peabody 1976.
55. The whip sheet comes from the Donald K. Rumsfeld Papers (http://library.rumsfeld.com/doclib/sp/954/Rumsfeld%20-%20Republican%20Congressmen%20-%201965%20-%2089th%20Congress%20-%20tally%20sheet%20for%20Ford-Halleck%20Race%20January%201965.pdf [accessed March 20, 2018]). The date of the tally is unclear, but it appears to have been taken the day before the election.
56. See for example Crowther 1965; R. Donovan 1964; and Peabody 1976. Ford's DW-NOMINATE score in the 89th Congress was 0.269, versus Halleck's 0.218.
57. Robert Peabody interview with John Anderson, January 11, 1965, RLP. See also Averill 1964a, 1964c; R. Donovan 1964; Kumpa 1964; and Peabody 1976.
58. Adding a dummy variable equal to one if a lawmaker was from any of the large state delegations targeted by Ford (California, New York, Ohio, and Pennsylvania) proves statistically insignificant. It is nonetheless worth noting that Pennsylvania Republicans were worried by rumors that the minority sergeant-at-arms, a Pennsylvanian, would be removed, and 78 percent of state delegation members who committed to either candidate pledged support to Ford (Peabody 1976, 134; Scheele 1966, 255).
59. Omitting the age variable results in weak statistical significance (p < .10) for terms in office in Model 4. Adding a squared term variable has no effect on the statistical significance of any of the variables.

60. DW-NOMINATE loses statistical significance when running the analysis without outlier values for term, two party vote, and DW-NOMINATE scores, and does so in just Model 4 when excluding freshmen. When rerunning the regressions with the excluded state delegation variables via a penalized log-likelihood model (see chapter 1, note 35), DW-NOMINATE loses its significance in Model 4 (and age loses its significance in both models). However, when replacing DW-NOMINATE scores with one of two proxy measures of ideology—membership in the Wednesday Group or voting against the 1964 Civil Rights Act—the former proves weakly significant and positive ($p < .10$) in Model 2, and the latter is weakly significant and negative ($p < .10$) in both models. Dropping lawmakers who ran unopposed in 1964 has no effect on the statistical significance of any of the variables.

61. Departures included two Indianans, Earl Wilson and Donald Bruce, and conservative Republicans Homer Abele (OH), Bruce Alger (TX), Ralph Beerman (NE), August Johansen (MI), and John Pillion (NY).

62. For an earlier analysis of this race, see Green 2006.

63. Majority Whip Hale Boggs (D-LA) also briefly considered challenging McCormack (Maney 1998, 243).

64. Morris K. Udall, Dear Democratic Colleague letter, December 26, 1968, Box 107, Folder: Speakership, JWM.

65. Udall, Dear Democratic Colleague, December 26, 1968. Udall was forty-six and finishing his fourth term in the House, whereas McCormack was finishing his twenty-first term and would be seventy-seven at the time of the election.

66. Udall's 1st dimension DW-NOMINATE score in the 91st Congress was −0.37, which was to the left of the party median score (−0.321).

67. Udall may have stuck it out, even as his odds of victory grew slim, because he nonetheless believed he might win, or because he was simply an inherent "risk-taker" (Carson and Johnson 2001, 105).

68. The six Democrats were John Blatnik (MN), Sam Gibbons (FL), Richard McCarthy (NY), Graham Purcell (TX), Lionel Van Deerlin (CA), and Charles Vanik (OH). They do not appear to share any observable characteristic that might explain their behavior. Counts were obtained from Head Count, Box 78, Folder 3, House Leadership Campaign Files 1969–71, MKU, and Caucus 1968–69 letters and telegrams, Box 107, Folder 6, JWM. One Democrat was absent (Rep. Richard Hanna [D-CA]) and it appears Udall and McCormack refrained from voting.

69. Age may also capture collective party concerns that McCormack was too old to be an effective Speaker or strong public face of the Caucus (see, e.g., Carson and Johnson 2001, 105; and King 1971, 41). Legislator age is positively correlated with seniority in Congress, but excluding it has no significant effect on the results in any of the models, nor does excluding outlier values of age or seniority.

70. This measure codes the six Democrats who pledged support to both candidates as having cast their votes for Udall.

71. When running Models 2 and 4 without the age variable, terms becomes statistically significant and negative.

72. Excluding outliers has no effect on the statistical significance of the variables in either model. Omitting unopposed Democrats results in statistical significance for the Massachusetts variable in Model 2, and the two-party vote variable becomes significant in Model 4. Substituting DW-NOMINATE with membership in the liberal Democratic Study Group (DSG) results in a statistically significant effect for the DSG variable in both models ($p < .05$), suggesting DW-NOMINATE is capturing ideological preferences. Running the analysis with a penalized log-likelihood model to include omitted variables (see chapter 1, note 35) does not alter the statistical (in)significance of the remaining variables.

73. Udall himself later identified one other factor that might have been in play: outgoing president Lyndon Johnson, who lobbied Democrats against him ("House Head Count," Box 78, Folder 3: House Leadership Campaign Files, 1968–71, MKU).

74. Other floor revolts include nine Republicans refusing to vote for Newt Gingrich (R-GA) for Speaker in January 1997, and nineteen Democrats failing to vote for Nancy Pelosi (D-CA) as her party's nominee for Speaker in January 2011.

75. Unlike other analyses, we include as party leaders fifteen lawmakers identified by news stories or other sources as being deputy or assistant Republican whips.

76. The four who were removed from committees were Justin Amash (R-MI) and Tim Huelskamp (R-KS) from the Budget Committee and Walter Jones (R-NC) and David Schweikert (R-AZ) from the Financial Services Committee.

77. Adding the omitted variables via a penalized log-likelihood model does not alter the statistical (in)significance of the remaining variables, nor

does omitting the age variable (which is moderately correlated with terms in office).

Chapter 7. Conclusion

1. This discussion excludes floor defections on speakership votes.

2. Of course, these accounts may involve some post-hoc rationalizations about the victors and losers in these races.

3. These averages include the change in relative probabilities of voting for candidates in the 1971 majority leader race on the first ballot, which are only partially reported in chapter 3. For fellow state delegates, these included a 54 percent change in the probability of voting for Sisk relative to Boggs, 47 percent for Hays, and 35 percent for O'Hara; for fellow committee members, 23 percent for Udall, -10 percent for Sisk, and 20 percent for Hays.

4. Interview with Republican leadership aide, May 4, 2016.

5. Interview with Republican leadership aide, May 2, 2016.

6. Interview with House Republican aide, June 3, 2016.

7. Interview with former Democratic leadership aide, May 4, 2016.

8. The averages are calculated by taking the mean PRE or R^2 of all models except limited ones (i.e. those that look only at the effect of professional connections or otherwise omit particular variables).

9. We note in chapter 5 that Murtha's campaign hoped to get one legislator's vote based on her relationship with a former lawmaker (whom she would later marry). We are also aware of at least one leadership race from the 1980s in which a lawmaker was dating one of the candidates, unbeknownst to the other candidates who fruitlessly tried to get the lawmaker's vote.

10. Interview with Republican aide, May 2, 2016.

11. Interview with Republican aide, June 9, 2016.

12. Interview with former Democratic leader, May 18, 2016.

13. Interview with Democratic member of Congress, July 8, 2016.

14. Robert Peabody interview with Robert Griffin, December 29, 1964, RLP.

15. There could also be second-degree effects, in which a candidate persuades a legislator to not only support her but lobby on her behalf with other friends or those with whom he has professional connections. This was more common in the past, when a larger number of state delegations

took the lead of their most senior member and some candidates targeted those "deans" of delegations in the hope that their connections would, in turn, yield votes (as happened in the 1965 race for Republican leader; see chapter 5).

16. For instance, Jim O'Hara (D-MI) claimed he got "a few" votes from "close personal friends *mainly from Michigan*" (Peabody 1976, 228, emphasis added).

17. See also Office Memo, "Leadership Wrap-Up," January 21, 1971, Box 78, Folder 17: Majority Leader's Race (1), MKU.

18. Interview with former Democratic leader, May 18, 2016.

19. Interview with Republican aide, June 3, 2016.

20. Interview with Republican aide, May 2, 2016.

21. In this respect, leadership elections might resemble elections for local public office, in which voters tend to be concerned primarily not with party or ideology but with "managerial competence" (Oliver 2012; see also Sides et al. 2012, ch. 10).

22. Interview with former Democratic leader, May 18, 2016; emphasis added.

23. Barber Conable Jr. to Guy Vander Jagt, November 12, 1980, Box 149, Folder: Leadership Races (97th Congress), 1981, GVJ.

24. Interview with House Republican aide, June 3, 2016.

25. Polsby (1962 [1992], 281–83) and Peabody (1976, 166) argued that outsider strategies do not work because vote commitments cannot be enforced, but as we note in chapter 1, nearly all lawmakers consider their commitments to be sacrosanct, even on a secret ballot.

26. Of the four multiround balloting elections we examine, the average R^2 statistic drops by 0.12 when comparing regression models of the first round of voting versus the second or third round.

27. Interview with Democratic member of Congress, July 8, 2016.

28. "House Head Count," Box 78, Folder 3: House Leadership Campaign Files, 1968–71, MKU.

29. Letter to Newt Gingrich from Mickey Edwards, April 2, 1987, Box 1077, Folder: Correspondence—Mickey Edwards, NLG.

30. Letter to Dan Rostenkowski from Jim Wright, November 15, 1976, DDR.

31. One of the only confirmed examples we could find was Dick Cheney, who said he voted for Bob Michel as leader in 1980 in part because "I thought he would win the Leader's job" (Cheney 2011, 134).

32. For a longer-term perspective on changes in the number of party leaders, see Nelson 1977.
33. Interview with former Republican leader, March 22, 2016.
34. Interview with former Republican member of Congress, March 22, 2016.
35. Interview with House Republican aide, June 3, 2016.
36. Ibid.

Appendix

1. Interview with House Republican leadership aide, June 3, 2016.
2. Ibid.
3. Interview with Republican leadership aide, May 2, 2016.
4. Interview with former Democratic leadership aide, May 4, 2016. See also Bonior 2018, 319.
5. A similar process is used in other countries' elections as well; see e.g. D. Farrell 2001.

BIBLIOGRAPHY

Albert, A., and J. A. Anderson. 1984. "On the Existence of Maximum Likelihood Estimates in Logistic Regression Models." *Biometrika* 71 (1): 1–10.

Aldrich, John H. 1995. *Why Parties? The Origin and Transformation of Political Parties in America.* Chicago: University of Chicago Press.

Anderson, Jack. 1970. "Money for Indian Children Diverted." *Washington Post*, December 19.

Arieff, Irwin B. 1980a. "Hill Democrats, Republicans Organize for 97th Congress." *Congressional Quarterly Weekly Report*, November 29, 3431–33.

———. 1980b. "House Democrats, GOP Elect Leaders, Draw Battle Lines." *Congressional Quarterly Weekly Report*, December 13, 3549.

Averill, John H. 1964a. "Early Parley Fight Won by GOP 'Young Turks.'" *Los Angeles Times*, December 3.

———. 1964b. "Halleck Fends Off Ouster as House Minority Leader." *Los Angeles Times*, December 17.

———. 1964c. "Rep. Halleck Haunted by Old Tactics in Leadership Fight." *Los Angeles Times*, December 20.

———. 1964d. "Halleck-Ford GOP House Duel Forced." *Los Angeles Times*, December 20.

Bachrach, Judy, and Donnie Radcliffe. 1976. "A Speaker's Celebration." *Washington Post*, December 7.

Bailey, Michael A. 2016. *Real Stats: Using Econometrics for Political Science and Public Policy.* New York: Oxford University Press.

Baker, Peter. 2000. *The Breach: Inside the Impeachment and Trial of William Jefferson Clinton.* New York: Scribner.

Baker, Ross K. 1989. *The New Fat Cats: Members of Congress as Political Benefactors.* New York: Priority Press.

Barber, James David. 1965. *The Lawmakers: Recruitment and Adaptation to Legislative Life.* New Haven: Yale University Press.

Barnett, Timothy. 1999. *Legislative Learning: The 104th Republican Freshmen in the House.* New York: Routledge.

Baron, Alan. 1976. "The Baron Report." November 30.

Barry, John M. 1989. *The Ambition and the Power.* New York: Penguin Books.

Becker, Lawrence. 2005. *Doing the Right Thing: Collective Action and Procedural Choice in the New Legislative Process*. Columbus: Ohio State University Press.

Beckler, John. 1970. "Udall, O'Hara Forces Map Leadership Fight." *Washington Post*, December 25.

Bibby, John, and Roger H. Davidson. 1967. *On Capitol Hill: Studies in the Legislative Process*. New York: Holt, Rinehart, and Winston.

Billings, Erin P. 2005. "Vice Chair Money Race Heats Up." *Roll Call*, October 17.

Blake, Aaron. 2015. "John Boehner Just Endured the Biggest Revolt against a House Speaker in More Than 150 Years." *Washington Post*, January 6.

Bolling, Richard. 1965a. *House Out of Order*. New York: E. P. Dutton.

———. 1965b. "Defeating the Leadership's Nominee in the House Democratic Caucus." *Inter-University Case Program*, no. 91. Indianapolis, IN: Bobbs-Merrill.

Bolton, Alexander. 2006. "Bass, Flake Press the 3 Candidates." *The Hill*, January 18.

Bonior, David E. 2018. *Whip: Leading the Progressive Battle during the Rise of the Right*. Westport, CT: City Point Press.

Bradshaw, Joel. 1995. "Who Will Vote for You and Why: Designing Strategy and Theme." In *Campaigns and Elections American Style*, 1st ed., ed. James A. Thurber and Candice J. Nelson, 30–46. Boulder, CO: Westview Press.

Brady, Henry E. Richard Johnston, and John Sides. 2006. "The Study of Political Campaigns." In *Capturing Campaign Effects*, ed. Henry E. Brady and Richard Johnston, 1–26. Ann Arbor: University of Michigan Press.

Bresnahan, John, and Jim VandeHei. 1998. "Democratic Leadership Race Heats Up." *Roll Call*, August 10.

Bresnahan, John, and Jennifer Yachnin. 2006. "Leader Race Heats Up." *Roll Call*, November 15.

Brown, Lynne P., and Robert L. Peabody. 1992. "Patterns of Succession in House Democratic Leadership: Foley, Gephardt, and Gray." In *New Perspectives on the House of Representatives*. 4th ed., ed. Robert L. Peabody and Nelson W. Polsby, 319–72. Baltimore: Johns Hopkins University Press.

Bullock, Charles S. III. 1971. "The Influence of State Party Delegations on House Committee Assignments." *Midwest Journal of Political Science* 15 (3): 525–46.

Burger, Timothy J. 1993a. "How Many Texans Are Too Many Texans in the Top Ranks of House Republicans?" *Roll Call*, September 27.

————. 1993b. "Gingrich Forces Declare Victory in Leader Race as All Eyes Turn to Hot Whip Battle." *Roll Call*, October 11.

————. 1994a. "Kolbe Joins GOP Leadership Sweepstakes, Challenges Hunter for Research Panel Chair." *Roll Call*, August 1.

————. 1994b. "In House GOP Whip Race, All Three Call in Outside Reinforcements to Woo Candidates." *Roll Call*, August 18.

————. 1994c. "In House GOP Whip Race, Vote Counts Don't Add Up." *Roll Call*, October 10.

————. 1994d. "On Road in Sooner State with Rep. Tom DeLay." *Roll Call*, October 24.

————. 1994e. "With GOP Whip Race Looming, California's Committee on Committees Slot Up for Grabs." *Roll Call*, November 3.

————. 1994f. "DeLay Claims Victory in GOP Whip Contest." *Roll Call*, December 1.

————. 1994g. "Leadership Slate Final." *Roll Call*, December 8.

Burger, Timothy J., and Mary Jacoby. 1994. "Leadership Showdowns This Week as Capitol Greets Two Congresses." *Roll Call*, November 28.

Calmes, Jacqueline. 1986. "Coelho Harvests the Fruits of His Labors In Vineyard of House Democratic Politics." *Congressional Quarterly Weekly Report*, December 13.

Camia, Catalina. 1994a. "Some Republican Contests May Hinge on Freshmen." *Congressional Quarterly Weekly Report*, November 11, p. 3329.

————. 1994b. "Detour Didn't Derail DeLay." *CQ Weekly*, December 10, p. 3491.

Cann, Damon M. 2008. *Sharing the Wealth: Member Contributions and the Exchange Theory of Party Influence in the U.S. House of Representatives*. Albany: State University of New York Press.

Cannon, James. 1998. "Gerald R. Ford: Minority Leader." From *Masters of the House: Congressional Leadership over Two Centuries*, ed. Roger H. Davidson, Susan Webb Hammond, and Raymond W. Smock, 259–88. Boulder, CO: Westview Press.

Cannon, Lou. 1980. "Convention 1980, the Republicans in Detroit." *Washington Post*, July 12.

Carney, Dan. 1998. "Impeachment: Seeking Closure?" *CQ Weekly*, November 7, p. 2986.

Carr, Rebecca. 2000. "Lewis Steps Up Majority Whip Campaign." *Atlanta Journal Constitution*, February 13.

Carsey, Thomas M. 2000. *Campaign Dynamics: The Race for Governor*. Ann Arbor: University of Michigan Press.

Carson, Donald W., and James W. Johnson. 2001. *Mo: The Life and Times of Morris K. Udall.* Tucson: University of Arizona Press.

Cassidy, J. P. 2001a. "Pelosi Wins More Support in Race with Hoyer for Democratic Whip." *The Hill*, August 1.

———. 2001b. "Bonior Supports Pelosi as Dem Whip Race Enters Homestretch." *The Hill*, October 3.

———. 2002. "Gephardt's Succession Struggle Shaping Up as a Vicious Contest." *The Hill*, March 6.

Casteel, Chris. 1998. "Largent, Watts Say Backers Increasing." *NewsOK*, November 11. Available at: http://newsok.com/article/2632850 (accessed August 5, 2015).

Caygle, Heather. 2016. "House Dems Court Votes in Leadership Battle." *Politico*, October 3.

Caygle, Heather, and Kyle Cheney. 2016. "Pelosi Beats Back Democratic Dissent." *Politico*, November 16.

"Censure of Rep. Diggs." 1980. In *Congressional Quarterly Almanac 1979*, 35th ed., 561–66. Washington, DC: Congressional Quarterly.

Champagne, Anthony, et al. 2009. *The Austin/Boston Connection: Five Decades of House Democratic Leadership, 1937–1989.* College Station: Texas A&M Press.

Chapman, William. 1982. "Bolling, near Retirement, Muses about a Battle That Never Was." *Washington Post*, August 24.

Cheney, Dick, with Liz Cheney. 2011. *In My Time: A Personal and Political Memoir.* New York: Threshold Editions.

Cheng, Simon, and J. Scott Long. 2007. "Testing for IIA in the Multinomial Logit Model." *Sociological Methods and Research* 35 (4), 583–600.

Chicago Tribune. 1964. "Goodell Raps Halleck for 'Lack of Zest.'" December 28.

Cicero, Quintus Tullius. 64 B.C. [2012]. *How to Win an Election: An Ancient Guide for Modern Politicians.* Trans. Philip Freeman. Princeton, NJ: Princeton University Press.

Cillizza, Chris. 2006. "Backing Dark Horse Boehner May Mean Big Payoff for a Few." *Washington Post*, February 5.

Clancy, Paul, and Shirley Elder. 1980. *Tip: The Biography of Thomas P. O'Neill, Speaker of the House.* New York: Macmillan.

Clapp, Charles L. 1963. *The Congressman: His Work as He Sees It.* Washington, DC: Brookings Institution.

Clift, Eleanor, and Tom Brazaitis. 1996. *War without Bloodshed: The Art of Politics.* New York: Scribner.

Clines, Francis X. 1998. "Armey Defends Post on Left and Right." *New York Times*, November 13.

Clymer, Adam. 2001. "Two Competing for Post of Democratic Whip in the House." *New York Times*, October 10.

Cohen, Richard E. 1999. *Rostenkowski: The Pursuit of Power and the End of the Old Politics*. Chicago: Ivan R. Dee.

———. 2001. "The Race for No. 2." *National Journal*, September 22.

Congressional Quarterly Weekly Report. 1978. "Anderson Re-elected to GOP Leadership Post." December 9, p. 3405.

———. 1979. "Rhodes to Leave Minority Post." December 15, p. 2866.

Connelly, William F. Jr., and John J. Pitney Jr. 1994. *Congress' Permanent Minority? Republicans in the U.S. House*. Lanham, MD: Rowman & Littlefield.

Contra Costa Times. 2000. "Update." July 28.

Cooper, Kenneth J. 1994. "GOP Formally Names Gingrich Speaker." *Washington Post*, December 6.

Costa, Robert, and Mike DeBonis. 2015. "Ryan Declares Official Candidacy for House Speaker." *Washington Post*, October 23.

Cottle, Michelle. 2016. "Pelosi Remains Leader, but the Democrats Are Restless." *The Atlantic*, December 1.

Cox, Gary W., and Mathew D. McCubbins. 1993. *Legislative Leviathan*. Berkeley: University of California Press.

———. 2005. *Setting the Agenda: Responsible Party Government in the U.S. House of Representatives*. New York: Cambridge University Press.

Crowther, Rodney. 1965. "Halleck Out; Ford Named GOP Leader." *Baltimore Sun*, January 5.

Currinder, Marian. 2003. "Leadership PAC Contribution Strategies and House Member Ambitions." *Legislative Studies Quarterly* 28 (4): 551–77.

———. 2009. *Money in the House: Campaign Funds and Congressional Party Politics*. Boulder, CO: Westview Press.

Curry, James M. 2015. *Legislating in the Dark: Information and Power in the House of Representatives*. Chicago: University of Chicago Press.

Davidson, Roger H. 1988. "The New Centralization on Capitol Hill." *Review of Politics* 50 (3), 345–364.

DeLay, Tom, with Stephen Mansfield. 2007. *No Retreat, No Surrender: One American's Fight*. New York: Sentinel.

Dinan, Stephen. 2006. "Boehner Wins the Majority." *Washington Times*, February 3.

Donovan, Beth. 1993. "Eyeing the Leadership Shuffle." *Congressional Quarterly Weekly Report*, October 9, p. 2715.

Donovan, Robert J. 1964. "Joe Martin Will Help Ford to Oust His Old Foe, Halleck." *Boston Globe*, December 19.

Dorment, Richard. 2014. "How to Fix Congress Now." *Esquire*, October 15.

Dow, Jay K., and James W. Endersby. 2004. "Multinomial Probit and Multinomial Logit: A Comparison of Choice Models for Voting Research." *Electoral Studies* 23, 107–22.

Drew, Elizabeth. 2007. "Democrats: The Big Surprise." *New York Review of Books*, January 11.

Dubose, Lou, and Jan Reid. 2004. *The Hammer: Tom Delay, God, Money, and the Rise of the Republican Congress*. New York: PublicAffairs.

Eaton, William J. 1989. "Gephardt, Gray Win Party Posts." *Los Angeles Times*, June 15.

Edwards, Willard. 1964. "House G.O.P. Meets and Harmony Rules." *Chicago Tribune*, December 17.

Eilperin, Juliet. 1998a. "Desire for New Face Puts Armey at Risk; GOP Members Want Telegenic Figure, Unifier." *Washington Post*, November 11.

———. 1998b. "Hastert May Be Drafted for House GOP Contest." *Washington Post*, November 15.

———. 2001a. "Bonior to Leave House, Run for Governor of Michigan." *Washington Post*, May 22.

———. 2001b. "House Whip Race Seen as Indicator of Democrats' Future." *Washington Post*, September 8.

———. 2001c. "Democratic Whip Hopefuls Rustle Up Votes." *Washington Post*, October 8.

———. 2001d. "Democrats Pick Pelosi as House Whip." *Washington Post*, October 11.

———. 2002. "The Making of Madam Whip." *Washington Post Magazine*, January 6, p. W27.

Elving, Ronald. 1997. "Molinari to Trade Congress for Career in Television." *Congressional Quarterly Weekly Report*, May 31, p. 1273.

Espo, David. 1998. "Livingston Takes Command of House Speaker's Race." *Associated Press*, November 9.

Evans, C. Lawrence, and C. Grandy. 2009. "The Whip Systems of Congress." In *Congress Reconsidered*, 9th ed., ed. L. Dodd and B. Oppenheimer, 189–216. Washington, DC: Congressional Quarterly Press.

Evans, Rowland, and Robert Novak. 1964a. "'Wednesday Group' May Turn to Action." *Los Angeles Times*, August 20.

———. 1964b. "Halleck Stays, but . . ." *Washington Post*, November 10.

———. 1964c. "The December Caucus." *Washington Post*, November 30.

———. 1967. "Move Grows in Democratic Party to Ditch McCormack as Speaker." *Washington Post*, November 13, A17.

———. 1970a. "McCormack Aims to Thwart Liberals By Supporting Boggs, Rostenkowski." *Washington Post*, July 20.

———. 1970b. "Nixon's Secret Adventure." *Washington Post*, November 29.

———. 1970c. "Cold Shoulder to Reagan." *Washington Post*, December 27.

Eversley, Melania. 2000. "John Lewis Drops House Whip Bid; Says He Would Fill Seat if Asked." *Atlanta Journal Constitution*, July 20.

Fagan, Amy. 2006. "Unlikely GOP Allies Back Shadegg." *Washington Times*, January 25.

Farrell, David M. 2001. *Electoral Systems: A Comparative Introduction*. New York: Palgrave.

Farrell, John A. 2001. *Tip O'Neill and the Democratic Century*. Boston: Little, Brown.

Faucheux, Ronald A. 2003. "Writing Your Campaign Plan." In *Winning Elections: Political Campaign Management, Strategy & Tactics*, ed. Ronald A. Faucheaux, 66–78. New York: M. Evans.

Fenno, Richard F. Jr. 1963. "The Appropriations Committee as a Political System." In *New Perspectives on the House of Representatives*, ed. Robert L. Peabody and Nelson W. Polsby, 79–108. Chicago: Rand McNally.

———. 1973. *Congressmen in Committees*. Boston: Little, Brown.

Ferrechio, Susan. 2002. "House Democrats Begin 'Anew.'" *CQ Weekly*, November 9, p. 2932.

Fiellin, Alan. 1963. "The Functions of Informal Groups: A State Delegation." In *New Perspectives on the House of Representatives*, ed. Robert L. Peabody and Nelson W. Polsby, 59–78. Chicago: Rand McNally.

Finkel, Steven E. 1993. "Reexamining the 'Minimal Effects' Model in Recent Presidential Campaigns." *Journal of Politics* 55 (1): 1–21.

Firth, David. 1993. "Bias Reduction of Maximum Likelihood Estimates." *Biometrika* 80 (1): 27–38.

Flippen, J. Brooks. 2018. *Speaker Jim Wright: Power, Scandal, and the Birth of Modern Politics*. Austin: University of Texas Press.

Foerstel, Karen. 1998. "GOP Freshmen Say Unity, Balance Matter Most in Picking Leaders." *CQ Weekly*, November 14, p. 3059.

———. 2000. "House: The Limits of Outreach." *CQ Weekly*, November 11, p. 2649.

———. 2001. "Democrats Already at Work Trying to Put House in Order." *CQ Weekly*, July 7.

Ford, Gerald R. 1979. *A Time to Heal: The Autobiography of Gerald R. Ford.* New York: Harper & Row.

Fowler, James H. 2006. "Connecting the Congress: A Study of Cosponsorship Networks." *Political Analysis* 14 (4): 456–87.

Fowler, Linda L., and Robert D. McClure. 1989. *Political Ambition: Who Decides to Run for Congress.* New Haven: Yale University Press.

Fram, Alan. 1998a. "Their Campaigns Over, Freshmen Enter House Maelstrom." *Associated Press*, November 13.

———. 1998b. "GOP Picks Livingston, Armey, Watts." *Associated Press*, November 18.

Franklin, Charles H. 1991. "Eschewing Obfuscation? Campaigns and the Perception of U.S. Senate Incumbents." *American Political Science Review* 85 (4): 1193–1214.

Freeburg, Russell. 1964. "Ford Seeks to Grab Job of Halleck." *Chicago Tribune*, December 20.

Frey, Lou Jr., and Aubrey Jewett, eds. 2009. *Political Rules of the Road: Representatives, Senators, and Presidents Share Their Rules for Success in Congress, Politics, and Life.* Lanham, MD: University Press of America.

Fuller, Jaime. 2014. "Elizabeth Warren and the Long History of Conveniently Invented Leadership Titles." *Washington Post*, November 13.

Fuller, Matt. 2014. "McCarthy Works Back Channels, While Labrador Tries Talk Radio in Majority Leader Race." *Roll Call*, June 16.

Gaddie, Ronald Keith. 2004. *Born to Run: Origins of the Political Career.* Lanham, MD: Rowman and Littlefield.

Gaddie, Ronald Keith, and Charles S. Bullock III. 2000. *Elections to Open Seats in the U.S. House.* Lanham, MD: Rowman & Littlefield.

Garrett, Major. 2005. *The Enduring Revolution: How the Contract with America Continues to Shape the Nation.* New York: Crown Publishing.

Garsson, Robert M. 1994. "Anti-Interstate Lobbyist Joins an Intraparty Battle." *American Banker*, November 29.

Gehrke, Joel. 2015. "Flawed Candidates Keep Majority Leader's Race Close." *National Review*, October 2.

Gimpel, James G. 1996. *Legislating the Revolution: The Contract with America in Its First 100 Days.* Boston: Allyn & Bacon.

Goldstein, Steve. 1994. "With Posts Secured, Legislators Vote for Power." *Philadelphia Inquirer*, December 4.

Graham, Fred P. 1970. "Ground Rules Bar a Dark Horse From House Leadership Race." *New York Times*, December 26.

Granat, Diane. 1984. "Obey Withdraws from Race for House Democrats' Post." *Congressional Quarterly Weekly Report*, May 26, p. 1265.

Green, Matthew N. 2006. "McCormack versus Udall: Explaining Intraparty Challenges to the Speaker of the House." *American Politics Research* 34 (1): 3–21.

———. 2008. "The 2006 Race for Democratic Majority Leader: Money, Policy, and Personal Loyalty." *PS: Political Science & Politics* 41 (1): 63–67.

———. 2010. *The Speaker of the House: A Study of Leadership*. New Haven: Yale University Press.

———. 2015. *Underdog Politics: The Minority Party in the U.S. House of Representatives*. New Haven: Yale University Press.

———. 2016. "The Multiple Roots of Party Loyalty: Explaining Republican Dissent in the U.S. House of Representatives." *Congress and the Presidency* 43 (1): 103–23.

Green, Matthew N., and Briana Bee. 2016. "Keeping the Team Together: Explaining Party Discipline and Dissent in the U.S. Congress." In *Party and Procedure in the United States Congress*, ed. Jacob Straus and Matt Glassman, 41–62. Lanham, MD: Rowman & Littlefield.

Green, Matthew N., and Douglas B. Harris. 2007. "Goal Salience and the 2006 Race for House Majority Leader." *Political Research Quarterly* 60 (4): 618–30.

———. 2015a. "Explaining Vote Choice in the 1976 Race for House Majority Leader." Presented at the Annual Meeting of the Midwest Political Science Association, Chicago, April 16–19.

———. 2015b. "Explaining Vote Choice in the 1965 Race for House Minority Leader." Presented at the Annual Meeting of the American Political Science Association, San Francisco, September 3–6.

———. 2016. "Explaining Vote Choice in the 1994 Race for House Majority Whip." Paper delivered at the Annual Meeting of the Midwest Political Science Association, Chicago, April 7–10.

Greenfield, Meg. 2002. *Washington*. New York: PublicAffairs.

Grofman, Bernard, William Koetzle, and Anthony J. McGann. 2002. "Congressional Leadership, 1965–1996: A New Look at the Extremism versus Centrality Debate." *Legislative Studies Quarterly* 27 (1): 87–105.

Grynaviski, Jeffrey D. 2010. *Partisan Bonds: Political Reputations and Legislative Accountability*. New York: Cambridge University Press.

Gugliotta, Guy, and Juliet Eilperin. 1998a. "Gingrich Steps Down in Face of Rebellion." *Washington Post*, November 7.

————. 1998b. "Livingston Appears to Seal Election as House Speaker; Republicans Turn Attention to Race for Majority Leader." *Washington Post*, November 10.

Hallow, Ralph Z. 1998. "Largent Targets Centrist Votes, Predicts Victory in House Race." *Washington Times*, November 12.

Hanmer, Michael J., and Kerem Ozan Kalkan. 2013. "Behind the Curve: Clarifying the Best Approach to Calculating Predicted Probabilities and Marginal Effects from Limited Dependent Variable Models." *American Journal of Political Science* 57 (1): 263–77.

Harris, Douglas B. 1998. "The Rise of the Public Speakership." *Political Science Quarterly* 113 (2): 193–212.

————. 2006. "Legislative Parties and Leadership Choice: Confrontation or Accommodation in the 1989 Gingrich-Madigan Whip Race." *American Politics Research* 34 (2): 189–222.

————. 2010. "Partisan Framing in Legislative Debates." In *Winning with Words: The Origins and Impact of Framing*, ed. Brian F. Schaffner and Patrick J. Sellers, 41–59. New York: Routledge.

————. 2013. "Let's Play Hardball: Congressional Partisanship in the Television Era." In *Politics to the Extreme: American Political Institutions in the Twenty-First Century*, ed. Scott A. Frisch and Sean Q. Kelly, 93–115. New York: Palgrave MacMillan, 2013.

————. 2014. "Sack the Quarterback: The Strategies and Implications of Congressional Leadership Scandals." In *Scandal! An Interdisciplinary Approach to the Consequences, Outcomes, and Significance of Political Scandals*, ed. Alison Dagnes and Mark Sachleben, 29–50. New York: Bloomsbury.

Harris, Douglas B., and Matthew N. Green. 2015. "Intra-Party Competition for Leadership Posts in the House of Representatives." Presented at the Annual Meeting of the New England Political Science Association, New Haven, CT, April 24–25.

————. 2017. "Selecting the Senate Leader: George Mitchell's Campaign for and Election as Senate Majority Leader." Presented at the Annual Meeting of the New England Political Science Association, Providence, RI, April 20–22.

Harris, Douglas B., and Garrison Nelson. 2008. "Middlemen No More?

Emergent Patterns in Congressional Leadership Selection." *P.S.: Political Science & Politics* 41 (1): 49–55.

Hastert, J. Dennis. 2004. *Speaker: Lessons from Forty Years in Coaching and Politics.* Washington, DC: Regnery.

Hearn, Josephine. 2006a. "Pelosi Pulls Out the Stops for Murtha." *The Hill,* November 16.

———. 2006b. "Dem Division and Dismay." *The Hill,* November 16.

———. 2006c. "Hoyer Targets Liberals after Pelosi's Blow." *The Hill,* November 14.

Hearn, Josephine, and Jonathan Allen. 2006. "Murtha Launches Bid for Majority Leader." *The Hill,* November 30.

Heberlig, Eric S., and Bruce A. Larson. 2012. *Congressional Parties, Institutional Ambition, and the Financing of Majority Control.* Ann Arbor: University of Michigan Press.

Herald Tribune. 1964. "Laird Seeks to Head House GOP Conference." December 30.

Herrnson, Paul S. 2012. *Congressional Elections: Campaigning at Home and in Washington.* 6th ed. Washington, DC: CQ Press.

Herszenhorn, David M., and Emmarie Huetteman. 2015. "Caucus Clears Path for Ryan to Be Speaker." *New York Times,* October 22.

The Hill. 2000. Interview with Rep. Nancy Pelosi. August 16.

Hinckley, Barbara. 1970. "Congressional Leadership Selection and Support: A Comparative Analysis." *Journal of Politics* 32 (2): 268–87.

Hohmann, James. 2016. "How Tim Ryan Decided to Challenge His Mentor, Nancy Pelosi, for Democratic Leader." *Washington Post,* November 21.

Hook, Janet. 1989a. "Battle for Whip Pits Partisans against Party Pragmatists." *Congressional Quarterly Weekly Report,* March 18, pp. 563–65.

———. 1989b. "Gingrich's Selection as Whip Reflects GOP Discontent." *Congressional Quarterly Weekly Report,* March 25.

———. 1989c. "Leadership Jockeying Starts as Party Shake-Up Nears." *Congressional Quarterly Weekly Report,* May 27, p. 1230.

———. 1993. "House GOP Hones a Sharper Edge as Michel Turns in His Sword." *Congressional Quarterly Weekly Report,* October 9, p. 2717.

Hook, Janet, and Pat Towell. 1986. "Other Shifts Follow Addabbo's Death: Rep. Chappell in Line to Chair Defense Appropriations Panel." *Congressional Quarterly Weekly Report,* May 3, p. 973.

Hornblower, Margot. 1980. "Reps. Michel and Vander Jagt Battling Fiercely to Lead House GOP." *Washington Post,* December 8, p. A2.

Hosler, Karen. 2001. "California's Pelosi Chosen as House Democratic Whip." *Baltimore Sun*, October 11.

Hulse, Carl. 2006. "In Election, a Fight to Lead the G.O.P. in a Crucial Year." *New York Times*, January 30.

Hunter, Marjorie. 1970a. "McCormack Says He Will Not Seek New House Term." *New York Times*, May 21.

————. 1970b. "7 House Democrats Begin Jockeying for Election as Floor Leader." *New York Times*, May 30.

————. 1970c. "House Elections Hold the Key To Democratic Leader Line-Up." *New York Times*, September 20.

————. 1970d. "House Democrats Vie for Top Post." *New York Times*, November 22.

————. 1971a. "House Democrats to Pick Leader." *New York Times*, January 18.

————. 1971b. "Democrats Name Albert and Boggs to Top House Jobs." *New York Times*, January 20.

Irish, Ann B. 2001. *Joseph W. Byrns of Tennessee: A Political Biography*. Knoxville: University of Tennessee Press.

Jackson, Brooks. 1986. "Passion for Detail and Drive to Win Enabled Coelho to Become Next House Majority Whip." *Wall Street Journal*, December 9.

Jacobs, John. 1995. *A Rage for Justice: The Passion and Politics of Phillip Burton*. Berkeley: University of California Press.

Jacobson, Gary C. 2015. "How Do Campaigns Matter?" *Annual Review of Political Science* 18, 31–47.

Jacobson, Gary C., and Samuel Kernell. 1983. *Strategy and Choice in Congressional Elections*. New Haven: Yale University Press.

Jacoby, Mary. 1998. "House GOP Must Pick an Identity." *St. Petersburg Times*, November 12.

Javers, Eamon. 1998. "Hazing the Freshmen; Armey, Largent and Dunn Are on the Phone." *The Hill*, November 18.

Jenkins, Jeffery A., and Charles Stewart III. 2013. *Fighting for the Speakership: The House and the Rise of Party Government*. Princeton, NJ: Princeton University Press.

Jessee, Stephen, and Neil Malhotra. 2010. "Are Congressional Leaders Middlepersons or Extremists? Yes." *Legislative Studies Quarterly* 35 (3): 361–92.

Kabaservice, Geoffrey. 2012. *Rule and Ruin: The Downfall of Moderation and *the Destruction of the Republican Party, From Eisenhower to the Tea Party.* New York: Oxford University Press.

Kane, Paul, and Ed O'Keefe. 2016. "Nancy Pelosi Chosen Again as House Democratic Leader—but Tally Suggests Deep Division." *Washington Post,* November 30.

Kantin, Kerry. 2002. "LaHood Drops Out of GOP Whip Race." *The Hill,* March 3.

Katz, Jeffrey. 1998. "Election '98: Shakeup in the House." *CQ Weekly,* November 7, p. 2989.

Katz, Jeffrey L., and Carroll J. Doherty. 1998. "Leadership Candidates." *CQ Weekly,* November 14, p. 3061.

Kazee, Thomas. 1994. *Who Runs for Congress? Ambition, Context, and Candidate Emergence.* Washington, DC: CQ Press.

Kelly, Sean Q. n.d. "A Generation of Change: Selecting the Senate Democratic Leader in the 104th Congress." Manuscript hard copy, Department of Political Science, California State University, Channel Islands.

Kenworthy, Tom. 1989a. "Wright's Book Was Different, Gingrich Says." *Washington Post,* March 21.

———. 1989b. "Gephardt Pushed for Majority Leader." *Washington Post,* May 26.

———. 1989c. "Gephardt Won't Compete with Coelho." *Washington Post,* May 27.

Kenworthy, Tom, and Don Phillips. 1989. "Intrigue in the House: Leadership Choices Loom." *Washington Post,* March 20.

Kiewiet, D. Roderick, and Mathew D. McCubbins. 1991. *The Logic of Delegation: Congressional Parties and the Appropriations Process.* Chicago: University of Chicago Press.

King, Larry L. 1971. "The Road to Power in Congress." *Harper's Magazine,* June.

———. 1980. *Of Outlaws, Con Men, Whores, Politicians, and Other Artists.* New York: The Viking Press.

———. 1999. *Larry L. King: A Writer's Life in Letters.* Fort Worth: TCU Press.

Kirn, Dorothy Nelson. 1980. "Hale Boggs: A Southern Spokesman for the Democratic Party." Ph.D diss., Department of Speech, Louisiana State University.

Kolodny, Robin. 1998. *Pursuing Majorities: Congressional Campaign Committees in American Politics.* Norman: University of Oklahoma Press.

Koopman, Douglas L. 1996. *Hostile Takeover: The House Republican Party, 1980–1995*. Rowman & Littlefield.

Kornacki, Steve. 2006. "Murtha Halts Bid for Leader." *Roll Call*, June 14, p. 1.

Koszczuk, Jackie. 1997. "Frustration Sparks Rebellion, Discontent Fuels Smoldering Fire." *Congressional Quarterly Weekly Report*, July 26.

Kraft, Joseph. 1971. "Larger Caucus Role." *Washington Post*, January 21.

Kumpa, Peter J. 1964. "Many in GOP Seen Set to Oust Halleck." *Baltimore Sun*, November 12.

Laitin, David D. 1994. "The Tower of Babel as a Coordination Game: Political Linguistics in Ghana." *American Political Science Review* 88 (3): 622–34.

Lawless, Jennifer. 2012. *Becoming a Candidate: Political Ambition and the Decision to Run for Office*. New York: Cambridge University Press.

Lawrence, John. 2016. "Why Pelosi Won, and What It Means." *DOMEocracy blog*, December 2, https://johnalawrence.wordpress.com/2016/12/02/why-pelosi-won-and-what-it-means (accessed June 21, 2017).

Leamer, Laurence. 1977. *Playing for Keeps: in Washington*. New York: Dial Press.

Lee, Frances E. 2009. *Beyond Ideology: Politics, Principles and Partisanship in the U.S. Senate*. Chicago: University of Chicago Press.

———. 2016. *Insecure Majorities: Congress and the Perpetual Campaign*. Chicago: University of Chicago Press.

Lee, Frances E., and Bruce I. Oppenheimer. 1999. *Sizing Up the Senate: The Unequal Consequences of Equal Representation*. Chicago: University of Chicago Press.

Lillis, Mike. 2016. "Tim Ryan to Challenge Pelosi for House Dem Leader." *The Hill*, November 17.

Lippmann, Walter. 1922. *Public Opinion*. New York: Harcourt Brace.

Loomis, Burdett. 1984. "Congressional Careers and Party Leadership in the Contemporary House of Representatives." *American Journal of Political Science* 28 (1): 180–202.

Lott, Trent. 2005. *Herding Cats: A Life in Politics*. New York: HarperCollins.

Lyons, Richard L. 1963. "68 in GOP Hit Halleck Rights Role." *Washington Post*, November 1.

———. 1976. "Soothing Bridge-Builder." *Washington Post*, December 7.

Mackaman, Frank. Forthcoming. "Robert H. Michel Biography: Preparing for Public Service." In *Leading the Republican House Minority: The Congressional Career of Robert H. Michel*, ed. Frank Mackaman and Sean Q. Kelly.

Mackay, Robert. 1980. "Michel, 58, Eyes GOP Minority Leader Post with Air of Confidence." *Peoria Journal Star,* March 3.

Maestas, Cherie, et al. 2006. "When to Risk It? Institutions, Ambitions, and the Decision to Run for the U.S. House." *American Political Science Review* 100 (2): 195–208.

Maisel, L. Sandy, and Walter J. Stone. 1997. "Determinants of Candidate Emergence in U.S. House Elections" *Legislative Studies Quarterly* 22 (1): 79–96.

Malecha, Gary, and Daniel J. Reagan. 2011. *The Public Congress.* New York: Routledge.

Maney, Patrick J. 1998. "Hale Boggs: The Southerner as National Democrat." In *Masters of the House: Congressional Leadership over Two Centuries,* ed. Roger H. Davidson, Susan Webb Hammond, and Raymond W. Smock, 223–58. Boulder, CO: Westview Press.

Martin, Joseph (as told to Robert J. Donovan). 1960. *My First Fifty Years in Politics.* New York: McGraw-Hill.

Mayhew, David R. 1974. *Congress: The Electoral Connection.* New Haven: Yale University Press.

———. 2000. *America's Congress: Actions in the Public Sphere, James Madison through Newt Gingrich.* New Haven: Yale University Press.

McGrory, Mary. 1969. "Congress Educates a Liberal." *Boston Globe,* 3 January.

———. 1989. "Adding Aye of Newt." *Washington Post,* March 23.

Meinke, Scott. 2016. *Leadership Organizations in the House of Representatives: Party Participation and Partisan Politics.* Ann Arbor: University of Michigan Press.

Menard, Scott. 2010. *Logistic Regression: From Introductory to Advanced Concepts and Applications.* Los Angeles: Sage Publications.

Merida, Kevin. 1998. "The House Speed-Dial Race." *Washington Post,* November 14.

"Michel Announces Retirement." 1994. In *Congressional Quarterly Almanac 1993,* 49th ed., 19–20. Washington, DC: Congressional Quarterly.

Miller, Judith. 1980. "2 Conservatives Vie to Lead House G.O.P." *New York Times* July 20, p. 15.

Miller, Norman C. 1970a. "McCormack Retirement Sets Off Battle between Democratic Factions in House." *Wall Street Journal,* May 21.

———. 1970b. "Carl Albert: What Kind of Leader?" *Wall Street Journal,* December 10.

Mintz, Morton. 1976. "The Speaker: Carl A. Albert to Retire." *Washington Post,* June 6.

Montgomery, Lori, and Juliet Eilperin. 2000. "Hoyer Sets Sights on Leadership Position." *Washington Post*, August 17.

National Center for Public Policy Research. 1998. *Scoop*, November 11, www.nationalcenter.org/Scoop205.html (accessed August 5, 2015).

Naughton, James M. 1976. "4 Seeking House Leadership Post Press Claims in the Election Today." *New York Times*, December 6.

Nelson, Garrison. 1977. "Partisan Patterns of House Leadership Change, 1789–1977." *American Political Science Review* 71 (3): 918–39.

———. 2017. *John William McCormack: A Political Biography*. New York: Bloomsbury.

New Republic. 1970. "House Battle." December 5.

———. 1971. "Udall and O'Hara." January 16.

Newhauser, Daniel. 2014. "Would-Be Whips Woo Conservatives, Reassure Moderates." *Roll Call*, June 17.

Newsweek. 1969. "Gamble for the Gavel." January 6, pp. 24–25.

"95th Congress Elected New Leaders." 1978. In *Congressional Quarterly Almanac 1977*, 33rd ed., 3–10. Washington, DC: Congressional Quarterly.

Noel, Hans. 2013. *Political Ideologies and Political Parties in America*. New York: Cambridge University Press.

O'Connor, Patrick. 2006a. "Blunt Takes Initial Lead." *The Hill*, January 11.

———. 2006b. "Candidates Try to Force Second Ballot." *The Hill*, January 25.

———. 2006c. "Boehner Pulls Off Victory on Second Ballot." *The Hill*, February 2.

Obey, David R. 2007. *Raising Hell for Justice: The Washington Battles of a Heartland Progressive*. Madison: University of Wisconsin Press.

Oliver, J. Eric, with Shang E. Ha and Zachary Callen. 2012. *Local Elections and the Politics of Small-Scale Democracy*. Princeton, NJ: Princeton University Press.

O'Neill, Tip, with William Novak. 1987. *Man of the House: The Life and Political Memoirs of Speaker Tip O'Neill*. New York: Random House.

Oppenheimer, Bruce I., and Robert L. Peabody. 1977. "The House Majority Leadership Contest, 1976." Paper prepared for delivery at the 1977 meeting of the American Political Science Association, Washington, DC, September 1–4.

Oreskes, Michael. 1989. "Wright Says He Has Backing of Fellow House Democrats." *New York Times*, March 16.

Ota, Alan K. 1998. "Majority Leader: Steve Largent Seeks Return to Limelight." *CQ Weekly*, November 7, p. 2979.

————, 2006. "The House Leadership Lineup." *CQ Weekly*, November 13, p. 2919.

Panetta, Leon, with Jim Newton. 2014. *Worthy Fights: A Memoir of Leadership in War and Peace*. New York: Penguin Press.

Patterson, Samuel C. 1963. "Legislative Leadership and Political Ideology." *Public Opinion Quarterly* 27 (3): 399–410.

Peabody, Robert L. 1967. "Party Leadership Change in the United States House of Representatives." *American Political Science Review* 61 (3): 675–93.

————. 1976. *Leadership in Congress: Stability, Succession, and Change*. Boston: Little, Brown.

Pearson, Kathryn. 2015. *Party Discipline in the U.S. House of Representatives*. Ann Arbor: University of Michigan Press.

Pellegrini, Pasquale A., and J. Tobin Grant. 1999. "Policy Coalitions in the U.S. Congress: A Spatial Duration Modeling Approach." *Geographical Analysis* 31 (1): January.

Pershing, Ben. 2006a. "House GOP Seeks New Direction." *Roll Call*, January 9.

————. 2006b. "Leader Race Goes to Wire." *Roll Call*, February 2.

————. 2006c. "Winner's Allies Stand to Benefit." *Roll Call*, February 6.

Peters, Ronald M. Jr. 2001. "Southern Party Leaders in the Postreform House." In *Eye of the Storm: The South and Congress in an Era of Change*, ed. John C. Kuzenski, Laurence W. Moreland, and Robert P. Steed, 109–34. Westport, CT: Praeger.

Peters, Ronald M. Jr., and Cindy Simon Rosenthal. 2010. *Speaker Nancy Pelosi and the New American Politics*. New York: Oxford University Press.

Petrocik, John R. 1996. "Issue Ownership in Presidential Elections, with a 1980 Case Study." *American Journal of Political Science* 40 (3): 825–50.

Phillips, Don. 1989a. "Reps. Madigan, Gingrich Vie for GOP Post." *Washington Post*, March 16.

————. 1989b. "Piggyback Entry into House GOP Race." *Washington Post*, March 17.

Phillips, Don, and Tom Kenworthy. 1989. "Gingrich Elected House GOP Whip." *Washington Post*, March 23.

Pianin, Eric. 2000. "Hopeful Democrats Jockey for No. 3 Post." *Washington Post*, April 24.

Polsby, Nelson W. 1962 [1992]. "Two Strategies of Influence: Choosing a Majority Leader, 1962." In *New Perspectives on the House of Representatives*, 4th ed., ed. Robert L. Peabody and Nelson W. Polsby, 260–90. Baltimore: Johns Hopkins University Press.

———. 2004. *How Congress Evolves: Social Bases of Institutional Change*. New York: Oxford University Press.

Poole, Keith T., and Howard Rosenthal. 1997. *Congress: A Political-Economic History of Roll Call Voting*. New York: Oxford University Press.

Posler, Brian D., and Carl M. Rhodes. 1997. "Pre-Leadership Signaling in the U.S. House." *Legislative Studies Quarterly* 22 (3): 351–68.

Powell, Eleanor Neff. 2009. "Partisan Entrepreneurship and Career Advancement in Congress." Ph.D. diss., Department of Government, Harvard University.

Preston, Mark D. 1998. "Gibbons Lobbying against Majority Leader Armey." *Las Vegas Sun*, November 13.

Purdum, Todd S. 2014. *An Idea Whose Time Has Come: Two Presidents, Two Parties, and the Battle for the Civil Rights Act of 1964*. New York: Henry Holt.

Raum, Tom. 1980. "Vander Jagt, Michel Claim Voters for House Minority Leader." Associated Press, December 2.

Reid, Jan. 2014. "Tom DeLay: Power and Hubris." In *Triumphs and Tragedies of the Modern Congress: Case Studies in Legislative Leadership*, ed. Maxmillian Angerholzer III, James Kitfield, Christopher P. Lu, and Norman Ornstein, 60–64. Santa Barbara, CA: Praeger.

Rennert, Leo. 1977. "For Californians, the House Is Not a Home." *California Journal*, January.

Reston, James. 1970. "Washington: Are the Democrats Serious?" *New York Times*, May 22.

Rhodes, John J., with Dean Smith. 1995. *John Rhodes: I Was There*. Salt Lake City: Northwest Publications.

Rice, Andrew. 1999a. "Three House Democrats Vie for Non-Existent Majority Whip Post." *The Hill*, August 11.

———. 1999b. "Whipped." *New Republic*, October 18.

Ripley, Randall B. 1967. *Party Leaders in the House of Representatives*. Washington, DC: Brookings Institution Press.

Robertson, Campbell. 2010. "After Party's Rout, a Blue Dog Won't Back Down." *New York Times*, November 13.

Rodgers, Wilfred C. 1964. "Halleck Faces GOP Revolt." *Boston Globe*, November 6.

Rohde, David W., and Kenneth A. Shepsle. 1987. "Leaders and Followers in the House of Representatives: Reflections on Woodrow Wilson's *Congressional Government*." *Congress and the Presidency* 14: 111–33.

Roll Call. 1999. "Morning Business." October 14.

Rosenthal, Cindy Simon. 2006. "En-gendering Choice in Congressional Leadership Elections." Paper presented at the National Symposium on Women and Politics. Institute for Governmental Studies, University of California, Berkeley, June 9–10.

Rothstein, Betsy. 1999. "Black Caucus Split over Bid by Rep. Lewis." *The Hill*, September 29.

Rumsfeld, Donald. 2011. *Known and Unknown: A Memoir.* New York: Sentinel.

Russell, Mary. 1976a. "The Struggle." *Washington Post*, June 6.

———. 1976b. "It's a Bitter 4-Man Race for House Majority Leader." *Washington Post*, November 22.

———. 1976c. "Rep. Wright Is Elected House Majority Leader." *Washington Post*, December 7, 1976.

———. 1979a. "Today's Vote on GOP Leadership Post Seen as Test of Freshmen's Influence." *Washington Post*, June 20.

———. 1979b. "Rhodes Will Step Down as House GOP Leader After Next Year." *Washington Post*, December 13.

Scheele, Henry Z. 1966. *Charlie Halleck: A Political Biography.* New York: Exposition Press.

Schelling, Thomas. 1978. *Micromotives and Macrobehavior.* New York: W. W. Norton.

Schlesinger, Joseph. 1966. *Ambition and Politics: Political Careers in the United States.* Chicago: Rand McNally.

Seeyle, Katharine Q. 1998a. "The Speaker Steps Down: The Overview." *New York Times*, November 11.

———. 1998b. "House Schedule, and Divorce, Become Issues in Race for Majority Leader." *New York Times*, November 13.

———. 1998c. "Armey's Rivals Maneuver in Leadership Race." *New York Times*, November 17.

———. 1998d. "Candidates Are Rounding Up Votes in Race for Majority Leader." *New York Times*, November 17.

———. 1998e. "The Republican Transition: The Overview." *New York Times*, November 19.

Sellers, Patrick J. 1998. "Strategy and Background in Congressional Campaigns." *American Political Science Review* 92 (1): 159–71.

"Session Summary, Party Leaders, Turnover in 1965." 1966. In *Congressional Quarterly Almanac 1965*, 21st ed., 24–27. Washington, DC: Congressional Quarterly.

Shaffrey, Mary. 2000a. "Rep. Lewis Insists He's Still in Race for House Dem Whip." *The Hill*, May 10.

———. 2000b. "Hoyer 'advantage' vexes Pelosi." *The Hill*, October 25.

Shannon, William V. 1971. "New Leadership in the House." *New York Times*, January 4.

Sheffner, Benjamin. 1994. "McCollum's Post-Election Blitz." *Roll Call*, December 19.

Sides, John, et al. 2012. *Campaigns and Elections: Rules, Reality, Strategy, Choice.* New York: W. W. Norton.

Simpson, Glenn R. 1994. "Rose Outpacing Foley in Gifts to Candidates." *Roll Call*, August 4.

Sinclair, Barbara. 1995. *Legislators, Leaders, and Lawmaking: The U.S. House of Representatives in the Postreform Era.* Baltimore: Johns Hopkins University Press.

———. 2006. *Party Wars: Polarization and the Politics of National Policy Making.* Norman: University of Oklahoma Press.

Smith, Steven S. 2007. *Party Influence in Congress.* New York: Cambridge University Press.

Smith, Zachary C. 2012. "From the Well of the House: Remaking the House Republican Party, 1978–1994." Ph.D. diss., Department of History, Boston University.

Steely, Mel. 2000. *The Gentleman from Georgia: The Biography of Newt Gingrich.* Macon, GA: Mercer University Press.

Steinhauer, Jennifer. 2015. "Lawmaker Weighs His Own House against Nation's." *New York Times*, October 22.

Steinhauer, Jennifer, and Emmarie Huetteman. 2015. "Ryan Now Open to Speaker's Job, But On His 'Own Terms.'" *New York Times*, October 21.

Sterne, Joseph R. L. 1964a. "Ford Seeks Halleck's House Post." *Baltimore Sun*, December 20.

———. 1964b. "Ford Deplores Halleck Tactics." *Baltimore Sun*, December 28.

Stoddard, A. B. 1998a. "GOP Melee as Davis Gains in NRCC Race." *The Hill*, November 11.

———. 1998b. "Dirty Tricks Charges Mar Leadership Race." *The Hill*, November 18.

Strahan, Randall. 2007. *Leading Representatives: The Agency of Leaders in the Politics of the U.S. House.* Baltimore: Johns Hopkins University Press.

Struck, Myron. 1976. "Survey Shows Burton Ahead in House Majority Leader Race." *Roll Call*, December 9.

Sweeney, William R. 1995. "The Principles of Planning." In *Campaigns and Elections American Style*, 1st ed., ed. James A. Thurber and Candice J. Nelson, 14–29. Boulder, CO: Westview Press.

Thorp, Frank. 2012. "GOP Strips 4 of House Committee Seats." First Read blog, NBC News, December 3, http://firstread.nbcnews.com/ _news/2012/12/03/15653445-gop-strips-4-of-house-committee-seats ?lite (accessed March 17, 2014).

Tolchin, Martin. 1980a. "Two Schools Contend." *New York Times*, September 28.

———. 1980b. "Michel of Illinois Elected House's Republican Leader." *New York Times*, December 9.

Toner, Robin. 1989a. "G.O.P. Focuses on Cheney Succession." *New York Times*, March 13.

———. 1989b. "Race for Whip: Hyperspeed vs. Slow Motion." *New York Times*, March 22.

Treul, Sarah A. 2017. *Agenda Crossover: The Influence of State Delegations in Congress*. New York: Cambridge University Press.

Truman, David B. 1959. *The Congressional Party: A Case Study*. New York: Wiley and Sons.

U.S. News and World Report. 1970. "House Speaker—Target of Rebels." March 2.

Van Atta, Dale. 2008. *With Honor: Melvin Laird in War, Peace, and Politics*. Madison: University of Wisconsin Press.

VandeHei, Jim. 1997. "Gingrich May Ask Ouster of Leaders." *Roll Call*. July 21.

———. 1998a. "House Democrats Line Up for Leadership Races." *Roll Call*, January 26.

———. 1998b. "GOP Plans to 'Break Out' in Fall Election." *Roll Call*, July 23.

———. 1998c. "Hastert Draft Seen for Majority Leader Race; Armey, Largent, Dunn Splitting Conference Vote." *Roll Call*, November 12.

———. 1998d. "Armey Claims Victory, Opponents Doubt Count; GOP Leadership Races Will Be Decided This Week." *Roll Call*, November 16.

———. 1998e. "Armey Survives Challenge; Livingston Calls for Unity after Largent, Dunn Fall Short." *Roll Call*, November 19.

VandeHei, Jim, and Shailagh Murray. 2006. "Post-Abramoff Mood Shaped Vote for DeLay's Successor." *Washington Post*, February 3.

Vander Jagt, Guy. 1980. "Planning for a Republican Majority." *Commonsense* 3 (3): 67–77.

Viebeck, Elise. 2015. "Why Nobody Wants the Job of House Speaker." *Washington Post*, October 14.

Vucanovich, Barbara F., and Patricia D. Cafferata. 2005. *Barbara F. Vucanovich: From Nevada to Congress, and Back Again*. Reno: University of Nevada Press.

Wallison, Ethan. 1998. "Democrats Launch Quixotic Bids for Majority Whip." *Roll Call*, September 3.

————. 1999a. "House Democrats Get Head Start On Whip Race." *Roll Call*, August 2.

————. 1999b. "Hoyer Claims Plenty of Votes in Potential Majority Whip Battle." *Roll Call*, November 22.

————. 2000a. "Pelosi, Hoyer Battling Californian Claims 'Aura of Inevitability.'" *Roll Call*, February 24.

————. 2000b. "Dingell Signs on with Hoyer in Whip Race." *Roll Call*, May 25.

————. 2000c. "Lewis Leaves Whip Contest." *Roll Call*, July 20.

————. 2000d. "Pelosi Claiming Victory in Whip Race." *Roll Call*, July 27.

————. 2000e. "Hoyer and Pelosi Take Their Whip Race Out West." *Roll Call*, August 14.

————. 2000f. "Gephardt to Stand for Leader Again." *Roll Call*, November 9.

————. 2001a. "Whip Race Ready to Go." *Roll Call*, August 16.

————. 2001b. "Whip Contest Goes to Wire." *Roll Call*, October 8.

Walsh, Edward. 1998. "A Republican Woman near the Top." *Washington Post*, November 13.

Washington Post. 1970. "Californians Boom Sisk for House Leadership." November 20.

————. 1971. "Udall Leads Race for Majority Leader." January 12.

"Washington Wire." 1974. *Wall Street Journal*, December 6.

Watts, J. C. Jr., with Chriss Winston. 2003. *What Color Is a Conservative? My Life and My Politics*. New York: HarperCollins.

Weaver, Warren Jr. 1970. "Race Wide Open for Albert Post." *New York Times*, May 22.

Wehrman, Jessica. 2006. "Boehner, Rivals Take Anti-Pork Stands." *Dayton Daily News*, January 31.

Weingast, Barry R. 1979. "A Rational Choice Perspective on Congressional Norms." *American Journal of Political Science* 23 (2): 245–62.

Weisman, Jonathan. 2006a. "Shadegg Enters GOP Contest." *Washington Post*, January 14.

————. 2006b. "Corruption Scandals Cast Shadow on GOP Leadership Race." *Washington Post*, January 30.

————. 2006c. "In an Upset, Boehner Is Elected House GOP Leader." *Washington Post*, February 3.

————. 2006d. "Pelosi Endorses Murtha as Next Majority Leader." *Washington Post*, November 13.

Weisman, Jonathan, and Lois Romano. 2006. "Pelosi Splits Democrats with Push for Murtha." *Washington Post*, November 16.

Welch, William M. 1998. "House GOP to Decide on its Leadership Today." *USA Today*, November 18.

Welch, William M., and Jim Drinkard. 1998. "Livingston Grabs Top Spot After House Rival Concedes." *USA Today*, November 10.

Wicker, Tom. 1965. "Goldwater Aftermath." *New York Times*, January 16.

Wicks, Aaron E. 2001. "Leadership Selection in the United States House of Representatives." Ph.D. diss., Department of Political Science, University of Rochester.

Willis, Derek. 2002. "Blunt Now Sole Candidate for GOP Whip." *CQ Weekly*, March 2, p. 576.

Winneker, Craig. 1994. "Heard on the Hill." *Roll Call*, May 5.

Wong, Scott. 2015. "Paul Ryan Elected Speaker." *The Hill*, October 29.

Wong, Scott, and Cristina Marcos. 2015. "Right Flexes Muscle ahead of Speaker Vote." *The Hill*, October 7.

Wright, Jim. 1996. *Balance of Power: Presidents and Congress from the Era of McCarthy to the Age of Gingrich*. Atlanta, GA: Turner Publishing.

Yachnin, Jennifer, and John Bresnahan. 2006. "Hoyer Defeats Murtha." *Roll Call*, November 16.

York, Anthony. 2002. "Harold Ford Crusades to Save the Democrats." Salon, November 9, www.salon.com/2002/11/09/pelosi_ford (accessed August 28, 2016).

Zorn, Christopher. 2005. "A Solution to Separation in Binary Response Models." *Political Analysis* 13 (2): 157–70.

INDEX

92 Group, 82
Adams, Brock, 121
Affordable Care Act, 52, 151
AFL-CIO, 58, 62
age, and influence on vote choice,
    200. *See also individual races by
    name*
Agnew, Spiro, 182
Albert, Carl, 29, 63–64, 237n18,
    237n26, 238n38; 1961–62 race
    for majority leader, 39, 120; 1971
    race for Speaker, 38, 56–57,
    250n1; retirement, 118, 119,
    251n10
Amash, Justin, 266n76
ambition, 199; expressive, 27,
    34–38; nascent, 27–34, 36. *See
    also individual races by name*
Americans for Democratic Action,
    62
Anderson, Glenn, 62
Anderson, John, 183, 245n35
Arends, Les, 180
Armey, Dick, 193, 248n74; 1994
    election as Republican leader, 37,
    44, 104; 1998 race for Republican
    leader, 35, 39, 159–77
Ashley, Thomas "Lud," 230n23,
    253n29
Aspinall, Wayne, 207–8, 237n24,
    251n9
Austin-Boston alliance, 121, 250n4

balloting, multiple-round. *See* selec-
    tion process for choosing party
    leaders
bandwagon strategy, 215–16, 225,
    232n37, 238n32. *See also indi-
    vidual races by name*
Barton, Joe, 140, 164
Bauman, Robert, 99
Bethune, Ed, 90, 91
Blue Dog Democrats, 46
Blunt, Roy, 22, 29; 2006 race for
    Republican leader, 138–47
Boehner, John, 36, 163, 206, 220,
    234n21, 248n74; 1998 race for
    Republican Conference chair,
    32–33, 160–61, 165, 168; 2006
    race for Republican leader,
    138–47, 206; 2013 floor chal-
    lenge against, 193, 194–96, 220;
    departure from House, 26, 193
Boggs, Hale, 29, 235n30, 265n63;
    1970–71 race for Democratic
    leader, 22, 35, 57–69, 77, 206–7
Boland, Eddie, 60, 62, 214, 236n10,
    237n23
Bolling, Richard, 29, 71, 236n10,
    240n53; 1961–62 race for major-
    ity leader, 39, 40; 1976 race for
    Democratic leader, 120–34, 199,
    207
Bonior, David, 213, 234n14; 1989
    race for Democratic whip, 38,